DESIGNING
FOR **PRIVACY**
AND RELATED NEEDS

DESIGNING
FOR **PRIVACY**
AND RELATED NEEDS

JULIE STEWART-POLLACK
ROCKY MOUNTAIN COLLEGE OF ART & DESIGN

ROSEMARY MENCONI
ROCKY MOUNTAIN COLLEGE OF ART & DESIGN

FAIRCHILD PUBLICATIONS, INC.
NEW YORK

Executive Editor: Olga T. Kontzias

Acquisitions Editor: Joseph Miranda

Assistant Acquisitions Editor: Jason Moring

Art Director: Adam B. Bohannon

Director of Production: Priscilla Taguer

Development Editor: Sylvia L. Weber

Production Editor: Amy Zarkos

Assistant Editor: Suzette Lam

Publishing Assistant: Jaclyn Bergeron

Copy Editor: Amy Jolin

Interior Design: Renato Stanisic

Cover Design: Adam B. Bohannon

Cover images: Top right: Bruce Forster/Getty Images, Bottom left: Courtesy of Herman Miller

Page ii: Designed by: DiLeonardo International, Inc. Photographer: Warren Jagger

Library of Congress Catalog Card Number: 2004101107

ISBN: 1-56367-340-1

GST R 133004424

Printed in Singapore

Contents

Extended Contents

Preface

The 21st century is living up to and exceeding many of the predictions made about how we would live, work, and communicate in the new millennium. Every day we learn more about the complexities of living in a global community. Diversity of cultures, beliefs, and values demand a broader perspective and a deeper knowledge base in

order to survive and presents us with challenges that previously were rarely considered or discussed. The potentials and problems associated with living in a world dominated by information and technology challenge our ability to integrate as well as to separate our personal and professional lives from one another. We are living longer and searching for more meaning in the act of living, even as we continue to expand the built environment into the last remaining wild places on earth. In the process we further isolate ourselves from the benefits of direct contact with the natural environment, often forgetting how important it is to keep that environment healthy.

Only recently have we begun to understand the delicate balance between the quality of the physical environment and the quality of human life. We know, however, that understanding this relationship becomes more important as our

population continues to grow. Today, the earth holds 418 cities of at least one million people and 22 mega cities of 10 million or more residents. By 2010 more than half of the nearly 7 billion people on Earth will inhabit cities in some form of built environment, *making the world more urban than rural for the first time in human history*. (Worldwatch Institute).

Billions of people crammed into the world's overcrowded cities on a planet already suffering from the effects of increased human population, decreased natural resources, and limited physical space could become the greatest challenge to our quality of life that we have ever faced as a species.

We know that quality of life issues dominate today's political and social discussions. These issues are also central to the definition of the interior designer: "The professional interior designer is qualified by education, experience and examination to enhance the function and quality of interior spaces for the purpose of *improving the quality of life*, increasing productivity and protecting the health, safety and welfare of the public." (Foundation for Interior Design Education Research).

Few professions are as affected by or required to respond to the physical, economical, social, political, and psychological changes in society as is interior design. The complex needs we have of our environments are diverse and dynamic, subject to both internal and external forces shaped by genetics, experience, culture, crisis, expectations, education, and lifestyles. Because the degree to which we experience quality of life is related to the satisfaction of our needs, it is essential that the interior designer understand the ways in which the built environment can be designed to support and to help satisfy those needs.

Privacy is not only one of these needs, but also a critical part of the larger body of human needs for survival that have deep roots in our evolutionary past. We argue in this book that the concept of privacy is an essential component of our physical and emotional health and well-being, and in turn, is a central consideration to be made by interior design professionals. In the complex world of the 21st century, ability to achieve privacy is no longer assured, yet perhaps it has never been needed more.

Acknowledgments

This book has two authors, but there were many contributors to the process, and we want to thank them all: Dr. Stephanie Clemons of Colorado State University, our mentor and good friend; Dr. Susan Rennie, another mentor and friend; and Roy Maddox, an inspiration to us in life and a beautiful memory since his untimely death.

We want to acknowledge other people and groups who contributed to this book: Dr. Gary Evans, whose work has inspired us as well as the research staffs at Haworth; Herman Miller, Inc.; Steelcase Inc.; and Knoll who graciously took the time to furnish us with text material and illustrations. We also owe a debt to Associates III, a sustainable interior design firm that believes in what we are doing and also contributed generously from their own portfolios for a number of photographs used in the book.

We wish to thank the interior design educators who generously gave time to participate in the Fairchild-sponsored round table discussion of interior design at the 2003 national IDEC conference. They are: Stephanie Clemons, Denise Guerin, Louise Jones, Lisa Waxman, and John Weigand. Other educators include the reviewers who were kind enough to read the first draft of this book. Your recommendations were invaluable, and we listened to all of them with respect and appreciation and made appropriate adjustments.

We also appreciate the encouragement of participants over the years in our CEU, "Privacy, the Universal Need." Many of you asked us to write a book about privacy, and so we did. A special thanks goes to Barbara Henn, former Director of Education, ASID, who gave us many opportunities over the years to present our seminars to groups of interior design practitioners, educators, and students.

There might never have been a book without our students, past and present. They have delighted and inspired us over the years, and they have educated us as well. During the process of writing this book, our publisher sponsored a project for interior design students at Rocky Mountain College of Art & Design to express their understanding of the concepts of privacy with written and graphic solutions to design problems in residential and commercial categories. Our special thanks to all who participated, and in particular the three students whose work is featured in this book: Seema Pandya, Miriam Hoffman, and Rachel Laessig. We also thank our illustrators, Lindsey Kruger and Miranda Nicholson, both recent graduates of Rocky Mountain College of Art and Design. Their talent and their professional interior design training have enhanced our book tremendously.

Our editors at Fairchild Books have encouraged us at every stage of the development of this book, and we are grateful to them for their help, their graciousness, and their willingness to answer our many questions.

We would also like to thank the following reviewers, selected by the publisher, for their helpful suggestions: Stephanie Clemons, Colorado State University; Denise Guerin, University of Minnesota; Cheryl Gulley, Watkins College of Art and Design; Jerry L. Nielson, University of Florida; Virgina North, Lawrence Technological University; Chris Priest, University of Minnesota; Roberto Rengel, University of Wisconsin—Madison; and Suzanne Scott, University of Wisconsin—Madison.

Finally, no list of acknowledgments would be complete without thanking our husbands, Rich Pollack and Larry Menconi, whose encouragement, loyalty, and patience were unswerving.

Introduction

One of the most significant challenges to interior designers today is the need to understand the range of physical and psychological consequences that design may have on massive human populations living their lives almost exclusively in artificial, densely populated human-made environments. How will these changes affect our quality of

life, and how will designers accommodate the diversity of human needs in such settings? These questions are central to the subject of this book.

This book is devoted to the exploration and examination of the concept of privacy—the universal need to control how much and what types of interaction we have with others—as an essential ingredient in the quality of life. It is our assertion that a greater understanding and appreciation of the concept of privacy will enable designers to more effectively meet some of the challenges resulting from expanding population and inevitable higher density living as well as some of the less dramatic challenges of modern life. Considerations for privacy needs are not new to the practice of interior design. However, this book places privacy at the center of the discussion of the relationship between quality of life issues and the design of the built environment by identifying the physical, psychological, and cognitive benefits of various types of privacy and the physical characteristics of environments that support privacy.

Although privacy is studied in a variety of disciplines, we have chosen to focus this book primarily upon the privacy theories developed in environmental psychology. Environmental psychology is concerned with the interactions and relationships between people and their environments and provides important research based information used by the design disciplines to create environments that work better for people. Our discussion of these environmental psychology theories is not meant to be all-inclusive. Rather, it is our intention to show relationships between selected privacy and related theories and the design of the built environment.

This book is intended for intermediate to advanced interior design students, as well as design educators, design professionals, and all those in related professions who are interested in the ways environments affect people and people affect environments. It is divided into two major topics: 1) privacy and related theories and how they correspond to the design of the built environment, and 2) applications of these theories to specific types of designs. Chapters 1–3 establish the theoretical and applicable framework for the book by examining the factors that cause us to need privacy, the benefits of privacy, how and why our privacy needs vary, and how the built environment can be designed to provide for diverse privacy needs.

We begin building this framework in Chapter 1 with the question "Why study privacy?" This is a legitimate question given the many issues and demands for which today's interior design professionals are responsible. While privacy may be a consideration in our design decisions, why is it important enough to warrant such in-depth examination? To answer the question, privacy is examined in Chapter 1 as a universal, complex human need that serves many purposes from the broad categories of survival and physical and psychological health to the more personal issues of self-identity and emotional release. We discover through this examination that the benefits attributed to the experience of privacy are far greater and more significant to overall well-being than perhaps previously recognized. One of the most compelling of these benefits is the ability of privacy to provide restoration from stress and mental fatigue. This restorative capacity of privacy is further expanded upon and discussed in each chapter of the book.

Chapter 2 continues to build the theoretical and applicable framework by exploring the concept of privacy and its role in our lives. We examine the work of major privacy theorists who have found that there are several "types" of privacy and that each type provides specific physical, psychological, and cognitive benefits. By exploring the ways people communicate their needs for and uses of privacy in physical settings, Chapter 2 introduces the possibilities and potential of design to significantly affect how environments can support the ability to achieve desired privacy.

The theoretical and applicable framework for the book is completed in Chapter 3. We explore how people evaluate environments for their needs and develop preferences for certain environments and environmental characteristics that support privacy. Through an examination of the restorative qualities of natural environments we gain insights into how physical characteristics of nature can enhance the restorative benefits of privacy in built environments. Finally, we identify and examine specific characteristics of physical environments that promote privacy when applied to the design of interiors.

Chapters 4 to 7 apply the framework established in the first three chapters to application in four areas of interior design: residential, work environment, healthcare, and hospitality. Each application chapter discusses the privacy theories and related concepts that apply to the particular specialty area of interior design, followed by interior design application. We also examine current applicable design research in each of the four areas of specialty as it relates to each area's specific privacy considerations.

Chapter 8 explores age-specific considerations for privacy and deals with the dynamic changes in privacy needs over a lifetime. The final chapter, Chapter 9, presents a model for designing for privacy that integrates privacy considerations into the three major phases of the design process: the intelligence phase, the concept development phase, and the design implementation phase.

Assignments are provided at the end of each chapter. They are structured to allow the reader to apply knowledge and concepts from the chapter together with the knowledge and concepts from the previous chapters to solve various designing for privacy problems. Using FIDER indicators as a model, each assignment describes the objectives and desired learning outcomes and presents a variety of opportunities to build awareness and understanding of privacy issues through direct application.

CHAPTER 1

Why Study Privacy?

OUR UNIVERSAL NEED FOR PRIVACY

Where do you go when you need privacy? Is it an indoor or outdoor environment? Do you need lots of space or an enclosure? Do you want to be hidden from the view of others but able to see them yourself, or do you prefer total seclusion? Do you want to

be away from all noise, or do you prefer natural sounds like ocean waves and wind in the trees. Or you would rather instead be able to select the sounds you hear such as music? Is your ideal private environment bathed in sunlight, or do you prefer it to be illuminated by controllable artificial light or a combination of both? Do you like to be in a familiar space surrounded by cherished items, or do you seek new and unusual private places? How much control do you need to have over your private place, and how do you feel when others invade it?

These questions and their answers can provide insights into the characteristics of our personal preferences for a private environment. They also reflect the complex, changing nature of our needs for privacy and reveal two interrelated patterns that form the foundation for an examination of privacy as it relates to interior design.

1. The ability to achieve privacy is very much dependent upon the physical environment.
2. The preferred environmental characteristics of a private place vary with the circumstances and the individual.

Although we often think of privacy as a physical separation from others that requires total seclusion, it is in fact a process that involves both a seeking of interaction and a control of interaction. Both of these privacy activities depend upon the opportunities provided by the physical environment, the circumstances that cause us to seek privacy, and our personal needs, motivations, expectations, and experiences.

Privacy is both a process by which we control access to ourselves or our group and a condition of selective distance or isolation (Altman 1975). It involves our continually changing needs to be with others and our need to be alone. Privacy cannot be viewed as an absolute condition, but rather as a dynamic need that motivates us to seek optimum levels of interaction as well as control over who has access to us or our group and under what circumstances. This optimizing feature of privacy means that too much privacy (such as social isolation) or too little privacy (such as crowding) at any given time is unsatisfactory and creates imbalances that may have serious consequences upon our overall well-being (Pederson 1997).

Privacy is also a complex human need that serves many purposes in our lives from the broad categories of survival and physical and psychological health to the more personal issues of self-identity and emotional release. The need for privacy is universal with many cross-cultural similarities (Newell 1998). The ways, however, that we express our desire for privacy vary with culture, society, age, gender, circumstance, and environment (Altman 1975). As a concept and as a universal need, privacy is closely related to other behavioral concepts and needs. These include concepts and theories of personal space, territoriality, and crowding as well as needs for friendship, love, belonging, personal autonomy, self-evaluation, restoration, and development of self-identity.

As with all attempts to address human needs, designing for privacy presents a challenge to interior designers to synthesize diverse information from many sources and translate that information into workable design solutions. The process begins by asking questions to help understand how our universal need for privacy works.

1. What factors cause us to need privacy?
2. What are the benefits of privacy?
3. How do our privacy needs vary and why?
4. How can the built environment be designed to provide for our diverse privacy needs?

These four questions provide the framework for this book. Each chapter will answer one or more of the questions. For example, this chapter discusses the first two questions—the factors that cause us to need privacy and the benefits of privacy. Chapter 2 discusses how our privacy needs vary and why. Chapter 3 discusses how the built environment must be designed to provide for our privacy needs. Chapters 4 through 8 apply design solutions to enhance privacy needs in the built environment. (See **Box 1.1**).

---

1. What factors cause us to need privacy?

2. What are the benefits of privacy?

3. How do our privacy needs vary and why?

4. How can the built environment be designed to provide for our diverse privacy needs?

Box 1.1 The four questions designers must ask in order to understand the diverse privacy needs of those for whom we design. Questions 1 and 2 will be addressed in this chapter.

WHEN WE NEED PRIVACY

Life is composed of many situations and circumstances that cause us to need privacy. We need privacy when we are ill, sad, grieving, angry, tired, and anxious. We need privacy for intellectual, ethical, spiritual, creative, and physical development. We need privacy for emotional release, for self-evaluation, for intimacy, for autonomy, for contemplation, and for rejuvenation. And we need privacy when we are stressed.

All of these privacy situations and circumstances are part of our lives at one time or another. Some occur more frequently than others, and some are experienced more intensely than others. They all have in common, however, the need to exert a degree of control over access to ourselves and our interaction with others. Without the kind of control that the process of privacy uniquely provides, we are less able to cope with or benefit from these situations and circumstances.

Controllability, therefore, is central to the privacy process. **Controllability** is a perceived relationship between the individual and his or her environment that is essential to effective functioning. This type of environmental control is defined as the ability to alter the physical environment to meet our needs or to regulate overexposure within the surroundings (Evans & McCoy 1998). As we will see throughout this book, controllability can be planned for and designed into our environments to facilitate privacy needs in a variety of ways.

Privacy as a Survival Mechanism

The need for privacy is not new, and it is not a luxury. Privacy is both genetically grounded and environmentally dependent (Harris, et al. 1995, Westin 1967). Its biological and evolutionary roots were originally formed during our earliest interactions with the only environment we had, the natural environment, in which privacy served as a survival mechanism. In order to survive in natural settings, early human beings needed the ability to recognize, respond appropriately to, and learn from the environmental characteristics that represented survival advantage and survival risk (Heerwagen & Orians 1993). Human sensory systems developed specifically for the task of survival. However, the ability to perceive accurately, to respond appropriately, and to learn effectively from these crucial environmental characteristics also required the ability and time to assimilate and process the information gained from the environment. Simply put, human beings needed time away from the immediacy of the survival struggle to be alone or to be with selected companions to process and share information necessary for survival.

Whether in the wilderness or in the city, the occasional condition of privacy still operates to promote our survival and development (Newell 1998). We need the time away from the demands of the modern world that privacy uniquely provides to regenerate, to process experiences, and to "put things into perspective."

Privacy as a Way to Satisfy Related Human Needs

The need for privacy is related to and influenced by other important human needs. The study of what human beings need involves the physical, behavioral, and social sciences. Research from these disciplines reveals that human needs—including privacy—motivate our behavior and affect our perceptions about ourselves, other people, other species, and our surroundings (Crooks & Stein 1991, Altman 1975).

The basic needs that we have of our environments to provide shelter, food, water, safety, and security are found in all forms of animal life. Human beings, however, have more complex needs of our environments. These needs are the result of biological, psychological, and social drives and motives. For example, the need for **personal autonomy**—our sense of individuality and integrity, the freedom to separate ourselves from others to be alone with our thoughts and feelings, to explore our capacities and limitations, to strive for independence, to think and act without coercion (Westin 1967)—has been shown as essential to the development of individuality and the ability to make personal choices in life. This type of complex human need contributes to the need for privacy because in order to achieve autonomy, our environments must provide the opportunity to achieve selective distance from others (Westin 1967).

The Hierarchy of Human Needs

Humanistic psychologist Abraham Maslow proposed that human needs exist within a five-level

LINK
How can autonomy be achieved in healthcare environments? See Chapter 6, page 134.

hierarchy of broad categories ranging from the lowest basic biological needs to the highest and most dominant motivating force in our lives: the need for self-actualization. (See **Figure 1.1**).

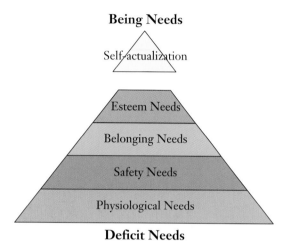

Being Needs

Self-actualization

Esteem Needs

Belonging Needs

Safety Needs

Physiological Needs

Deficit Needs

Figure 1.1 According to psychologist Abraham Maslow, we must achieve our most basic needs before we can achieve our higher needs. Maslow links the highest of these needs—self-actualization—to an increased desire for privacy.

Self-actualization, according to Maslow, is the natural inclination that humans have to strive to fulfill our potential. Among the characteristics of a self-actualized individual are superior perceptions of reality; increased acceptance of one's self, of others, and of nature; increased desire for privacy; and increased autonomy (Maslow 1968). Maslow's premise is that all of these characteristics are associated with a higher quality of life. However, before we can pursue our higher level needs, Maslow asserts that we must first fulfill our basic needs for food, water, shelter, safety, and security. Only then do we move onto the higher level needs, such as affiliation and self esteem; the need to know, to understand, and to explore; needs for aesthetic experiences; and ultimately the need for self-actualization.

Each of Maslow's needs is in some way environmentally dependent. Some are obvious, such as shelter. Other needs may not, on the surface, seem to be dependent upon the physical environment. Yet these needs can be supported or denied by environmental conditions. For example, the

need for **affiliation**—to form friendships, to communicate and interact with others, to be a part of a group, and to love—is a need that demands a great deal from our physical environments. In order to form friendships, our paths must cross but must not be perceived as threatening, and we must be able to communicate and interact effectively. In order to explore, develop, and express our love for another person, we require physical elements that provide for intimate interaction. Without these characteristics of the physical environment that help us to choose our levels of interaction with others (an important part of the privacy process), it becomes more difficult to develop affiliation relationships.

Maslow's hierarchy reflects the dual properties of privacy: Although humans are social beings requiring interaction, affiliation, friendship, and love, we also have the need to retreat and reflect, to decompress, and to be off stage. If these needs are not met, our quality of life can be compromised.

Quality of Life and Privacy

Quality of life is a phrase often used to describe the features or characteristics of the personal, social, psychological, and physical environments as well as the conditions and circumstances that affect our ability to satisfy human needs. Some social scientists assert that the measure of quality of life is the extent to which our happiness requirements are met (McCall 1975), i.e., those requirements that humans must have to be truly happy. This perspective suggests that there may be "universals" or general happiness requirements that do not vary from person to person or from culture to culture.

One such universal is personal freedom. In an oppressed society, the basic physical needs of food, water, and shelter may be met. However, without the freedom to make choices about how one lives his or her life—such as making privacy decisions about how and when to interact with others or what information about oneself is available to others—there is little happiness and a lesser quality of life. The opportunities for choice and control afforded by environments designed to support privacy needs may therefore contribute to the quality of life.

FYI Because quality of life issues dominate today's political and societal discussions, these issues are also central to the study of interior design. This point is illustrated by the official definition of the interior designer:

"The professional interior designer is qualified by education, experience and examination to enhance the function and quality of interior spaces for the purpose **of improving the quality of life**, increasing productivity and protecting the health, safety and welfare of the public." (emphasis added)

(Foundation for Interior Design Education Research)

PRIVACY CHALLENGES OF HIGH-DENSITY LIVING

The design of the built environment has and will continue to play a major role in quality of life issues as we continue to expand the built world in order to meet our growing material needs for shelter, recreation, commerce, and a variety of other human activities dependent upon structures. We see the physical results of the unprecedented expansion of the built world all around us. They include urban sprawl, pollution, traffic congestion, depletion of natural resources, and degradation and loss of natural environments. The physical results of this ever expanding built environment present many new challenges to design professionals. One of the most significant challenges is the need to understand the range of physical and psychological consequences that design may have on massive

human populations living their lives almost exclusively in artificial, densely populated, human-made environments.

Growth and progress, although a necessary part of society, have often resulted in conditions of compromised privacy. Urban planners focus increasingly upon high-density living as a solution to urban sprawl and its detrimental effects upon the environment and quality of life. High-density living is already a reality for billions of people in the world's poorer cities for whom urban planning was not an option, creating the perception that poverty and chaos are the inevitable results. If, as anticipated, over half of the earth's population lives in cities in the very near future, high-density living will become a reality for many more millions.

Advantages and Demands of High-Density Living

Our perception of high-density or urban living is often negative, attributing density to traffic congestion, crime, lower property values, and loss of green space. However, historically well planned and designed densely populated environments are actually preferred by the majority of human beings (Rybczynski 1995). The collective benefits of urban living, including strong networks of social relationships and access to cultural, entertainment, and social services, have attracted the majority of the human population to cities throughout history. Additionally, urban environments that concentrate their products, services, support, wealth, and economic opportunities are more sustainable than their suburban counterparts because urban populations consume less energy and reduce dependency upon road transportation.

However, increased density demands a greater need to understand the complex relationships between people and environments. The close presence of others can sometimes interfere with our ability to perform tasks, to interact effectively, to cope with unpredictable and uncertain situations, and to attain our goals (Aiello and Baum 1979). For example, if we need to have a confidential conversation with someone but can find nowhere to do so out of the visual and acoustical range of others, we tend to perceive that environment as uncontrollable. We may respond negatively to such an environment in part because the space we require for effective interaction is not available, is beyond our control, or does not have the physical features necessary to accommodate our needs for privacy.

Balancing Interaction and Controllability for Privacy Needs

High-density environments require a careful balance between interaction and controllability to meet privacy needs. As population density increases, control and predictability tend to decrease. Therefore, even if we were able to find a relatively private place for that confidential conversation amid the crowds of people surrounding us, the chances of our privacy being invaded and our conversation being interrupted are much greater in high-density environments. This kind of unpredictability in our

surroundings can create feelings of helplessness by restricting our behavioral options and our ability to make choices. This resulting feeling of helplessness may create additional problems including psychological distress, which could lead to physical disease (Evans & McCoy 1998).

If possible, we generally avoid an environment that we perceive as unpredictable and/or uncontrollable for our needs (Mehrabian 1976). High-density living, however, makes avoidance more difficult, whether it is within a home, dorm room, restaurant, theater, hospital, or any other public or private place. (See **Figure 1.2**).

Densely Populated Environments and Crowding

Lack of control within densely populated environments contributes to the psychological condition of

LINK
What is avoidance behavior, and how is it affected by our needs for privacy? See Chapter 3, page 39.

crowding. Density and crowding, however, are two different experiences. **Density** is a physical condition involving space limitations and the number of people within that space. **Crowding** is a psychological response to overstimulation

Figure 1.2 Although high-density is not always a negative experience, high-density environments require a careful balance between interaction and controllability to meet privacy needs. David Joel/ Getty Images.

caused by too much interaction with others within a perceived limited space. High density is usually, but not always, necessary for crowding. For example, if we are on a deserted beach expecting to be alone and someone approaches us, we may feel crowded, even though the density is low. Conversely, if we are at an exciting standing-room-only concert, the density is high, but we may not feel crowded. However, both of these examples refer to short term experiences. Research indicates that living and working in high-density environments is very different than spending a few hours in densely populated spaces.

Crowding is a personal and subjective reaction causing us to look for ways to alleviate the perceived restrictions of space and the feelings of infringement (Stokols 1972). A significant effect of crowding is the tendency to withdraw from social interactions and to become less responsive to the needs of others. Studies indicate that long-term effects of crowding lead to a breakdown of socially supportive relationships and in turn increase psychological distress (Evans, et al. 1999).

FYI
Environments that we perceive as inflexible, where users lack the ability to control environmental elements, such as lighting and climatic conditions, and that also lack the space and resources necessary to function effectively contribute to our feelings of crowding.

(Evans et al. 2001)

Both population density and crowding are difficult to measure and vary greatly when considering such distinctions as "inside" and "outside." However, high density inside is more closely related to stress and crowding than outside (Veitch & Arkkelin 1995). As we will discuss in Chapter 2, although density contributes to crowding, many other factors contribute to this psychological state, including restriction of movement and the lack of privacy (Stokols 1972).

STRESS AND PRIVACY NEEDS

Earlier in this chapter we said that we need privacy when we are stressed. We cannot avoid the condition of stress in our lives. This is because stress is the result of many different influences and can be defined by a number of different physical and psychological responses. Seyle (1974) perhaps offers the broadest definition of stress as, "the nonspecific response of the body to any demand made upon it" (p. 14). Stress is, in fact, a necessary part of survival because it arouses the senses, the mind, and the body, preparing us to take necessary action in certain situations. Stress is more commonly discussed in modern society as the result of too many physical and psychological demands placed upon us, causing us to respond by exerting tremendous energy to cope or adapt. According to Seyle (1974), stress becomes negative when our ability to cope or adapt becomes exhausted.

This type of negative stress has become the number one health problem in the United States, a major contributor to heart disease, and often the source of numerous psychological problems. In addition, stress can suppress the immune system, cause high blood pressure, create ulcers, increase fatigue, and reduce tolerance for frustration. Stress is a major cause of absenteeism at work, and it has been shown to decrease overall satisfaction with life.

Stress is an enormous subject, the causes and effects of which are studied in a variety of disciplines. However, for the purposes of studying the effects of privacy on stress, we will examine how the physical environment can contribute to the negative experience of stress and why privacy helps to alleviate stress.

LINK
How are the issues of density and crowding addressed in the design of residential environments? See Chapter 4, page 85.

Environmental Stress and Environmental Load

Environmental stress occurs when the demands of the environment exceed our capacity to cope with or adapt to them (Veitch & Arkkelin 1995). The "environment" in this case includes the physical, psychological, cultural, and social settings for behavior. Within this context, research has identified stimulation as an architectural dimension linked to stress (Evans & McCoy 1998). **Stimulation** is the amount or rate of information in an environment at any given time, also called the **environmental load** (Mehrabian 1976). Levels of environmental stress vary depending upon the environmental load. The more information that we must process, the higher the perceived environmental load becomes.

A survey of research suggests that the two major contributors to environmental stress are

1. lack of control over the levels and types of stimuli in the environment
2. constant, rapid change within the environment

These contributors to environmental stress increase as population density increases. Greater density also increases the complexity of a setting. **Complexity**—how many elements, features, or changes an environment contains—in turn, affects the perceived environmental load. (See **Figure 1.3**). Complexity comprises physical characteristics of the environment such as spatial organization, patterns, scale, colors, and movement as well as the presence of people in the setting. People are, in fact, the greatest source of uncertainty and unpredictability in an environment (Mehrabian 1976), which helps to explain why high-density environments can contribute to environmental stress. The process of privacy—the ability to control how much interaction we have with others—helps to reduce environmental stress by providing a degree of control over the levels and types of stimuli in the environment and by providing a break from the constant, rapid change in the environment.

Some sociologists suggest that in our society today, many people suffer from overstimulation resulting from too many changes as well as

Figure 1.3 The physical characteristics of the environment such as spatial organization, patterns, scale, colors, and movement as well as the presence of people in the setting create complexity. The greater the complexity, the greater the environmental load tends to be. © Joseph Sohm; Visions of America/CORBIS.

cognitive and decision overload. For example, many of us spend a great deal of our lives sitting in massive traffic jams; racing to important meetings; being bombarded by noise, fumes, and angry motorists; listening to our radios tell us about another world crisis; and finding ourselves helpless to control any of these situations. These levels and types of stimulation, changes, and demands upon our ability to make effective decisions are unprecedented. Our traditional ways of coping simply may not be adequate for the high levels of stimulation and rapid change that we must deal with now on a daily basis. In such a world, the occasional condition of privacy can serve as a sanctuary, a respite from complex, high load environments.

Stress and Control

Responses to the environmental load vary from person to person and situation to situation. However, human beings function optimally with moderate levels of stimulation (Evans & McCoy 1998). While too little stimulation can lead to boredom or, if extreme, to sensory deprivation, too much stimulation becomes distracting, making it difficult to focus attention. We need enough stimulation to provide the necessary information about our environment in order to learn and to function effectively. We do not want so much stimulation, however, that our capacity to process that information is exceeded or overloaded.

Privacy is a major contributor to a sense of control in our environments (Evans & McCoy 1998) because it is an optimizing process whereby we choose and selectively control the levels and types of interactions that we have with others as well as how much information we reveal about ourselves to others. One feature of this optimizing process is the ability to regulate accessibility and interaction as circumstances change and according to individual needs. We experience crowding and stress differently under different circumstances. Similarly, we do not all require the same levels of privacy under the same circumstances. Each one of us engages continually in a personal adjustment process, balancing our desire for privacy with our desire for interaction and communication. This process takes place in and is affected by the environmental conditions and the social norms of the society in which we live (Altman 1975). When considerations for privacy needs are integrated into the design of our environments, they can help to modify the levels of stimulation that we require to function at optimum levels by regulating the amount and types of interactions that we have with others. Spaces designed to respond to privacy needs can also provide the ability to control properties of complexity within the environment that influence stimulation levels.

BENEFITS OF PRIVACY

The benefits or functions of privacy have been identified by Altman (1975), Westin (1967), Pederson (1997), Evans and McCoy (1998), Newell (1998), and others. Central to these theories involving the benefits of privacy is the ability to enhance feelings of well-being and to facilitate the development of our self-identity.

Privacy and Well-Being

Establishing and maintaining healthy internal physiological and cognitive functioning, described as "well-being" (Newell 1998), is widely considered to be a necessary condition for a high quality of life. As discussed earlier, stress from overstimulation, rapid change, and perceptions of crowding can produce detrimental effects upon our physical and psychological health. The often heard declaration, "I just need to get away from it all," expresses an inherent human understanding that the best way to relieve stress is to remove ourselves from the stressful environment. It is a survival mechanism telling us that we need time and space to recover our depleted coping capacity.

The ability to choose and to achieve a desired level of privacy is essential to this process because privacy is therapeutic. Studies show that by preventing excessive stimulation, privacy has a relaxing and refreshing effect upon us. This therapeutic benefit appears to be cross-cultural with the effect of "being more relaxed" as the primary consequence of achieving a desired level of privacy (Newell 1998). According to Newell, "A period of privacy provides an opportunity for restabilization, or system maintenance" (p. 359). System maintenance in this context is equated with well-being, and the desire for well-being is described as a "strong underlying motive for seeking privacy" (p. 359).

Privacy also functions therapeutically by providing restoration from mental fatigue and giving us the ability to control a major source of environmental stress: stimulation levels. Additionally, environments designed to accommodate privacy needs provide a refuge that has been shown to promote healing by providing rest, recovery, and contemplation (Evans & McCoy 1998, Ulrich 1995). Pederson (1997) describes two similar benefits of privacy: **rejuvenation**, which he describes as the opportunity to recover from a personal social injury or injustice or loss of self-esteem and to make plans for future social interactions; and **recovery**, which is similar to rejuvenation but has a stronger sense of refuge and relaxation.

Privacy and Self-Identity

The development of self-identity is an ongoing process that is related to both our interactions with others and to our time alone. According to Altman (1975), the primary functions of privacy are to regulate social interaction and the development of our sense of self. These interpersonal functions of privacy enable us to achieve "the very central goals of self-definition and self-identity" (p. 46). Altman asserts that ". . . self-identity is critical to human existence. For a person to function effectively in interaction with

others requires some understanding of what the self is, where it ends and begins, and when self-interest and self-expression can be exhibited" (p. 50). Through our interactions with others, we discover our interpersonal strengths, boundaries, and limitations, as well as how to control those interactions so that we can deal competently with the world. However, the development of our sense of self involves the processes of self-evaluation and self-observation which, Altman asserts, are best accomplished in private.

Privacy facilitates the development of self-identity by allowing us to establish physical boundaries. When we are "off stage" and out of the presence of others, we can reflect upon, explore, and evaluate our behavior, our strengths and weaknesses, our capacities and limitations, our emotions and reasoning, and our beliefs and disbeliefs (Altman 1975). Through private self-observation, we can experience emotional release and more fully imagine who we can be. Westin (1967) also views privacy as part of our need to develop self-identity. He describes privacy as "an instrument for achieving individual goals of self-realization" (p. 39).

FYI

Social worker and author Leontine Young (1966) explains the critical importance of privacy to the development of self-identity in children in her book *Life Among the Giants: A Child's Eye View of the Grown-up World:* "Without privacy there is no individuality. There are only types. Who can know what he thinks and feels if he never has the opportunity to be alone with his thoughts and feelings?" (p. 32)

Specific Benefits or Functions of Privacy

Westin (1967) identified four specific benefits or functions of privacy that facilitate the development of self-identity.

- *Personal autonomy: our sense of individuality and integrity; the freedom to separate ourselves from others to be alone with our thoughts and feelings, to explore our capacities and limitations, to strive for independence, to think and act without coercion*
- *Emotional release: relief from the pressures and stimulation associated with life, the ability to withdraw from public view to release our emotions*
- *Self-evaluation: the ability to process the variety of information constantly bombarding us and to consider the consequences of our behaviors, to plan, to develop ideas, to decide what information about ourselves we want to reveal to others*
- *Limited and protected communication: to control the mental and physical distance that we keep from others, enabling us to choose the depth of communication that we wish to have with them*

Westin's four functions or benefits of privacy demonstrate that we engage continually in an attempt to find the right levels of privacy to help us interact effectively with others as well as to serve our individual privacy needs. Achieving this two-fold purpose, says Westin, is essential because "either too much or too little privacy can create imbalances which seriously jeopardize the individual's well-being" (p. 40). As you will recall, Altman (1975) refers to this concept as the optimization factor.

Pederson (1997) conducted studies and expanded upon Westin's four functions to create seven categories of privacy functions based on their specific benefits to both well-being and self-identity.

- *Contemplation serves many purposes, including self-discovery and the ability to plan future social interactions in environments where we feel free to express ourselves.*

- *Autonomy provides the opportunity for self-discovery and to experiment with new behaviors without judgment of others.*
- *Rejuvenation provides the opportunity to recover from a personal social injury or injustice or loss of self-esteem and to make plans for future social interactions.*
- *Creativity allows us to explore possibilities of expression and mental process that lead to the formulation of solutions, ideas, theories, conceptualizations, and artistic expression.*
- *Recovery is similar to rejuvenation but has a stronger sense of refuge and relaxation.*
- *Catharsis is an emotional release of tension and anxiety.*
- *Concealment allows us to control social interaction by withholding personal information.*

The benefits of privacy to our overall well-being and the development of self-identity also include the ability to facilitate intellectual, ethical, and spiritual development (Newell 1998) as well as to enhance the ability to concentrate and make decisions (Edney & Buda 1976, Pedersen 1997). These benefits of privacy resulting from the ability to control interaction and access to ourselves provide a strong rationale for the study of privacy as it applies to the design of the built environment. (See **Figure 1.4**).

We now return to the questions posed at the beginning of this chapter. Where does one go to "get away," and what characteristics do we want in our private places? Because privacy is a voluntary and temporary process by which we control access to ourselves, it is dependent upon our personal ability to choose the way that we retreat. Closed doors and do-not-disturb signs provide little privacy in a technological world of pagers, emails, faxes, and cell phones. For some of us in certain circumstances, nothing less than physical separation and isolation will do. For others a redirection of attention toward something pleasant to which we can affiliate and relate

Figure 1.4 The qualities of a personal private place vary with the individual and the circumstances.

may be sufficient, such as the view of a garden through the window.

We have learned that privacy is not static, but rather is subject to our personal needs and to the circumstances as well as the conditions within which we must interact. We continually seek different levels of privacy; therefore, attempting to create a "private place" to serve all functions is impractical. As we will learn in the following chapters, the physical characteristics of an environment that support our privacy needs must reflect this varied, circumstantially dependent reality.

Spaces designed to accommodate the experience of privacy that allow people to choose how much social interaction they experience, how much visual and acoustical exposure they

LINK

For more information about redirected attention and privacy see Chapter 3, page 37.

have, and how much environmental stimulus reaches them can help to alleviate many of the problems associated with high-density living, crowding, and overstimulation, including stress. These spaces can also provide the opportunity to heal, to restore our coping abilities, to create, and to develop our self-identity.

The complex needs that we have of our environments are diverse and dynamic, subject to both internal and external forces shaped by genetics, experience, culture, crisis, expectations, education, and lifestyles. Because the degree to which we experience quality of life is related to the satisfaction of our needs, it is essential that interior designers understand the ways in which the built environment can be designed to support and to help satisfy those needs. Privacy is central to this understanding because it can provide both the choice and control necessary to meet many of these needs.

KEY CONCEPTS

1. Privacy is both a process by which we control access to ourselves or our group and a condition of selective distance or isolation. Privacy is also a complex human need that serves many purposes in our lives.

2. The ability to achieve privacy is very much dependent upon the physical environment. The preferred environmental characteristics of a private place vary with the circumstances and the individual.

3. Choice and control are key interrelated concepts of privacy. Choice involves the ability to decide how much interaction we have with others and under what circumstances. Control involves the ability to adjust the physical environment or regulate exposure to our surroundings. Choice without control is meaningless.

4. Lack of control within densely populated environments contributes to the negative psychological condition of crowding.

5. Environmental stress occurs when the demands of the environment exceed our capacity to cope with or adapt to those demands. Two major contributors to environmental stress are the lack of control over the levels and types of stimuli in the environment and constant, rapid change within the environment.

6. Privacy is a major contributor to a sense of control in our environments.

7. The overall benefits of privacy include the ability to enhance feelings of well-being and to facilitate the development of self-identity.

ASSIGNMENT
OBSERVATIONAL STUDY:
HIGH LOAD/LOW LOAD ENVIRONMENTS

Learning Objectives:
- To develop an understanding of the relationship between human behavior and the environment through observation
- To formulate conclusions about the effectiveness of the design based upon the relationship between the physical characteristics of the environment and observed behaviors of those using that environment

Learning Outcomes:
- Increased awareness of the complex nature of the physical features that make up environments, their interrelatedness, and their effects upon behavior
- Development of observational abilities

Description:
Choose two environments: one high load and one low load. Create an observational form that allows you to compare the significant physical elements and characteristics of each space, as well as the behavior of those using each space. The form should include a breakdown of the complexity (elements, features, and changes) of the observed environments. For example:

- Apparent function of the space
- Approximate number of people in the space
- Apparent ages of the people in the space
- Scale of the overall space: relative to human size, relative to expected scale for this type of space
- Scale of the architectural and interior elements
- Dominant materials used for architectural and interior elements

- Dominant and subordinate colors
- Dominant and subordinate patterns
- Dominant and subordinate textures
- Light source(s) and direction
- Types of furniture used (scale, style)
- Placement of furnishings relative to the function of the space
- Traffic patterns
- Noise levels
- Quality of the air (fresh, types of smells)
- Temperature
- Visual and physical access to the exterior (views, adjoining gardens, etc.)

Observe and describe the following behaviors:

- Movement of people in and out of the space as well as movement within the space
- How people position themselves within the space (the distances they maintain between themselves and others, as well as the differences in these distances among apparent friends, family members, and strangers)
- Levels and types of conversations (intimate, friendly, informational, confrontational, businesslike)
- Preferred areas (those areas within the space in which people seem to prefer to congregate, sit, stand, interact)
- If and how people modify the space (move furniture, adjust window treatments, change lighting, open or close doors)
- Whether space is perceived overall as positive, negative, or neutral

REFERENCES

Abercrombie, S. (1990). *A philosophy of interior design.* New York: Harper & Row.

Aiello, J. R., Baum, A. (1979). *Residential crowding and design.* New York: Plenum Press.

Altman, I. (1975). *The environment and social behavior: Privacy, personal space, territory, crowding.* Monterey, CA: Brooks Cole Publishers.

Crooks, R. L. & Stein J. (1991). *Psychology: Science, behavior, and life.* Ft. Worth, TX: Holt, Rinehart and Winston, Inc.

Cohen, S.; Evans, G. W.; Stokols, D.; & Krantz, D. S. (1986). *Behavior, health, and environmental stress.* New York: Plenum Press.

Edney, J. J. & M. A. Buda. (1976). Distinguishing territoriality and privacy: Two studies. *Human Ecology,* 4, pp. 283–296.

Evans, G. W.; L. E. Maxwell; & B. Hart. (1999). Parental language and verbal responsiveness to children in crowded homes. *Developmental Psychology,* 35, 1020–1023.

Evans, G. W.; Lepore, S. J.; & Schroeder, A. (1996). The role of interior design elements in human responses to crowding. *Journal of Personality and Social Psychology,* 70, 41–46.

Evans, G. & McCoy, J. M. (1998). When buildings don't work: the role of architecture in human health. *Journal of Environmental Psychology,* 18, 85–89.

Evans, G. W. (2001). Environmental stress and health. In A. Baum, T. A. Revenson, & J. E. Singer. *Handbook of health psychology.* Mahwah, NJ: Lawrence Erlbaum Associates.

Gauvain, M.; Altman, I.; & Fahim, H. (1983). Homes and social change: A cross-cultural analysis. In N. Feimer & S. Geller (Eds.). *Environmental psychology: Directions and perspectives.* New York: Prager.

Harris, P. B.; Werner, C. M.; Brown, B.; & Ingebritsen, D. (1995). Relocation and privacy regulation: A cross cultural analysis. *Journal of Environmental Psychology*, 15, 311–320.

Heerwagen, J. & Orians, G. H. (1993). Humans, habitats, and aesthetics. In S. Kellert and Wilson, E. O. (Eds.). *The biophilia hypothesis*. Washington: Island Press.

Kaplan, R. & S. Kaplan. (1989). *The Experience of nature: A psychological perspective*. Cambridge: Cambridge University Press.

Maslow, A. H. (1968). *Toward a psychology of being*. New York: Van Nostrand Reinhold.

McCall, S. (1975). Quality of life. *Social Indicators Research*, 2, 229–248.

Mehrabian, A. (1976). *Public places and private spaces*. New York: Basic Books, Inc.

Newell, P. (1998). A cross-cultural comparison of privacy definitions and functions: A systems approach. *Journal of Environmental Psychology*, 18, 357–371.

Pawlukiewicz, M. & Myerson, D. L. (2002). ULI/NMHC/AIA Joint Forum on Housing Density. Urban Land Institute.

Pedersen, D. M. (1997). Psychological functions of privacy. *Journal of Environmental Psychology*. 17, 147–156.

Rybcznski, W. (1995). *City life: Urban expectations in a new world*. New York: Touchstone.

Seyle, H. (1974). *Stress without distress*. New York: Signet Books.

Stolkos, D. (1972). A social psychological model of human crowding phenomena. *American Institute of Planners*, 38, 72–83.

Ulrich, R. (1995). Effects of healthcare design on wellness: Theory, and recent scientific research. In S. O. Marberry (Ed.), "Innovations in healthcare design." New York: Van Nostrand Reinhold, 88–104.

Veitch, R. & Arkkelin, D. (1995). *Environmental psychology: An interdisciplinary perspective*. New Jersey: Prentice Hall.

Westin, A. F. (1967). *Privacy and freedom*. New York: Antheneum.

Worldwatch Institute. (2000) *The State of the World*. New York: W. W. Norton & Company.

Young, L. (1966). "Life among the giants." New York: McGraw Hill.

What was once commonplace—the possibility of escape from the crowd for privacy and rest—has all but vanished. The crowds, once restricted to the streets and borders of the public domain, now follow unbidden into the solitary, private domain.

**CHERMAYEFF AND ALEXANDER
(1963, P. 74)**

CHAPTER

2

The Concept of Privacy and Its Role in Our Lives

EVOLUTION OF THE CONCEPT OF PRIVACY

The concept of privacy is studied and discussed with great interest in science, literature, and even politics. Certain rights to privacy are protected by the Constitution of the United States, which ensures our "rights to be secure in persons, houses,

papers and effects against unreasonable searches and seizures." However, the concept of privacy as it relates to the design of the built environment is relatively new. Architect Witold Rybczynski (1986) reminds us that historically, even in our most intimate spaces, privacy has not always been a factor. He writes "it was unusual for someone in the 16th century to have his own room. It was more than a hundred years later that rooms to which the individual could retreat from public view came into being—they were called 'privacies'" (p. 18). Rybczynski describes privacy as an essential component of comfort, without which "our dwellings will indeed be machines instead of homes" (p. 232).

A number of privacy theorists have studied this perspective of privacy as a necessary quality of our environments. We will discuss four of them in this chapter: Alan F. Westin, Irwin Altman, Darhl Pederson, and Patricia Brierley

Newell. These four privacy theorists provide explanations about what privacy is, what it does, how we express our needs for privacy, and how our privacy needs vary and why. (See **Box 2.1**).

---

1. What factors cause us to need privacy?

2. What are the benefits of privacy?

3. How do our privacy needs vary and why?

4. How can the built environment be designed to provide for our diverse privacy needs?

Box 2.1 The four questions designers must ask in order to understand the diverse privacy needs of those for whom they design. Question #3 will be addressed in this chapter.

Chapter 2 also defines the types of privacy and how each type provides specific psychological benefits. Finally, we will examine behaviors that we use to achieve desired levels of privacy called privacy mechanisms, and what happens when our privacy mechanisms fail to work and we have more interaction with others than desired.

Privacy Theorists

Political scientist Alan Westin (1967) is one of the first contemporary authors to explore the concept of privacy and its benefits in the context of modern society. Westin identified four types of privacy and their related benefits to human health and well-being. His work has been expanded upon by a number of psychologists including Altman, Newell, and Pederson.

Environmental psychologist Irwin Altman (1975) developed an influential contemporary theory concerning the concept of privacy. Altman views privacy as the central motivational force driving our needs for personal space and territorial behavior, as well as our responses to crowding. Altman's perspective helps to place the concept of privacy in a contemporary context for designers.

Both Westin (1967) and Altman (1975) established privacy as a universal need by cross-cultural examination of behaviors used to communicate the need for and to achieve desired levels of privacy. Psychologist Patricia Brierley Newell (1998) has extended these studies of cross-cultural comparisons of privacy, and Newell's research findings support the assertion that the need for privacy is universal. Her findings also reveal that privacy needs are expressed and recognized differently according to culture. Central to Newell's explanations about privacy is the assertion that privacy is essential to the maintenance of overall well-being.

Psychologist Darhl M. Pederson (1997) studies how privacy needs are met through the various types of privacy that we seek. Pederson expanded upon Westin's theories to provide a more comprehensive explanation of how privacy contributes to our physical and psychological health and development.

Each of these privacy theorists offers an important piece to the puzzle of how our privacy needs vary and why. We will now take a more in-depth look at their contributions to the knowledge base of privacy information.

Alan F. Westin

Westin (1967) asserts that our basic needs for privacy are genetically based and therefore universal. However, he views our modern attitudes towards privacy and our changing needs for privacy as the result of the conditions, demands, and sociopolitical influences of contemporary society. He explains that although primitive societies rely upon the close physical presence of others in the tribe, family, or larger community for survival, most contemporary societies—especially the United States—tend to emphasize the rights and needs of individuals.

Westin examined the findings of anthropological studies of the lifestyles of primitive societies. These findings suggest that privacy, in the sense that it means physical separation from others, simply does not exist. This does not mean that individuals within primitive societies have no privacy needs. These studies indicate that the need to interact with others, to control the degree of that interaction as well as the need for personal privacy, is common among all societies. The ways or cultural norms, however, with which different individuals within societies express these needs and the ways that their cultures accommodate these needs have varied greatly throughout history.

Westin explains some of the reasons privacy needs are different in the modern world: "The developments associated with the rise of modern industrial societies—such as the nuclear family living in individual households, urbanization and the anonymity of city life, mobility in work and residences, the weakening of religious authority over individuals—all provide greater situations of physical and psychological privacy than do the milieu and belief-system of primitive man.

But modern societies have also brought develop-ments that work against the achievement of pri-vacy: density and crowding of populations; large bureaucratic organizational life; popular moods of alienation and insecurity that can lead to desires for new 'total' relations; new instruments of physical, psychological, and data surveil-lance . . ." (p. 21). Westin equates the ability to choose and to achieve one's desired levels of pri-vacy in modern society with personal and politi-cal freedom, which, as we discussed in Chapter 1, have been equated by other theorists with quality of life issues associated with privacy and related human needs.

Irwin Altman

According to Altman (1975), privacy is essential to understanding the relationships between environments and human behavior. He explains that "environment and behavior are closely intertwined, almost to the point of being insep-arable" (p. 205). In this context, Altman's theory examines not just how the environment acts upon people, but also how people act upon the environment. Because this process is dynamic, always changing, and subject to social, cultural, and individual differences, we use a variety of behaviors to interact with the environment and with other people in that environment. These behaviors, termed *privacy mechanisms* by Altman (1975) will be discussed later in this chapter as they relate to how we communicate our needs for privacy.

Altman places privacy at the center of the discussion of environment and behavior. Instead of the traditional view of privacy as an excluding process, Altman (1975) views it as "a changing self/other boundary-regulation process in which a person or group sometimes wants to be separated from others and sometimes wants to be in contact with others" (p. 207). This per-spective calls for designers to create what Altman refers to as **responsive environments** that provide the opportunity to alter one's sur-

roundings to accommodate changing needs for togetherness and separateness. These respon-sive environments, says Altman, should be designed to be flexible in such a way that they allow control over interaction with others and thus respond to our changing needs for privacy.

Patricia Brierley Newell

Newell (1998) developed a systems model of pri-vacy in which privacy is viewed as part of a group or system of behaviors used to promote survival and physical, psychological, and cognitive devel-opment. Newell explains that a systems approach is useful in studying privacy because it allows us to consider the effects of interacting variables, such as time, as well as the physical, psychologi-cal, and social changes occurring within the indi-vidual and the environment. This systems approach enables Newell to structure the multi-disciplinary ideas, assumptions, concepts, and theories involving privacy into a model that can be used for further research.

Central to Newell's systems model of privacy is the hypothesis that the need for privacy is both genetically grounded and environmentally dependent. Newell asserts that the desire for privacy is universal because it helps establish and maintain "healthy internal physiological and cognitive functioning, subjectively des-cribed as 'well-being'" (p. 359). Using this model, Newell studied cross-cultural compar-isons of the reasons that we seek privacy and the benefits of privacy. The studies reveal that ". . . there are cultural universals operating to promote survival and development and that an occasional condition of privacy, as and when required, contributes to the process" (p. 358).

Dahrl M. Pederson

Pederson (1997) examined how and why people seek privacy. He asserts that the various types of privacy that we desire provide different benefits, and that some types of privacy provide these benefits better than do other types (see Types of

FYI Cross-cultural studies were conducted to determine definitions of privacy, qualities of privacy, and benefits of privacy among male and female college students in Ireland, Senegal, and the United States. The findings from this study support the theory that privacy is therapeutic and helps us to recover from psychological distress. These findings emphasized the ability of the individual to choose whether or not to interact with others. People from different cultures indicated that they need privacy when they are sad, anxious, angry, tired, or grieving, as well as when they need to focus and concentrate. They also agreed that the most important quality of privacy is "not being disturbed" and that the primary aftereffect of the experience of privacy is a feeling of being more relaxed followed by feeling refreshed. Newell explains, "For those who were stressed or distressed initially, to feel relaxed after enjoying a period of privacy does indeed indicate a positive therapeutic effect."

(Newell 1998, p. 367)

Privacy). Pederson (1997) further asserts that one important reason we seek privacy is because privacy behaviors can be used to meet important psychological needs such as autonomy, confiding, rejuvenation, contemplation, and creativity.

Similar to Westin, Altman, and Newell, Pederson (1997) concludes that although there are commonalities in our needs for privacy, individual differences affect the ways in which we use privacy. Therefore the psychological benefits are also likely to vary according to these individual differences as well as from circumstance to circumstance and from time to time.

Both Westin (1967) and Pederson (1997) defined the types of privacy that appear to be universal as well as the functions or benefits of privacy. Westin first identified four privacy

types, and Pederson later expanded upon Westin's model to identify six types. The benefits of privacy, discussed in Chapter 1, will be reviewed and discussed here in the context of these privacy types.

TYPES OF PRIVACY

Westin's four types of privacy are

- *Solitude: the need to be alone and free from observation by others.*
- *Intimacy: the need to be alone with others such as friends, lovers, or family without interference from unwanted intrusions.*
- *Anonymity: the freedom to be in public while at the same time free from identification or surveillance by others.*
- *Reserve: the need to limit communication about ourselves, which is protected by the cooperation of others.*

Based upon his research of Westin's four types of privacy, Pederson separated Westin's definition of "solitude" into two more distinctive types of privacy: solitude and isolation. He also separated Westin's "intimacy" into two types: intimacy with friends and intimacy with family.

Pederson's six types of privacy are

- *Solitude refers to situations in which others cannot hear or see what we are doing— retreating to our bedrooms or offices and closing the door.*
- *Isolation involves separating ourselves physically from others by means of physical distance—going for a long drive alone, hiking deep into the wilderness, or walking along a deserted beach.*
- *Intimacy with family involves being alone with our family and excluding others— going to a family "getaway" location such as a beach house or mountain cabin.*

- ***Intimacy with friends** is the same as intimacy with family except that we are alone with friends to the exclusion of others.*
- ***Anonymity** is the experience of being "lost in a crowd." For example, when we are surrounded by strangers and therefore don't expect to be recognized, such as when we go to a movie, sporting event, or concert alone.*
- ***Reserve** is verbally controlling information about ourselves such as withholding our feelings, opinions, and ideas rather than expressing them to others.*

Both Westin's and Pederson's descriptions of the types of privacy have this in common: solitude, anonymity, reserve, and isolation. These types of privacy involve our desire to be separate from others, while intimacy (with family, lovers, or friends) involves our desire to be alone with selected individuals or groups away from the intrusions of others. (See **Figure 2.1**).

You will recall that the general benefits of privacy for well-being and self-identity discussed in Chapter 1 were divided into more specific benefits by both Westin (personal autonomy, emotional release, self-evaluation, limited and protected communication) and Pederson (contemplation, autonomy, rejuvenation, creativity, recovery, catharsis, and concealment). Pederson (1997) takes this process one step further to describe how the six types of privacy provide these specific benefits.

According to Pederson, *solitude* provides the best opportunity for creativity and contempla-

tion. Solitude also contributes to rejuvenation and feelings of autonomy. *Isolation* also provides the opportunity for contemplation and autonomy as well as for rejuvenation. The most common benefit of *anonymity* is recovery, followed by autonomy. *Reserve* also contributes to feelings of recovery as well as providing for concealment. Finally, *intimacy with family* and *intimacy with friends* can provide for recovery and rejuvenation. (See **Table 2.1**).

Information about the types of privacy we seek and the specific benefits that each type helps designers to plan spaces that meet various individual privacy needs, thus helping to create the type of responsive environments to which Altman (1975) refers. For example, according to Pederson's research, if the goal is to design a hospital patient lounge that helps to promote recovery and rejuvenation, it should be designed to provide spaces for *intimacy* with patients' families and friends. Although this may appear at first to be a general, common sense consideration, it is often rare to find such spaces in hospital patient lounges. However, when designers are aware of the benefits of this type of privacy to the patients' health, as well as an understanding of the physical qualities that can provide intimacy, these spaces can be designed with sensitivity and skill.

The next step in understanding how and why our privacy needs vary involves the behaviors that we use to communicate our privacy needs to others and to achieve our desired levels of interaction. These behaviors illustrate both the universal qualities of the privacy process as

Figure 2.1 The six types of privacy can be categorized according to the goals of privacy.

Goals of Privacy:	***To be separate from others***	***To be alone with selected individuals***
Types of Privacy that meet goals:	*Isolation, Solitude Anonymity, Reserve*	*Intimacy with family Intimacy with friends*

Benefits of Privacy

TYPES OF PRIVACY	MAJOR BENEFITS
Isolation	contemplation, autonomy, rejuvenation, emotional release, self-evaluation, catharsis
Solitude	creativity, contemplation, autonomy, rejuvenation, emotional release, self-evaluation, catharsis
Intimacy	recovery, rejuvenation
Anonymity	personal autonomy
Reserve	recovery, concealment, limited and protected communication

Table 2.1 Each type of privacy provides specific benefits.

well as the differences in the ways we express our privacy needs. By developing an awareness of how people use these behaviors, designers can better understand what types of privacy to plan for in their designs.

Behaviors That We Use to Achieve Desired Levels of Privacy

How do we let others know when we need privacy? What behaviors do we use to achieve our desired levels of privacy? How do we use our physical environments to help us achieve privacy?

These questions are central to Irwin Altman's (1975) privacy theories. Altman points out that it is important to make the distinction between desired privacy and achieved privacy. **Desired privacy** is our subjective feeling about the ideal level of interaction we wish to have with others at any given time. **Achieved privacy** is the actual amount of contact we have with others as a result of those interactions.

Altman describes a variety of privacy mechanisms that enable us to communicate to others the types of privacy that we desire. These mechanisms also help us to actually achieve our desired types or levels of privacy. These four privacy mechanisms are: verbal behavior, nonverbal behavior, use of cultural patterns of accepted behavior, and use of the physical environment (personal space and territoriality).

Verbal Behavior

The spoken word is our primary means of social interaction. As with all types of human communication, the way that we use words to convey our desired levels of privacy are complex. When we tell others, "Go away," or, "Leave me alone," the meaning of the words is clear. We want to be away from contact and interaction with them. Equally clear is the meaning of "Please come in," and, "Let's talk," as an indication that we want to interact. In this way, verbal behavior helps us to decide whether to approach or avoid another person or a setting. Often, we use verbal behavior to communicate that our desired levels of privacy were not achieved. We may say, "I thought I told you to leave me alone," or, "Can't you read the do-not-disturb sign?" Or we may negotiate for privacy by saying, "Give me a few minutes, and I'll get back to you," or, "If I can just have a few minutes of your time, then I promise to leave you alone."

Altman (1975) asserts that it is not just the *content* (what we say) but also the *structure* (how we say it) that truly communicates our needs for privacy. Structural aspects of our verbal behavior are more subtle than content aspects. We use the structure of our speech to emphasize or mask our intentions. The pitch of our voices, rate and loudness of our speech, and the vocabulary that we choose all contribute to the meaning of our words. Using code words or a different language so that we can communicate with a friend or lover while excluding others is another example of structure.

Nonverbal Behavior

Nonverbal behavior involves using the complex positioning and movement of the body, commonly called "body language," to communicate. Using the body to convey messages is our oldest form of communication. Whether we use facial expressions, head movements, posture, gestures, or arm and leg positions, the body communicates on levels both obvious and subtle. We lean toward someone with whom we want to communicate and away from someone we wish to avoid. We smile and nod to indicate our openness and agreement, and we frown and shake our heads to indicate that we are closed to discussion or dislike the interaction. We position ourselves in a doorway, arms crossed across our chest, feet wide apart, our body rigid to send the unmistakable message, "Do not enter." Or we stand in that same doorway, arms open wide to say, "Do come in."

Perhaps the most interesting nonverbal behavior that humans use to communicate is eye contact. If someone stares at you intensely you may perceive one of two messages: that they desire to interact with you or that they pose a threat. When combined with other nonverbal behaviors, however, such as posture and gestures, the message becomes more clearly defined. By avoiding eye contact, we communicate that we don't want to be disturbed or that we are uncomfortable. In this way we use eye contact to symbolically regulate interpersonal distances (Veitch & Arkkelin 1995).

Cultural Patterns of Accepted Behavior

Altman (1975) describes behaviors and practices considered typical or representative of a group or society as cultural patterns of accepted behavior. All societies have behaviors and practices that are considered typical or representative of the society's usage to regulate interaction. The rules and standards of conduct that specify what is appropriate and what is inappropriate within a society typically include rewards for conforming to these norms and punishments for violating them. Privacy is often dependent upon these norms. When an individual or group desires privacy, they let it be known by using a variety of privacy mechanisms. They may verbally state their desire for privacy, use body language, or manipulate the physical space according to their accepted cultural norms. Response to these cues may also depend upon cultural norms. To afford others privacy, we may avoid the individuals and the space they occupy. We may lower our eyes, look away, or maintain a culturally accepted distance. If someone is having a private telephone conversation, we may behave as if we do not hear it, even though we can hear it clearly. In some cultures, it is not acceptable to touch strangers casually while in other cultures it is common practice, especially in crowded situations. Displays of intimacy between lovers in public may be totally accepted in one culture but considered inappropriate in others.

It is important that interior designers understand the cultural norms that define and regulate privacy as they apply to those for whom they design. For example, cultural norms apply not only to societies but also to groups. Families may have rules governing respect of the individual privacy needs of family members. Clubs, sororities, and fraternities may have practices that are entirely different from the dominant cultural norms. Close friends may forgo many of the accepted cultural norms that facilitate privacy in lieu of their own code of behavior. For example, a very close friend may enter another friend's home without observing the territorial markers of ringing a doorbell or knocking on the door first.

Use of the Physical Environment

Use of the physical environment involves the ways that we position ourselves in a space relative to others as well as the ways in which we manipulate the physical qualities of spaces to control interaction. The ways that we use our surroundings to communicate who we are, what we want, and how we feel are of special interest to design professionals. Altman's view that a reciprocal connection exists between people and environments recognizes the complex person-to-person and person-to-environment interactions constantly taking place within the spaces that we design.

Two environmental behaviors identified by Altman as privacy mechanisms are personal space and territoriality. Each of these privacy mechanisms helps us to use the physical environment to control interactions with others.

to the body and we take it with us wherever we go. The term *personal space bubbles* has been widely accepted to describe these invisible boundaries. However, the term has been called misleading by some researchers (Aiello 1987, McAndrews 1993) in part because it evokes images of bubbles bouncing off of one another as people interact, when in fact these invisible boundaries are always changing to accommodate the changing needs of the individual.

Proxemics

Edward T. Hall's (1969) concept of **proxemics**, the study of how we use space to communicate based upon social and cultural influences, examines the spacing or distance that we naturally place between ourselves and others in different situations. The concept of personal space is closely related to Hall's distance zones because the size of our invisible boundaries changes depending upon the circumstances and the environment. These distance zones or personal space bubbles extend from the body creating a

PERSONAL SPACE AND TERRITORIALITY

Both personal space and territoriality allow us to personalize and position the environment to regulate interaction and communication. Personal space also helps regulate physical access to our bodies.

Personal Space

The physical distances that we naturally place between ourselves and others is not random, but rather a reflection of the dynamics that occur between people within their environments (Hall 1969, Sommer 1969). Robert Sommer (1969) uses the term **personal space** to describe the "invisible boundaries surrounding a person's body into which intruders may not come" (p. 26). Sommer refers to personal space as a "portable territory" (p. 27) because it is attached

FYI Hall (1969) speculates that human beings may be categorized as belonging to either a contact culture or a noncontact culture. According to Hall, contact cultures (specifically Arab, Asian, and Latin) prefer closer personal space distances than noncontact cultures (Northern European and North American). Territoriality is also expressed differently between contact and noncontact cultures with contact cultures relying primarily upon physical barriers and symbols to mark and control territories, while noncontact cultures rely more upon social norms and practices. Based upon these observations, Hall reasons that contact cultures may be more tolerant of crowding than noncontact cultures.

boundary around us that we use to regulate how open and accessible we are to others. These bubbles are not necessarily spherical. They tend to extend further from the front of our bodies and are narrower at the sides and back. They are not static; they expand and contract according to our levels of comfort and ever changing needs for interaction and regulation of access to our bodies. Although all cultures exhibit some form of this natural spacing, Hall asserts that the actual distances vary from culture to culture. Hall's distance zones are based upon studies of middle-class, healthy adults, mainly from the north-eastern United States. He identified the four spatial zones that most Americans use for social interaction. Each distance zone has a near and a far phase. (See **Figure 2.2**).

Hall's Distance Zones

- *Intimate distance* is an area extending zero to 18 inches from the body, providing a great deal of sensory information about us to others. Sounds, smells, physical contact, and communication via body language are all considerable at this distance. Intimate distance is typically reserved for interaction between lovers, as well as for comforting and protecting. It is also the distance used between parents and infants or very young children. Intrusion by unwanted persons into our intimate zone is considered unpleasant and often offensive. When forced into this close range physical contact with others such as in a crowded elevator, we tend to compensate for the intrusion by standing rigid, staring either up or down, or holding our brief cases, handbags, or shopping bags close and in front of our bodies.

- *Personal distance* extends 18 inches to approximately four feet from the body. It is the common distance for interaction among friends, and it is characteristic of the spacing we naturally place between ourselves and others in pleasant circumstances. Physical contact is possible but sounds and smells are

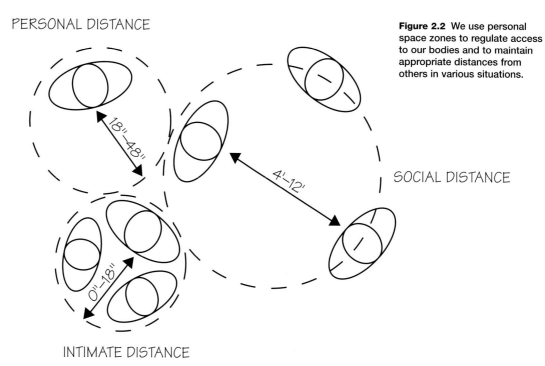

Figure 2.2 We use personal space zones to regulate access to our bodies and to maintain appropriate distances from others in various situations.

PERSONAL DISTANCE

SOCIAL DISTANCE

18"–48"

4'–12'

0"–18"

INTIMATE DISTANCE

PERSONAL SPACE BUBBLES

less noticeable than in the intimate zone. We use personal distance as a transition between the intimate zone and more formal social and public zones.

- **Social distance** *is a zone from four to twelve feet from the body. Within the closer phase of this zone (four to seven feet) we conduct impersonal business and have casual social contact. This zone is often used to determine placement of furniture in offices and public settings. The far phase of this distance (seven to twelve feet) is more formal, and physical details are less noticeable.*

- **Public distance** *is a zone extending 12 to 25 feet from the body. It is the distance we maintain in formal situations or when we feel the need to maintain a defensive or evasive position with strangers. This is the distance usually maintained by public speakers or those we regard as high-status. Many adjustments in communication are made at a public distance, including raising one's voice and exaggerating gestures. Subtle communication via eye contact and body language are less effective within this zone.*

We use these zones to regulate interaction with others and to communicate the levels of privacy that we desire when in the presence of others. According to Hall, these zones literally become an extension of our personalities. For this reason, it is important that designers consider how these zones work when designing environments that require a great deal of interaction. The space that we need to function, to be comfortable, and to maintain a sense of control over access to ourselves far exceeds the actual physical space that we occupy. As high-density and high-load environments become an increasingly large part of our everyday lives, affecting our ability to achieve our desired levels of privacy, these distance zones may provide important insights into how we can plan for privacy more effectively.

Functions of Personal Space

Because we use personal space to regulate the physical distance between ourselves and others, it is a powerful mechanism for communicating our privacy needs and achieving certain types of privacy. We especially use personal space to regulate our more intimate interactions with others.

From a functional-evolutionary perspective, it is likely that personal space served a variety of survival functions for our species throughout history. Personal space can help protect us from physical and emotional harm. For example, larger personal space zones enable us to prepare to flee from or avoid danger and lessen the impact of emotional threats. Larger personal space zones also help us regulate the amount of sensory information that we receive from others, thereby reducing the environmental load. (McAndrews 1993).

Personal Space Factors

Altman (1975) created three categories of factors that affect or are affected by our needs for personal space: individual factors, interpersonal factors, and situational factors. These factors help to explain further why our needs for privacy vary.

- **Individual factors** *include demographic characteristics, such as age, sex, socioeconomic, racial, and ethnic backgrounds; personality characteristics, such as our level of extroversion or introversion, our needs for achievement and affiliation, our personality disorders or abnormalities; personal skills, such as intelligence and creativity, our past experiences, and our current psychological and physiological states.*

- **Interpersonal factors** *include the nature of our relationships with others and our affiliation with them, including whether or not we like those with whom we are interacting or can identify with them. Interpersonal factors involve group composition, such as sex and* *ethnic backgrounds, as well as status and group size.*

- ***Situational factors*** *include the physical characteristics of a setting—the complexity, environmental load, and details, as well as the function of the space and the tasks to be performed.*

Some General Personal Space Observations

- Children have smaller personal space bubbles than adolescents or adults. Children learn gradually through interaction in different social situations the appropriate distances that they should maintain.

- Males tend to have larger personal space bubbles than females, and people tend to maintain greater distances from males as well. However, this generalization can be affected by whether the interaction is between men and women, men and men, or women and women, as well as by sexual orientation and cultural backgrounds.

- High-status individuals and groups are afforded larger personal space bubbles than lower-status individuals and groups.

- We tend to have smaller personal space bubbles when interacting with those with whom we have a positive interpersonal relationship.

- Formal environments cause us to maintain larger personal space bubbles, while familiar environments cause us to be more willing to be in close physical contact with others.

- Northern and Western European cultures as well as Americans tend to have larger personal space bubbles than Middle Eastern, Latin, and Mediterranean cultures.

(Altman 1975, Hall 1969, Sommer 1969)

Territoriality

Territoriality involves the need to control a fixed geographical location by laying claim to it in a variety of ways. Our motives for territorial behavior as well as the ways that we actually claim and control our territories vary according to the individual and the circumstances. While both humans and animals exhibit territorial behaviors for biological and social reasons, human territories are more complex. Human territories can range from our favorite chair, to our own room, to our neighborhood, and expand all the way to our country and even our planet. There are few places or things that humans have not claimed as theirs either individually or in groups. The history of humanity is often told through the acquisition and control of territory.

Human territoriality is multilayered. It provides for a variety of needs, including safety and security, mating, raising of children, acquisition of food, development of self-identity, and even indicator of status. One of the major functions of territorial behavior for humans is the acquisition and regulation of privacy (Altman 1975). We use territorial behavior to regulate social interactions by controlling physical space. Through personalization of our territories, we develop, manage, and communicate our self-identity. Additionally, as illustrated by the concept of "home field advantage," we tend to perform tasks better, feel more comfortable, and have a greater sense of well-being in our own territories.

Territorial Markers

We use **territorial markers** to define physical boundaries for ourselves and others (Altman 1975). From a practical viewpoint, territorial markers are used to communicate ownership and to personalize a space. These markers can be as subtle as leaving a newspaper on our seat to save our place, or as obvious as a "private property: do not enter" sign. Fences, walls, gates, doors, locks, landscaping, signs, personal

Figure 2.3 We use territorial markers to mark boundaries and restrict access to ourselves. Often, we use personal objects to extend our territories. Courtesy of Michael Littrel.

belongings, and human presence all serve as recognized territorial markers. Interior design students may occupy the same drafting table in a certain studio every day, spreading their belongings (markers) to adjacent tables to indicate their need for space and to communicate the level of interaction they want. (See **Figure 2.3**).

Design, when used to personalize and differentiate spaces, is a powerful tool to create and organize territorial markers. In this way, territorial markers reflect the values and personal characteristics of the individual or group.

Types of Territories

Human beings have multiple types of territories. The territories differ depending upon how central and important they are to the owners, the functions they serve, their degree of ownership and control, and their relative permanence. The type of privacy that we desire, as well as the ability to achieve desired privacy, is affected by the type of territories that we occupy at any given time. Altman (1975) identified three basic types of territories that account for these differences: primary, secondary, and public territories.

Primary territories are owned and controlled exclusively by the occupant(s) on a relatively permanent basis making these territories

central to the lives of the occupant(s). Our home is the most commonly recognized primary territory, and it is protected by law against invasion. Other spaces that are often considered to be primary territories include a private office or work space (whether at or away from home).

Altman asserts that violation of a primary territory can affect our self-identity, especially if it is repeated and we are unable to make the adjustments necessary to prevent the violation. This is because primary territories are considered an extension of the self. As illustrated by the plight of the homeless in modern society, the lack of a primary territory means that they have no place to call home, little control over access to themselves, and therefore nowhere to retreat for the basic human needs of safety and security. Primary territories are also our most common indicators of status. In general, the larger the primary territory, the greater is the perception of status.

Primary territories are powerful regulators of privacy. As a primary territory, the home is usually made up of a combination of types of territories controlled by different individuals within the family or group. There may be several smaller primary territories such as bedrooms or offices and multiple secondary territories such as the kitchen, family room, and living room. Each of these rooms symbolizes a certain level of expected privacy as defined by the culture, society, and individuals using the spaces.

Secondary territories are less central to the lives of the users because the users are not the exclusive owners or may have only perceived ownership. Occupancy in secondary territories is temporary. These territories often have public availability but are privately controlled, making them a bridge between the total control of primary territories and the relative lack of control of public territories. Therefore, secondary territories have greater potential for misunderstanding and conflict of use.

Examples of secondary territories include the neighborhood bar, entranceways and corridors of buildings, reception areas in offices, classrooms, and the areas mentioned earlier within the home. Occupancy of secondary territories is often equated with temporary ownership and control. If the territorial markers, verbal and nonverbal behaviors, or the social norms governing behavior in secondary territories are misunderstood or ignored, conflict is often the result. Objects within secondary territories are often claimed and used as primary territories. One's usual seat at the bar and a student's favorite desk in the classroom are common examples.

Personal space zones are commonly used to restrict interaction in secondary territories. Verbal and nonverbal behaviors are also frequently used in secondary territories to communicate one's desired level of privacy.

Public territories are generally available to anyone on a temporary basis. They include beaches, parks, libraries, shopping malls, playgrounds, and most facilities defined as "public." Use of these territories is restricted by laws, codes, customs, and regulations. For example, a public beach may have open access during the day but not overnight. Similar to

secondary territories, occupancy is often equated with temporary ownership. Once we have placed our blanket or towel on the beach, we have marked our territory and expect that territory to be "ours" for as long as we have it marked. We rely on social norms and customs to regulate privacy in public territories, but control in these settings is fragile and subject to invasion with little recourse except to defend it verbally or physically or to relocate.

Defending Our Territories

The ways that we defend our territories depend upon the type of territory, the type of encroachment, and the cultural norms and practices that apply. When a self or group boundary is unwarrantedly crossed, we may behave aggressively (defending our home against a break-in), or we may simply move to another location (when someone sits too close to us in the theater). In environments where relocation is not possible, such as on an airplane or other high-density spaces, we may withdraw psychologically and physically into a tighter personal space bubble. Regardless of the boundary violation, the result is that our achieved privacy is less than our desired privacy, and we will usually take action to remedy the situation (Altman 1975).

Using Territoriality to Achieve Desired Privacy

Territoriality provides ways to use our environments to regulate social interaction and therefore to help us achieve our desired types of privacy. *Solitude* and *intimacy with family* and *intimacy with friends* are usually easier to achieve in primary territories because these territories offer the best opportunity to control the environment and interactions. The ability to control our environments by either modifying or adjusting the physical elements or by regulating our exposure to the environment is more easily achieved in primary territories. It is expected that we can exert some degree of control over our homes or our room, which in turn contributes to our ability to achieve privacy.

Intimacy, either with family or friends, is often also achieved in secondary territories, especially those offering the opportunity to use privacy mechanisms effectively. Control is possible in some secondary territories if they have been designed to provide choices of spatial availability and control over the degree of visual and acoustical exposure.

Anonymity is best achieved in public territories where free access provides the ability to become lost in the crowd. However, control of the environment is much more difficult to achieve in public territories, and that difficulty can cause anonymity to be a temporary experience.

Since *reserve* involves limiting communication about ourselves and withholding information about ourselves, our feelings, opinions, and ideas rather than expressing them to others, it may be achieved in any type of territory. Primary territories provide greater opportunities for control and therefore greater ability to achieve reserve. However, reserve can also be achieved in secondary and public territories with the cooperation of others. (See **Table 2.2**).

DENSITY AND CROWDING

When our privacy mechanisms fail to work and we have more interaction with others than desired, the result is often a negative psychological state called crowding. Chapter 1 introduced the concept of crowding as it relates to population density and control of the environment. We will now explore this relationship further as it relates to the use of privacy mechanisms.

Density

You will recall that density is a physical condition involving space limitations and the number of people within that space. Density is increasing as the human population continues to grow dramatically and move to urban areas. Higher density urban living is necessary to provide housing to this rapidly increasing segment of

LINK
For information about how *reserve* is accommodated by the recently legislated Health Insurance Portability and Accountability Act (HIPAA), see Chapter 6, page 147.

Table 2.2 This table illustrates how privacy mechanisms are used to achieve desired levels of privacy.

Desired levels of privacy, privacy mechanisms, and achieved levels of privacy

DESIRED PRIVACY	PRIVACY MECHANISMS	ACHIEVED PRIVACY
ability to control access to oneself	personal space, verbal and nonverbal behavior	solitude, intimacy, territoriality, cultural norms
ability to separate ourselves physically from other people	personal space, territoriality	isolation, solitude, intimacy
ability to control information about ourselves	verbal and nonverbal behavior, cultural norms, personal space, territoriality	anonymity, reserve
ability to interact with selected individuals	verbal and nonverbal behavior, personal space, territoriality, cultural norms	intimacy with family and friends

society, making the effects of crowding a concern among urban planners, architects, and interior designers.

The higher the density or more people within a space, the greater the environmental load. As the level of uncertainty and unpredictability about our environments increase with density, the ability to control the levels of stimulation and the interactions we experience in these high load environments usually decreases. Higher density increases the probability that we will have physical contact with and will have to interact with others. As a result, there is also an increased probability that our personal space will be violated, our territories encroached upon, and ultimately that we will be less likely to achieve our desired privacy.

Two types of density have been identified by environmental psychologists: social density and spatial density. While both refer to the number of people per unit of space, **social density** refers to changes in the number of people in a fixed space, and **spatial density** refers to the same number of people occupying spaces of different sizes (McAndrews 1993).

To illustrate the difference between social density and spatial density, suppose you are waiting at the airport—a public territory—to board a flight that is late. You claim a temporary secondary territory, a seat away from the main traffic area to provide your desired type of privacy in this environment: anonymity. It is important to note that the type of privacy you desire in this environment depends upon whether you are alone, with a friend or loved one, or with a group of people. However, since you are alone and do not expect or want to be recognized by others in this environment, you pull out a book and wait. The ebb and flow of people as they arrive and depart the waiting area creates a constant change in *social density*. When a plane arrives, the area fills with people in motion, interacting, and communicating. The noise levels rise and the environmental load increases dramatically. Then, as

the travelers disperse, the area becomes almost deserted and the environmental load decreases. As a temporary observer, you may experience the changes in social density in the waiting area differently from someone who works there. The airport worker will most likely have adapted to the constant changes in social density, while you may find it distracting or even interesting.

Now, suppose you have finally boarded your flight, taking your seat in the middle of the row with strangers on both sides. During your flight, you establish—or try to establish—your seat as a primary territory. However, because the airplane is a secondary territory, you do not have complete control over your environment, and your personal space may be invaded repeatedly. Upon arrival, you and the 400 other passengers move through the airport to baggage claim where the *spatial density* may decrease. Later, you may go to a restaurant or to a concert that also seats approximately 400 people. Each time you share a different sized space with the same number of people, the *spatial density* changes. Four hundred people in an airplane provide for a very different physical and psychological experience from 400 people in a restaurant or 400 people in a concert setting. As *spatial density* changes, you must adjust to the corresponding changes in available personal space, territory, and privacy. (See **Figure 2.4**).

Social density changes with the number of people with whom we must deal in a given environment while *spatial density* changes with the size of the environments in which we must deal with a fixed number of people. *Social density* will vary in most environments. Rarely do the same number of people always occupy a given space. Often, as with many office environments, more people are added to an existing limited space, requiring adaptation, adjustment, and a reconfiguration of territories. When *social density* increases, the interpersonal distances between people usually decrease. This means we have less personal space, smaller territories, or may

Figure 2.4 The ebb and flow of people as they arrive and depart the waiting area of an airport creates a constant change in *social density.* Keystone/Getty Images.

lose our territories altogether. The result is often a feeling of lack of control, loss of privacy, and crowding. (Naz Kaya 1999).

Spatial density varies with the type of environment, specifically with its size relative to its function. The function and use of space will change considerably when a family of four moves from a four-bedroom home to a one-bedroom home. Physical and psychological adaptations and adjustments must be made to accommodate the changes in density. Personal space zones overlap, territories are invaded, and the ability to achieve privacy is greatly diminished. If the family of four moves instead from a one-bedroom home to a four-bedroom home, adaptations and adjustments must also be made. But greater spatial resources will provide more options for establishing territory, maintaining personal space, and achieving privacy. (See **Table 2.3**).

Table 2.3 Differences in social density and spatial density.

Social Density and Spatial Density

SOCIAL DENSITY	SPATIAL DENSITY
Changes in the number of people in a fixed space	The same number of people occupying spaces of different sizes
Is rarely a constant number	Changes with the size of environments in which we must deal with fixed numbers of people
Interpersonal distances decrease as social density increases resulting in less personal space, smaller territories, feeling of lack of control, loss of desired privacy, and crowding*	Requires that we adjust to changes in available personal space, territory, and privacy

*American Architecture Academy

Crowding

Changes in social density and spatial density can affect stress levels and contribute to feelings of crowding. These effects are dependent upon the number of people in the space, the size of the space, function and activities within the space, and individual and cultural factors. As discussed in Chapter 1, crowding is a psychological response to overstimulation caused by too much interaction with others within a given space. The interpersonal dimension of privacy and the multipurpose use of privacy mechanisms to alleviate crowding illustrates that privacy is used for other purposes than just "being alone." We use privacy mechanisms (individually or in combinations) to attempt to control or alleviate feelings of crowding. For example, we may tell others to give us more room or to leave us alone (verbal behavior); we may turn away from others or avoid eye contact with them (nonverbal behavior); we may attempt to place greater interpersonal distance between ourselves and others (personal space); and we may try to expand the space that is under our control by using territorial markers such as personalization (territorial behavior). If our privacy mechanisms work, feelings of crowding may be controlled or even eliminated (Altman 1975).

The Effects of Crowding

Crowding is experienced and studied on many levels: in countries, cities, neighborhoods, public or private gatherings, large and small buildings, landscapes, homes, rooms, and even areas within individual rooms. It can occur with one other individual, in small or large groups, with family, friends, acquaintances, or strangers. Similar to the need for privacy, the effects of crowding are also influenced by a variety of personal, social, cultural, and situational factors.

Social psychologist Jonathan L. Freedman (1975) argues that crowding in human beings is neither good nor bad. He suggests that higher-density environments increase the intensity of our responses to others and to the environment. Freedman's intensity-density theory of crowding suggests that if we expect to have a good time at the concert and the concert is crowded, we will have a good time. But if we expect to have a bad time, crowding will produce a negative response. However, Freedman (1975) fails to make a distinction between density and crowding, using the terms interchangeably. As we have seen thus far, more recent research indicates that density and crowding are related but are not the same experience.

Crowding and Gender

Freedman (1975) also studied the effects of crowding based upon gender, asserting that crowding may have different effects on men than on women. For example, research comparing the differences in response between groups of men, groups of women, and mixed gender groups reveals that when placed in crowded conditions, the all-male groups became more competitive and disliked other members of the group more than women did in the same conditions. Related studies (Epstein & Karlin 1975) found that women often respond to crowded conditions with greater cooperation, while men respond by being less cooperative and more competitive. Interestingly, Freedman (1975) found that crowding produced a relatively small effect upon mixed gender groups. Specific differences in the effects of crowding upon men and women remain to be confirmed. As Freedman points out, other factors beyond gender may contribute to the responses in these studies, making a conclusion about gender differences difficult.

The Physical and Psychological Effects of Crowding

Recent studies of human responses to crowding indicate that the condition of crowding is detrimental to our physical and psychological health (Evans 2001; Evans, Rhee, Forbes, Mata Allen, Lepore 2001). Environmental psychologist

Gary W. Evans's research of the physical and psychological implications of crowding on diverse populations is among the most applicable to the design of the built environment. (Specific applications of Evans's research will be discussed in Chapter 3 as we examine the characteristics of the physical environment that promote privacy). Evans (2001) links residential crowding to environmental stress, asserting that children and individuals in captive environments, such as prisons and refugee camps are the most vulnerable to physical health problems associated with crowding. Evans (2001) also associates psychological distress with crowding. Psychological distress can be caused by social withdrawal, the principal coping strategy that we use when dealing with chronically crowded environments. Without the ability to regulate our interaction with others through the use of privacy mechanisms, we withdraw from others and are less responsive to their needs (Evans, Rhee, Forbes, Mata Allen, Lepore 2001).

**Crowding as a Temporary and
as a Chronic Condition**

Crowding can be a temporary or a chronic condition. Research on short-term crowding indicates that this experience has numerous negative effects, including affecting our ability to perform complex tasks (McAndrews 1993). Although we may be able to cope with short periods of crowding, continuous conditions of crowding can lead to psychological distress (Evans, et al. 2001). The following description of chronic crowding is an illustration: "Overcrowding means never a moment of privacy for husband and wife to build an emotional life together, never a night's sleep unbroken by crying, fretful children in a crib next to the bed, in the kitchen, in the living room, never more than 15 feet away. . . . It's nowhere to go to rest and relax. It's a television set on a broken table in the living room—the only furniture that isn't for sleeping or eating— but who can watch it, the children must go to sleep. It's nowhere to drink a glass of beer—but out in the bar. . . . It's no place to cook three meals a day but a broken stove and a leaky sink, and no place to serve them. It's nowhere for children to do homework. . . . It's no place to pretty up to call one's own. . . . It's children sent out to the streets . . . anything for a minute's peace . . . but no way to get it" (Goodwin 1964, p. 4).

FYI   Evans, Lepore, and Allen (2000) conducted research to test Hall's reasoning that because contact cultures have closer interpersonal space zones, they will also be more tolerant of crowding and that the opposite is true for noncontact cultures. The research, conducted among Anglo-Americans and African Americans (noncontact), and Vietnamese Americans and Hispanic Americans (contact), and controlled for income, reveals that crowding tolerance (the ability to cope with the negative effects of high-density living) is not necessarily related to the size of one's personal space zones. The ability of a contact or noncontact culture to tolerate crowding is not necessarily equal to their perceptions of crowding. For example, although Hispanic Americans and Vietnamese Americans perceive crowding differently from Anglo-Americans and African Americans (with people of Asian and Latin descent perceiving their homes as less crowded), they did not differ from the noncontact groups in psychological distress (levels of depression and tension) associated with crowding. All groups experienced increased levels of psychological distress in environments of higher density. Evans, et al., conclude that although different cultures may perceive crowding differently, the psychological distress experienced in relation to density does not vary by culture.

How crowded is overcrowded? There is no magical ratio of number of people to size of physical space to indicate crowding because unlike density, which is a physical condition, crowding is a psychological response. While there may be an optimal number of people to function well in any given setting (social density), and optimum sizes for different types of environments that must accommodate a given number of people (spatial density), there is no formula to determine those numbers.

Perceived Control and Crowding

If higher density environments are our future, designers must understand how environments can be designed to help mediate the effects of crowding. Psychologists Sherrod and Cohen (1979) assert that mediation of crowding requires that environments be designed to provide the perception of controllability. They explain, "Perceived control may result from actual control, but it can also result from prior control experiences, from information suggesting that control is potentially available, from self-inferences, or from any social or physical intervention that makes the environment appear more manageable or predictable" (p. 223). Perceived control may indeed be only a perception; however, according to Sherrod and Cohen, it can have significant effects on human behavior.

Environments designed to provide the ability to achieve our desired levels of privacy not only enhance our perception of controllability, but also provide real, physical options to help us control our environments and reduce the potential for feelings of crowding and its negative effects.

FINAL THOUGHTS ON THE CONCEPT OF PRIVACY

The concept of privacy as a universal need—a need shared by all human beings regardless of gender or age, social, cultural, racial, economic, or educational backgrounds—is supported by most privacy theorists. Cross-cultural studies of privacy and privacy mechanisms used by human beings confirm that the need for individual and group privacy is indeed universal. All people in all societies, regardless of the many personal and cultural variables that distinguish us, need privacy to function effectively, to develop self-identity, and to maintain well-being. These studies also confirm, however, that individual, situational, and cultural differences cause us to use privacy mechanisms to regulate access to ourselves and our interaction with others differently. Designing for privacy requires an understanding of these differences as well as an understanding of how the physical characteristics of the built environment can be designed to accommodate these differences by providing both choice and control.

KEY CONCEPTS

1. Privacy is a universal need with commonalities across cultures.

2. The space that we need to function, to be comfortable, and to maintain a sense of control over access to ourselves far exceeds the actual physical space that we occupy.

3. Types of privacy have been identified by research. Each type has been shown to provide certain psychological benefits.

4. We use privacy mechanisms (verbal, nonverbal, and environmental behaviors) to achieve our desired levels of privacy and to communicate those desires to others.

5. The ways in which we use privacy mechanisms vary according to individual, social, and cultural differences.

6. One of the major functions of territorial behavior for humans is the acquisition and regulation of privacy.

7. When our privacy mechanisms fail to work, the result is often the negative psychological condition called crowding.

8. Density and crowding are related concepts but different experiences.

ASSIGNMENT
USING PRIVACY MECHANISMS TO ALLEVIATE CROWDING

Learning Objectives:
- To use observational skills to gather information about how privacy mechanisms are used to achieve desired levels of privacy and alleviate crowding in a secondary territory
- To work as a team to organize information and apply that information to the analysis of the privacy needs of diverse populations in a secondary territory

Learning Outcomes:
- Development of observational skills
- Development of an understanding of the relationship between human behavior and the built environment
- Development of an understanding of the designer's ability to affect people and the environment
- Development of creative thinking and analysis skills
- Development of teamwork skills

Description:
Divide into teams of 3 to 5 and visit one of the following types of environments that can serve as temporary secondary territories:

1. Hospital or clinic waiting rooms

2. Hotel lobbies

3. Airport, train or bus waiting areas

Note: Each team should choose a different location.

Observation:
- The changing density levels and apparent levels of crowding that exist in the space over a one hour period.
- The types of privacy that can be accommodated by the space (solitude, anonymity, intimacy, reserve)
- The relative sizes of personal space zones and how they differ during the one hour period and according to age, gender, and group affiliation
- How territories are defined and marked according to age, gender, and group affiliation
- How effective the use of personal space zones and territoriality appear to be in alleviating conditions of crowding.

Presentation:
- Prepare quick sketches of the space observed indicating how privacy is accommodated or denied by the physical elements of the space.
- Using the sketches, prepare for the class a discussion of your observations
- Compare and contrast the observations of each team based upon the type of secondary territory observed and the individual factors of the people occupying the space.

REFERENCES
Aiello, J. R. & Baum, A. (1979). *Residential crowding and design*. New York: Harper & Row.

Aiello, J. R. (1987). Human spatial behavior. In D. Stokols and I. Altman (Eds.), *Handbook of environmental psychology*. New York: John Wiley & Sons, 359–504.

Altman, I. (1975). *The environment and social behavior: Privacy, personal space, territory, crowding.* Monterey, CA: Brooks Cole Publishers.

Chermayeff, S. & Alexander, C. (1963). *Community and privacy: Toward a new architecture of humanism.* New York, Doubleday.

Epstein, Y. M. & Karlin, R. A. (1975). Effects of acute experimental crowding. *Journal of Applied Social Psychology,* 5, 34–53.

Evans, G. W. (1979). Design implications of spatial research. In J. R. Aiello & A. Baum, (Eds.), *Residential crowding and design.* New York: Harper & Row.

Evans, G. W. (2000). Cross-cultural differences in tolerance for crowding: Fact or fiction? *Journal of Personality and Social Psychology,* 79 (2), 204–210.

Evans, G. W.; Lepore, S. J.; & Mata Allen, K. (2000). Cross-cultural differences in tolerance for crowding: Fact or fiction? *Journal of Personality and Social Psychology.* (79), 2: 204–210.

Evans, G. W.; Rhee, E.; Forbes, C.; Mata Allen, K.; & Lepore, S. J. (2001). The meaning and efficacy of social withdrawal as a strategy for coping with chronic residential crowding. *Journal of Environmental Psychology.* 20 (4), 336–342.

Evans, G. W. (2001). Environmental stress and health. In A. Baum, T. A. Revenson & J. E. Singer, (Eds.), *Handbook of health psychology.* New Jersey: Lawrence Erlbaum Associates.

Freedman, J. L. (1975). *Crowding and behavior.* San Francisco: W. H. Freeman.

Goodwin, J. (1964). What is a slum? *The Independent* (1964, February) p. 4, (permission from Lyle Stuart, Inc.) In R. Sommer, *Personal space: A behavioral basis of design.* Prentice Hall: 1969.

Hall, Edward T. (1969). *The hidden dimension.* New York: Anchor, Doubleday.

Harris, P. B.; Werner, C. M.; Brown, B.; & Ingebritsen, D. (1995). Relocation and privacy regulation: A cross-cultural analysis. *Journal of Environmental Psychology,* 15, 311–320.

Hopstock, P. J.; Aiello, J. R.; & Baum, A. (1979). Residential crowding research. In J. R. Aiello & A. Baum, (Eds.), *Residential crowding and design.* New York: Plenum Press.

Kaya, N. & Feyzan, E. (1999). Invasion of personal space under condition of short term crowding: A case study on an automatic teller machine. *Journal of Environmental Psychology.* 19 (2), 183–189.

Maslow, A. H. (1968). *Toward a psychology of being.* New York: Van Nostrand.

McAndrews, F. T. (1993). *Environmental psychology.* Belmont, CA. Brooks Cole.

Newell, P. (1998). A cross-cultural comparison of privacy definitions and functions: A systems approach. *Journal of Environmental Psychology,* 18, 357–371.

Pedersen, D. M. (1997). Psychological functions of privacy. *Journal of Environmental Psychology.* 17, 147–156.

Pedersen, D. M. (1999). Model for types of privacy by privacy functions. *Journal of Environmental Psychology.* (19) 4, 397–405.

Rybczynski, Witold. (1986). *Home: A short history of an idea.* New York: Viking Penguin Inc.

Sherrod, D. R. & Cohen, S. (1979). Density, personal control, and design. In J. R. Aiello & A. Baum, (Eds.), *Residential crowding and design.* New York: Plenum Press.

Sommer, R. (1969). *Personal space.* Englewood Cliffs, NJ: Prentice-Hall.

Westin, A. F. (1967). *Privacy and freedom.* New York: Antheneum.

No matter what happens in the world of human beings, it happens in a spatial setting, and the design of that setting has a deep and persisting influence on the people in that setting.

EDWARD T. HALL (1969)

CHAPTER 3

Characteristics of Physical Environments That Promote Privacy

Privacy occurs in physical environments, or as Hall refers to them in the above quote, "spatial settings." We rely upon those environments, whether they are natural or human-made settings, to provide us with the physical resources that we need to achieve our desired levels of privacy. However, effective privacy, the kind from which

we receive the physical and psychological benefits that help us to live more fulfilling lives, doesn't happen in just any environment or in a closed box. If they are to contribute to our well-being and facilitate the development of our self-identity, environments that support privacy must also be rich in meaning. They must provide positive distractions and opportunities to choose how much interaction we have with others. Finally, private environments must provide the opportunity to control the environment so that we can truly experience the broad range of benefits from different types of privacy as they are needed.

A common thread running through the concepts and theories discussed in chapters 1 and 2 is the assertion that the experience of desired privacy is restorative. Privacy provides the opportunity to reflect, contemplate, recover, and rejuvenate. It provides an escape from the

stress and pressures of the fast paced, demanding world with which most people must deal on a daily basis. Privacy is effective in providing both physical and psychological restoration for several reasons. First, it is an expression of both choice and control, essential factors in the development and maintenance of a healthy self-identity. Second, it can promote recovery from stress and mental fatigue by providing the opportunity for rest, recovery, and contemplation (Evans and McCoy 1998). Third, through providing for desired levels of intimacy, privacy facilitates positive social interaction with those from whom we need social support (Ulrich 1995, 2000). This restorative capacity of privacy is the focus of our discussion of the physical qualities of environments that promote privacy.

We have learned thus far that environmental conditions such as density, complexity, and environmental load affect the ability to achieve

privacy, and that we use elements of our environments as privacy mechanisms to establish personal space zones and to mark and control our territories. Creating environments that facilitate privacy while also providing for the many other needs and functions of any given space requires that we translate the privacy theories discussed in chapters 1 and 2 into design solutions that utilize elements of the physical environment to actually facilitate privacy. It is, therefore, important for designers to identify and examine qualities of both the natural and built environments that have been shown to be effective in supporting the experience of privacy. Research in this area is limited and tends to address more directly the subjects of environmental preference, restorative environments, personal space, territoriality, stress, and crowding. Most of the available research involves how physical environments affect our behaviors, but often it stops short of providing information that is directly applicable to design. However, some studies have translated this information successfully into concepts that we can apply to the design of the built environment.

This chapter examines the relationship between the physical environment and privacy. First, we will discuss how certain concepts and theories of environmental evaluation and environmental preference can help designers better understand how people respond to and use the physical environment to meet their privacy needs. Second, we will examine the qualities of natural environments that have been shown to provide restorative experiences that may enhance the experience of privacy. Finally, we will expand upon our understanding of environmental evaluation and preference and the relationship between natural environments and privacy to identify and examine characteristics of the built environment that facilitate privacy. (See **Box 3.1**).

1. What factors cause us to need privacy?

2. What are the benefits of privacy?

3. How do our privacy needs vary and why?

4. How can the built environment be designed to provide for our diverse privacy needs?

Box 3.1 The four questions designers must ask in order to understand the diverse privacy needs of those for whom we design. Question 4 will be addressed in this chapter.

EVALUATING ENVIRONMENTS FOR PRIVACY

Theories of environmental evaluation seek to explain the processes that we use to make judgments about environments. The process of environmental evaluation occurs both on a conscious and unconscious level. Although we may find ourselves drawn to one setting but wanting to avoid another, we often are not aware of why we find a setting pleasant or unpleasant or why we feel comfortable in some places and uncomfortable in others. We do know, however, that we often have these responses, and we have experienced the effects they have on how we use space and how we interact with others within that space. To help us understand how we evaluate an environment favorably or unfavorably for privacy needs, we will examine the environmental psychology theories of Albert Mehrabian (1976).

Approach and Avoidance Behavior

Whether we evaluate an environment favorably or unfavorably affects our responses to that environment. According to Mehrabian (1976), the process of environmental evaluation determines our most fundamental responses to that

Figure 3.1 Our preferred qualities of the physical environment that promote privacy may have originated in our deep history living in natural environments. © Access Stock Photography.

space—whether we evaluate it as positive or negative, the degree to which we are aroused by the space, and whether we are drawn to the space or try to avoid it. Mehrabian asserts that our reactions to environments fall into one of two broad categories, which he terms "approach and avoidance." **Approach behavior** is a positive response to an environment involving our desire to be in that environment, to explore it, to interact with it and with other people. We tend to approach environments that we perceive as supportive of our needs and our performance of activities. **Avoidance behavior** is a negative response to an environment that we perceive as unsupportive of our needs and performance of activities. We avoid these environments by withdrawing from them physically. When we cannot withdraw physically, we may respond in a variety of ways. For example, we may turn psychologically inward or exhibit other types of avoidance behavior, such as choosing to ignore others, focusing our attention upon a book or magazine, or even closing our eyes to avoid interacting with the environment. These behaviors are all variations of privacy mechanisms as discussed in Chapter 2.

As designers, we want people to approach rather than avoid the environments that we create. Environments that support privacy should be designed to be especially "approachable." We therefore need to examine factors associated with our privacy needs and responses that affect how we evaluate and decide whether or not to approach environments. They include the environmental load, arousal, stimulus screening, and relationships between novelty and familiarity.

High Load and Low Load Environments

Environments with high information rates are termed *high load*, and environments with low information rates are termed *low load*. **High load environments** are those in which a great deal of novel, varied, intense, and complex information is contained or perceived at any given time. A crowded emergency room is an example of a high

Figure 3.2 Spas are designed to be low load environments to enhance the experience of restoration and rejuvenation. Allegria Spa at Park Hyatt, Beaver Creek. Courtesy of Associates III, Denver, Colorado.

load environment where one is bombarded with high levels of unfamiliar, rapidly changing sensory information. **Low load environments** are those in which the information rate is slower, more familiar, and less complex. A spa is an example of an environment designed specifically to be low load, to provide relaxation and rejuvenation. High load environments demand more of us than low load environments because they contain a great deal of information that must be processed by our sensory systems in order to function effectively. (See **Figure 3.2**).

Arousal

These demands upon our physical, cognitive, and psychological processes increase our levels of arousal. **Arousal** is our level of attention, excitement, tension, and readiness to respond. Our bodies and minds are on alert and prepared for action when we become aroused. Blood pressure rises, our hearts beat faster, we breathe more rapidly, our muscles grow tense, and our attention is focused. Typically, settings with lower environmental loads tend to produce lower arousal levels while settings with higher environmental loads tend to produce higher arousal levels. Unfamiliar, crowded, and complex environments increase our arousal levels while environments that are familiar, less complex, and have a slower rate of information tend to produce lower arousal levels.

Psychologists have developed several theories about how our levels of arousal affect our behaviors and our states of mind. The common denominator in these theories is that we seek optimal levels of arousal—neither too high nor too low—which enable us to perform at our best. Too much stimulus raises our arousal level, and we may become anxious, nervous, distracted, or stressed. Too little stimulus lowers our arousal level, and we may become bored, sluggish, tired, and unable to focus.

The optimal level of arousal varies with the task or goal. In general, more difficult tasks—those that are new to us, complex, detailed, and that require concentration—are performed more effectively and efficiently with lower levels of arousal and therefore may benefit from certain types of privacy. Tasks that are familiar, easy, and that require more physical and less mental concentration are performed more effectively and efficiently with higher levels of arousal.

Stimulus Screening

In order to maintain optimal levels of arousal and to prevent us from becoming overwhelmed by high environmental loads, Mehrabian (1976) asserts that human beings select or filter the environmental stimuli automatically on an unconscious level according to our survival needs. Mehrabian calls this process **stimulus screening**. Stimulus screening enables us to literally filter out the less relevant parts of our environments and reduce the environmental load.

According to Mehrabian, human beings are either screeners or nonscreeners, depending upon how much we, as individuals, characteristically tend to filter the information in our environments. **Screeners** are better able to select what they respond to while nonscreeners are less selective. **Nonscreeners** tend to sense more stimuli within an environment and therefore may experience it as more complex and the environmental load as higher than do screeners.

Using Mehrabian's reasoning, a crowded party with loud music, in an unfamiliar setting in which the guests are all strangers will be experienced very differently by screeners and nonscreeners. Because nonscreeners tend to sense more stimuli than screeners, they may experience the party as a high load environment and may be more likely to avoid the setting or to seek certain types of privacy to reduce the load. Screeners are better able to filter out unwanted or unnecessary stimuli and tend to adapt to this type of environment more quickly; therefore, the perceived environmental load of the party may be less for screeners. If we extend this reasoning to our understanding of privacy, nonscreeners may be more likely to need and prefer environments that offer more choice and control, thus enabling them to reduce the environmental load.

Complexity and Novelty

According to Mehrabian (1976), "the environmental load is equivalent to the level of uncertainty about what a place is about or what is happening there" (p. 13). He describes the environmental load as a combination of complexity and novelty. In Chapter 1, we learned that complexity is the number of different elements contained within environments as well as the configurations, interactions between, and changes in those elements. The more different types of elements and changes that an environment contains, the higher the environmental load becomes. Mehrabian (1976) explains, "Elements that are asymmetrical rather than symmetrical, intermittent rather than continuous, random rather than patterned, in motion rather than at rest, different rather than alike, crowded rather than uncrowded, or close up rather than distant, all have more load" (p. 13).

The environmental load is made up of elements that are novel as well as elements that are familiar. Novelty and familiarity are actually complementary components of the environmental load. **Novel** elements are those with which we have had little or no prior experience. **Familiar** elements are those that we understand because we have encountered them before. According to Mehrabian, we seek a balance of novelty and familiarity in our environments.

The relative uncertainty about novel elements and environments contributes to a higher environmental load. Novel environments may be interpreted and responded to in a variety of ways. We may experience them as mysterious, risky, uncertain, or exciting, depending upon how well we can make sense of them and predict what might happen in them. We may be attracted to or fearful of novel elements in environments depending upon how much information and new knowledge we believe we can gain from them. If we feel that the risk is not too great and that we can learn by exploring the novel elements, we are more likely to be attracted to or to approach the environment.

Familiar elements contribute to one of the most basic of human needs, the need for safety and security, as defined by Maslow (1968) and others. Familiarity is the result of experience and memory. Familiar elements were originally novel elements that we were able to organize and give meaning to so that we now know—or believe we know—what to expect from them as part of an environment. Therefore, familiar elements and environments can either reassure us or alert us by evoking memories and responses that affect how we evaluate and interact with the space and with others in that space. In general, because we know what they are and what they mean, familiar elements can reduce the environmental load. However, without novelty to help balance the experience, familiar environments can be experienced as too predictable and sometimes even boring.

A balance between novelty and familiarity in environments provides important opportunities to learn and gain new experiences while remaining relatively safe and secure. This balance also contributes to our ability to achieve desired levels of privacy. We know that privacy involves both the seeking of interaction and the control of interaction. Novel elements may promote interaction by requiring communication between people to better understand and learn from the new information. Nonthreatening familiar elements may provide the predictability as well as the sense of safety, security, and comfort that we need to help control the degree of interactions that we have.

Factors Used to Predict Approach/Avoidance Behaviors

Environmental evaluation and the tendency to approach or avoid certain environments, depend upon several factors described by Mehrabian.

- *The environmental load: If the perceived environmental load is too high to process the information effectively or too low to gain new information, we may avoid the space.*
- *The ratio of novelty to familiarity: If novelty is perceived as a threat or risk, we may avoid the environment. However, if the environment has a balance of novelty to familiarity that allows us to feel safe and comfortable, we may exhibit approach behaviors, including exploration of the environment.*
- *Our individual ability to screen stimuli: If the load is too high, nonscreeners may avoid the space or desire certain types of privacy to help control the levels of stimuli with*

which they must deal, while, if the environmental load is too low, screeners may avoid it.

- **Our attitudes, expectations, memories, and motivations:** *We often have preconceived ideas and beliefs about certain elements or types of environments that may cause us to like and therefore approach them or dislike and avoid them.*

- **Our feelings of affiliation with others in the environment:** *If we have a positive affiliation with others, we are likely to want to interact with and communicate with them. If we do not have a positive affiliation, we may want to avoid interaction and communication. Both behaviors are demonstrated by verbal and nonverbal behaviors, such as eye contact and body language.*

- **Our perception of performance:** *If the environment appears to have the qualities that will support our performance of a necessary, required, or desired task, we may exhibit approach behavior. But if that environment does not appear to support our performance of a task, we may exhibit avoidance behavior.*

Mehrabian asserts that the high load, unpleasant environments that characterize many of today's cities increase the need for privacy. However, he also asserts that we can tolerate higher environmental loads, perform unpleasant tasks more successfully, and tolerate higher density in pleasant or preferred environments.

ENVIRONMENTAL PREFERENCES FOR PRIVACY

The perspective of privacy as being essential to the maintenance of overall well-being suggests that settings that help us achieve privacy require careful considerations for environmental preferences. The intimate and personal nature of many private places means that these environments must not only support our individual needs for privacy, but also be pleasant, comfortable, and approachable. Can we, however, actually predict preferences for environments? If so, what characteristics of an environment would be preferred for the different types of privacy that we need? (See **Figure 3.3**).

The ability to predict environmental preference has been examined in a variety of studies that relate to the theories of privacy discussed in this book. Preference for certain qualities or characteristics of environments has been linked to the environment's ability to support effective functioning by psychologists Rachel and Stephen Kaplan (1989). Suggestions that familiarity is associated with preference were made by Mehrabian (1976) and by others (Veitch & Arkkelin 1995). Preference has also been linked to aesthetic judgments (Appleton 1996, S. Kaplan 1979, Heerwagen & Orians 1993).

Preferences for environmental characteristics that have been shown to promote privacy are those that are perceived to provide control by allowing us to establish desired visual,

Figure 3.3 Preferred physical characteristics that support privacy include prospect and refuge. Courtesy of Associates III, Denver, Colorado.

acoustical, and physical territories and personal space, and that provide the opportunity to redirect our attention away from stress producing stimuli. Although we often need privacy to concentrate and focus our attention upon a specific task (such as studying or writing), research has shown that prolonged periods of this type of directed attention produces mental fatigue (Kaplan & Kaplan 1989). Well designed private places provide the appropriate territories and personal space distances to not only accommodate the need to concentrate but also provide environmental characteristics that provide what the Kaplans refer to as involuntary attention or positive distractions.

Involuntary Attention

Directed attention is a fact of life, but it is also one from which we must escape occasionally if we are to maintain our ability to function effectively and maintain our overall well-being. **Directed attention** is required when we must focus and avoid distractions to effectively perform mental tasks. Studying, writing, planning, formulating solutions, and solving problems are some examples of mental tasks that require directed attention. Maintaining directed attention requires that we screen out stimuli that are not necessary to the task. If this task must be performed in a high load environment, a great deal of effort is required to screen the unwanted stimuli and maintain directed attention. This can be especially difficult for nonscreeners in environments that do not provide adequate resources to achieve privacy.

We need to be able to call upon directed attention when the circumstances require us to focus. The Kaplans (1989) assert that while directed attention was essential to the survival of our ancestors, it is even more essential to effectively function today. Whether it is driving in heavy traffic; preparing a report; creating a work of art; dealing simultaneously with multiple demands of work, society, and family;

following complex directions; or any of the many tasks that our modern world demands of us; we must be able to use directed attention when necessary. Some of the effects of too much directed attention include an inability to concentrate, increased irritability and aggression, and less responsiveness to others (Kaplan & Kaplan 1989).

Because our capacity for directed attention is limited, however, we experience mental fatigue when we exceed that capacity. The Kaplans (1989) assert, "If mental fatigue is the result of an overworked capacity for directed attention, then resting this capacity would seem to be the route to recovery. . . . Achieving this requires environments and tasks that make minimal demands on directed attention" (p. 182). One way to accomplish this is to create environments that redirect our attention away from the sources of stress by providing characteristics that evoke involuntary attention.

Involuntary attention requires little or no conscious effort. It is often the result of feeling as if we have escaped into a "whole other world" where we can experience feelings of connectedness with something larger than our immediate surroundings. We can experience involuntary attention through elements that fascinate us. The Kaplans (1989) explain, "fascination is important to the restorative experience not only because it attracts people and keeps them from getting bored but also because it allows them to function without having to use directed attention" (p. 184). We are fascinated by many diverse things within our environments. Novelty (if it is not overwhelming), the opportunity to learn new information, mystery (if it is not perceived as threatening), and, as previously mentioned, a sense of connection are all contributors to the experience of fascination.

Ulrich (2000) stresses the importance of involuntary attention, or what he terms "positive distractions," to the healing process.

According to Ulrich, nature is the most effective positive distraction for this purpose.

Many studies on the origins of human environmental preferences involve the evaluation of landscapes (Appleton 1996, Kaplan & Kaplan 1989, Kellert 1993, Wilson 1989). This makes sense when we consider that the human species evolved in natural settings. Until very recently, our "home" was nature. A growing body of research indicates that because our sensory systems and perceptual abilities developed in response to the information found in natural environments, our preferences for certain environmental characteristics may also be linked to the experience of nature (Appleton 1996; Heerwagen & Orians 1993; Kaplan & Kaplan 1989; Kellert 1993; Wilson 1989, 1993). Other theories assert that environmental preferences are learned responses, influenced by our life experiences and cultural values (Lyons 1983, Tuan 1979). The view of environmental preference taken by the authors of this book is that, like privacy, our preferences for environments are grounded in our need for information to survive but such preferences can be shaped by our experiences and culture.

LINK
For more information about privacy, positive distractions, and healing, see Chapter 6, page 124.

The Functional–Evolutionary Perspective of Environmental Preference

According to Rachel and Stephen Kaplan (1989), if the sensory information contained in an environment is going to help us survive, "it is essential that (we) not only perceive what is safe but also prefer it" (p. 41). Survival information in nature can take many forms. The presence of water, natural light, colorful plants, other species, and places from which to observe these elements in relative safety are examples (Heerwagen & Orians 1993). The functional–evolutionary perspective of environmental preference holds that because these natural elements provided important survival information, early humans found these and other natural nonthreatening elements aesthetically pleasing. They preferred environments rich in these elements, and we continue to do so today (Heerwagen & Orians 1993, Kaplan & Kaplan 1989). (See **Figure 3.4**).

Figure 3.4
Characteristics that provide survival information in natural settings are generally perceived as aesthetically pleasing.
© J. A. Kraulis/Wonderfile.

Characteristics of Preferred Environments

Certain identifiable characteristics and conditions of natural environments that influence preference appear to aid human perception and enhance the opportunity to explore and understand (Kaplan & Kaplan 1984, 1989). These characteristics also appear to be effective in reducing the environmental load and redirecting attention away from the sources of stress, which can enhance the restorative experience of privacy. These characteristics are:

- *Complexity: the amount and variety of elements found in an environmental setting. If the complexity of a setting is not too extreme, we tend to prefer environments with higher levels of complexity because they provide more information. We interact with, explore, and learn from environments rich in information. In this way, complexity that interests us but does not demand a great deal of focused attention can be helpful in removing us psychologically from the sources of environmental stress.*

- *Coherence: patterns of elements that help to provide a sense of order and direct our attention. Greater coherence within an environment leads to stronger preference. Designers use the elements and principles of design to create coherence in environments. Repetition of line, form, color, texture; progression of scale; and balance are examples of elements and principles that provide order and help us make sense of the complexity.*

- *Legibility: characteristics that aid the ability to understand and remember an environment. We tend to prefer more legible environments over less legible ones. Identifiable or familiar elements provide wayfinding and help to us to function more effectively in an environment. Performance of tasks is enhanced by legibility.*

- *Mystery: characteristics that provide the opportunity to learn something that is not obvious or apparent when we first perceive the space. If it is not accompanied by the perception of danger, a heightened sense of mystery is preferred. Mystery encourages exploration and involvement.*

According to the Kaplans, environments that provide these four characteristics are likely to be preferred over environments lacking these characteristics, in part because they aid effective functioning. We are simply better able to function physically, cognitively, and emotionally in environments that are rich in complexity, are coherent and legible, and that provide mystery.

These characteristics may also enhance the restorative experience of privacy and therefore be preferred characteristics for private environments. We have learned that effective, restorative privacy does not mean removing oneself from all environmental stimuli. Rather, privacy is best accomplished in settings with lower environmental loads in which the complexity is made up of a balance of novel and familiar elements. Private environments should not demand a great deal from us. They should be easy to organize and to understand. Private environments should also have the ability to redirect our attention away from sources of stress. Mystery, as described by the Kaplans, contributes to an important quality of restorative environments, the ability to redirect attention. (See **Figure 3.5a** and **3.5b**).

Historically we have designed interiors, leaving the natural world to the landscape architects, the environmentalists, and the poets. However, whether designing for privacy or other goals that enhance positive experiences in built environments, we cannot overlook the role that nature plays in all of our lives. We turn next to an examination of the intimate relationship between the natural environment and experiences of privacy.

LINK
How is mystery used to enhance privacy in residential environments? See Chapter 4, page 88.

Figure 3.5a & 3.5b Mystery is a positive distraction implying that if we explore further we will be rewarded with information to help us better understand our environment. Courtesy of Associates III, Denver Colorado and © Peter Griffith/Wonderfile, respectively.

LESSONS LEARNED FROM NATURE

Nature has been the exclusive home of our species until very recently. Only in the last few generations have we more or less completely moved indoors, effectively cutting ourselves off from the benefits that only nature can provide. Our sensory systems evolved in natural settings, determining what information our ancestors needed to respond to so they could survive and pass on their DNA to us. However, our inherited abilities to learn and benefit from nature may not be equally well adapted to the built world. A few generations' worth of living in an artificial, indoor world are not enough time for human beings to lose the need to experience and affiliate with nature. We need that ongoing relationship with nature to continue to develop and maintain our physical and emotional health and well-being. What can we learn from nature to help us design environments that offer the benefits of restoration, aesthetic experiences, privacy, and well-being?

Wilderness Solitude

Writers, poets, artists, and philosophers have long recognized the power of retreating alone to nature to restore their creativity, inspire their work, and provide spiritual renewal. So valued is wilderness solitude that conservation of natural places is often justified by the exceptional opportunity that they provide modern people to experience the unique benefits of being alone with nature.

Research to identify benefits of wilderness solitude, conducted in a variety of disciplines including the U.S. Forest Service, reveals that we experience personal autonomy, emotional release, reflective thought, self-evaluation, and personal growth when we are alone in the wilderness (Altman 1975; Hammit 1982; Hammit & Brown 1984; Hollenhorst, Frank, & Watson 1994; Westin 1967). William Hammit (1982) asserts that "a very desirable feature of wilderness is that compared to the pressing demands of everyday urban life, it allows us to control what we pay attention to and which activities we engage in" (p. 210). In other words, wilderness can provide involuntary attention, and a respite from the mentally fatiguing directed attention demanded by our daily lives.

FYI

Phillip Koch (1994), in his work *Solitude: A Philosophical Encounter,* identifies five virtues or benefits of wilderness solitude:

1. Freedom from the social norms and constraints that control interpersonal life
2. Attunement to self as compensation for the scattering and submersion of the self that occurs in social life
3. Attunement to nature, as opposed to our daily preoccupation with social attunement
4. Reflective perspective, including introspection, recollection, and contemplative analysis
5. Creativity, or the "programmic ordering" of the first four benefits/virtues into original expression (p. 60)

Some researchers view the positive benefits from wilderness solitude as being hierarchical in structure, similar to Maslow's (1968) hierarchy of needs discussed in Chapter 1. This hierarchy of benefits from wilderness solitude begins with physical renewal at the lower level and progresses toward self-discovery and self-realization at the highest levels (Hollenhorst, Frank, & Watson 1994).

The experience of wilderness solitude is unique. The difference between wilderness and nearby or backyard nature lies in the dominance of nature in wilderness settings and the lack of human influences. With the right conditions, we can experience some degree of involuntary attention and restoration necessary for privacy in nearby nature. However, nearby nature usually has been altered by some type of human intervention. Above all, the criterion that distinguishes wilderness from other natural settings is solitude without human influences (Hollenhorst, Frank, & Watson 1994). In the strictest sense of the concept, solitude involves physically removing ourselves from the influence and observation of others. While this may be accomplished by going to our room and closing the door or sitting in our backyard, the benefits of solitude found in the wilderness are not likely to be found behind the closed doors of most rooms nor even in our own nearby nature. Wilderness provides a distance barrier between us and the demands and stressors of the rest of the world. It also provides a rich, meaningful, private environment for us to experience involuntary attention. (See **Figure 3.6**).

Transcendent Experiences

Think about hiking in the mountains on a sunny, autumn day. You have exerted some effort to reach a spot high on the golden, aspen-covered mountainside with magnificent views of a lake and the mountains beyond. You stop there and take in the sensory information: the sun filtering through the shimmering leaves, the cool breeze blowing through the trees, and the birds calling to one another. You are alone. Time becomes irrelevant as you lose yourself in the moment. You feel an extreme sense of happiness, lightness, freedom, and harmony with the earth.

This singular experience is what psychologists call a **transcendent experience**, a phenomenon characterized by strong positive feelings, overcoming the limits of our physical lives, a sense of timelessness, and connection or oneness with the universe or a higher power. Research studies tell us that such experiences are

Figure 3.6 The experience of wilderness solitude is unique because of the relative lack of human intervention. © Digital Vision/Wonderfile Corporation.

often caused by direct interaction with natural and wilderness environments. The research into transcendent experiences reveals that the phenomenon is cross-cultural, and in all cultures, seems to have a special association with the experience of nature (Williams & Harvey 2001).

Transcendent experiences are the result of complex interactions between the individual and the environment. In many cultures, natural elements such as trees, mountains, water, as well as other species possess strong symbolic and spiritual meaning that may trigger transcendent experiences. Environmental psychologist Joachim Wohlwill (1983) explains, "This failure of the wilderness to be in any way moved by the person entering it may indeed be at the heart of the restorative powers claimed for it. More particularly, it could readily account for the feeling of freedom and oneness with nature engendered by the wilderness—where the individual experiences so little reaction or acknowledgment of his or her own presence that the boundaries between the self and the environment become muted and lose definition" (p. 25).

Restoration

The theory most directly related to the universal need for privacy holds that natural environ-

ments are restorative. The Kaplans (1989) assert that restorative natural environments are also aesthetically pleasing environments. Their research indicates that aesthetic natural settings not only give pleasure and are satisfying to experience, but also

- *Support human functioning*
- *Provide a context in which sensory information and complexity can be managed effectively*
- *Permit people to move about and explore with comfort and confidence*
- *Provide for recovery from mental fatigue*

These characteristics of nature make it a "restorative environment." Many scientists believe this restorative function is the most important physical and psychological benefit we enjoy from our experience of nature.

Research conducted by Ulrich (1993) found that visual exposure to natural settings such as grassy, park-like landscapes that also included a prominent water feature aided in recovery from stress and lowered levels of anger, aggression, and fear. Additionally, viewing these settings lowered blood pressure and reduced muscle tension.

THE BENEFIT OF NATURAL ENVIRONMENTS TO PRIVACY

The benefits of natural environments to our health and well-being make them also important considerations when designing for privacy. The experience of nature has the unique capacity to "take us away" physically and mentally from the stressors and circumstances that cause us to seek privacy. This is because many nonthreatening natural environments offer rich opportunities for both involuntary attention and for an experience known as prospect and refuge.

Involuntary Attention

Several qualities of natural environments that contribute to involuntary attention have been identified (Appleton 1996, Kaplan & Kaplan 1989, Orr 1993, Heerwagen and Orians 1993).

- *The relationship of novelty to familiarity:* *Unthreatening natural environments have the ability to redirect our attention through an elegant balance of new, varied, changing information, with information that is comfortable and known.*
- *Connectedness: Strong connections with nature can yield the kind of "deep privacy" that rejuvenates us so completely that we emerge with greater coping energies. Often, connectedness in nature is achieved by observing other species. We are fascinated by other species engaging in the ordinary or extraordinary tasks of their lives (whales or geese migrating, birds feeding, building nests, wild animals playing). Connectedness is also achieved by participating in physical activates associated with nature (gardening, hiking, biking, sailing). The less reliant we are upon technology for these activities, the greater the experience of connectedness and the greater the rejuvenation.*
- *Mystery: The quality of mystery provides important information about an environment,*

including the promise that if we proceed and explore we will discover something more. Mystery also provides a pleasant challenge for our imagination by refocusing our attention. To have mystery, the environment must have partially hidden information, something in the scene that tempts us to explore further. This is often accomplished by partially screening the view, the use of light to draw the eye, and the configuration of the circulation path.

- *Symbolic content/meaning: Humans have, over the millennia, attributed such strong symbolic meaning to other forms of life that they exert strong influences upon our emotional states of being. The symbolic content of the natural world is one of the primary ways that we learn to attribute meaning to our surroundings. Many symbols are ancient; some are archetypal or common to all humans; others are associated with individual cultures, eras, and religions. It is impossible to enter any environment—built or natural—without being affected consciously or unconsciously by the environment's symbolic content. These universal natural symbols have the greatest impact upon our emotional responses. They include*

  1. *Water a prime archetypal symbol of life and survival—calming and connecting*
  2. *Fire symbolic of security, survival, mystery, magic—hypnotic and contemplative*
  3. *Wind symbolic of change and transience—ephemeral qualities (breeze blowing through the trees or sheer curtains)*
  4. *Light symbolic of renewal, energy, light, enlightenment, knowledge, brilliance, spirituality—representing wisdom with dramatic power to direct the eye and our attention*
  5. *Trees symbolic of the connection between heaven and earth—sheltering and protective*

6. *Mountains symbolic of ascent to the heavens—representing omnipotence*

The symbolic content of these natural elements can be effective positive distractions when integrated in or used as part of the design of private places. They infuse the private setting with meaning that can enhance the restorative experience of privacy.

Prospect and Refuge

One of the most interesting physical qualities and use of natural environments associated with privacy is called prospect and refuge. Prospect is the ability to see what is around us, a vantage point. Refuge is the presence of a shelter, backup element, camouflage, or a symbol of security. The English geographer Jay Appleton (1996) defined **prospect and refuge** as environmental conditions that provide the ability to see without being seen. It is standing at the mouth of the cave or on the cliff overlooking the water; climbing the broad canopied tree or the tree-studded mountainside. From these vantage points we can survey our surroundings, observe those who approach long before they reach us, watch activities without having to participate, and experience a connection to the larger world.

Environments that provided prospect and refuge enabled our ancestors to explore new environments with relative safety and security. As a result, environments with characteristics of prospect and refuge would have been experienced as both pleasurable and preferred (Appleton 1996). We need only look at the history of the built environment to observe that these characteristics still are pleasurable and preferred. Think of the castle, the church tower, the tree house, the home with a view, and the penthouse office or apartment.

Evolutionary biologist E. O. Wilson (1984) examined the attraction and preference that we have for places of prospect and refuge by asking, "What was the prevailing original habitat in which the brain evolved? Where would people go if given completely free choice?" (p. 106) The answer, says Wilson, is places of prospect and refuge. He explains "it seems that whenever people are given a free choice, they move to open tree-studded land on prominence overlooking water. Those who exercise the greatest degree of choice, the rich and powerful, congregate on high land above lakes and rivers and along ocean bluffs. On such sites they build palaces, villas, temples, and corporate retreats" (p. 110). According to Wilson, we are attracted to and prefer these types of natural environments because we are "responding to a deep genetic memory of mankind's optimal environment" (p. 111). Although we no longer prefer characteristics of prospect and refuge solely because of their survival advantage, the tendency to prefer these characteristics appears to be very strong even today.

One reason we prefer environments that provide prospect and refuge is because they offer opportunities to achieve privacy by controlling access to ourselves and experiencing involuntary attention. Complex environments are also perceived as more coherent when viewed from a position of prospect and refuge because the novelty or new information within the environment can be studied from a position of relative familiarity. The experience of prospect and refuge can also evoke fascination and mystery.

THREE VARIABLES TO CONSIDER WHEN DESIGNING FOR PRIVACY

Designing for privacy requires an understanding of the relationship between three variables: individual needs (discussed in chapters 1 and 2), environmental opportunities, and the interactions between the two. Individual needs represent the problem (for example, the universal need for privacy and the variety of ways it is expressed as discussed in chapters 1 and 2), environmental opportunities represent the physical elements of environments capable of manipulation to support the experience of privacy (discussed later in this chapter), and the interaction between the two represents the pattern. The "pattern" in this context is the way that we respond, based upon privacy needs, to certain physical qualities of the environment.

Identifying Patterns

In 1977, architect and educator Christopher Alexander and colleagues introduced a groundbreaking philosophy for the design of towns, landscapes, buildings, and interiors entitled *A Pattern Language*. Alexander describes patterns as "timeless, observable interactions between human beings and environments that occur again and again, each time in a slightly different but recognizable way." These patterns, explains Alexander, are often archetypal, "so deeply rooted in the nature of things, that it seems likely they will be a part of human nature and human actions as much in five hundred years, as they are today" (p. xvii). The 253 identified patterns, with evocative names such as "Tapestry of Light and Dark," "High Places," and "Circulation Realms" represent universal ways that we perceive and respond to our environments in a positive manner and how the physical elements of environments can be configured to provide for these positive responses. The almost infinite combination of possible patterns creates a "pattern language" that can be used to create environments rich in meaning.

Patterns for Privacy

When we examine Alexander's patterns together with the theories of privacy discussed previously, we find that many of the patterns refer to environmental opportunities for privacy. For example, the pattern titled "Intimacy Gradient" states, "Lay out the spaces of a building so that they create a sequence which begins with the entrance at the most public parts of the building, then leads into the slightly more private areas, and finally to the most private domains" (p. 613). The Intimacy Gradient pattern suggests the possible interactions—and control of those interactions—between individuals, between groups of people, and between people and the environment as they move through a sequence of spaces. Certain aspects of individual needs for privacy can be accommodated using this pattern because it affords environmental opportunities to select the desired level of interaction with others.

Using patterns to help understand how human needs translate into environmental solutions provides a useful model for the creative process of designing for privacy. For example, by combining Intimacy Gradient with other patterns that also directly or indirectly facilitate privacy, designers can create "pattern language for privacy" that can help them develop effective privacy solutions.

Each pattern describes a universal way that we use environments to meet our needs and enhance our experience. By using multiple patterns, we create a language of design that is both symbolic and literal.

> **LINK**
>
> For examples of how the pattern Intimacy Gradient can be combined with other patterns and applied to create private spaces, see Chapter 7, page 164.

As Alexander (1979) reminds us, however, "the mere use of pattern language alone does not ensure that people can make places live" (p. 229). Environments must evolve, and people must participate in that evolution. The details of environments must have meaning, and people must understand and share that meaning. While these observations are true of all well designed environments, they are essential to private environments. If we are to experience the restoration of our weary minds, frayed nerves, and tired bodies; if we are to evaluate ourselves effectively and develop our self-identity; if we are to satisfy our needs for intimacy and interaction; and if we are, ultimately, to have the ability to control our environments to meet our privacy needs, we must feel connected to those environments.

We will now turn to an examination of physical characteristics of the built environment that promote privacy. These characteristics combine the information we have learned about environmental evaluation and preference and the privacy benefits of certain qualities of nature with certain patterns we have identified that facilitate privacy.

CHARACTERISTICS OF BUILT ENVIRONMENTS THAT PROMOTE PRIVACY

Designing for privacy means looking beyond the obvious design elements commonly used to physically separate us from others. Doors, walls and window treatments, for example, do indeed separate us, but they can also become physical constraints that limit the flexibility of a space. By relying on physical barriers alone, we ignore the psychological dimensions of privacy: the needs for involuntary attention, restoration, and meaning. The dynamic nature of privacy requires that our built environments respond to our changing physical and psychological needs to interact with others or to be alone.

Design Elements and Architectural Dimensions Linked to Privacy

A number of design elements and architectural dimensions may reduce stress and the effects of crowding (Evans, Lepore, & Schroeder 1996; Evans & McCoy 1998; Kaplan and Kaplan 1989). Some are directly related to qualities of natural environments; others are related indirectly. The design elements and architectural dimensions that follow are closely linked to privacy, and when used together with certain patterns, they can enhance the meaning and function of private spaces.

Spatial Hierarchy

The sequences of spaces through environments should progress from the less private to the more private. This technique is similar to the design methods used by ancient monument builders and medieval architects. Their structures drew people ever deeper into the setting while the spaces became more and more sacred until one reached the center, the place of ultimate sanctity. This is also the Intimacy Gradient pattern of Alexander et al. (1977) discussed previously. Alexander describes how this pattern functions: "Where there is a gradient of this kind, people can give each encounter

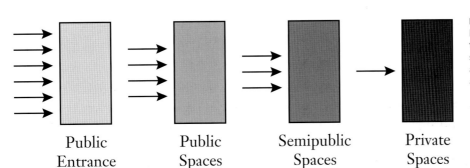

Figure 3.7 The pattern Intimacy Gradient shows the recommended spatial relationships and adjacencies between less and more private areas.

Public Entrance   Public Spaces   Semipublic Spaces   Private Spaces

SPATIAL HIERARCHY
(Intimacy Gradient)

different shades of meaning, by choosing its position on the gradient very carefully" (p. 610). When environments are designed with a sense of spatial hierarchy, we are able to make choices about where we want interaction or where we might prefer solitude. (See **Figure 3.7**).

Spatial Depth

Spatial depth is closely related to spatial hierarchy. Spatial depth refers to the number of spaces we must go through to get from one point in an environment to another. This appears to be an effective architectural element to regulate perceptions of crowding in residential environments (Evans, Lepore, & Schroeder 1996). The deeper the spatial depth, the less the perception of crowding is. Deeper spaces provide a greater sense of privacy and enhance our ability to regulate interaction with others (Evans & McCoy 1998). Research suggests that within high density environments with greater spatial depth, there is less need to withdraw socially to cope with crowding (Evans, Lepore, & Schroeder 1996). (See **Figure 3.8**).

Circulation Paths

Circulation paths bring us to a setting, guide us through the setting, and lead us to our goal within that setting. We can pass through a sequence of spaces or around them. The arrangement of spaces affects how we move between them. Alexander's et al. (1977) pattern "The Flow through Rooms" states, "The movement between rooms is as important as the rooms themselves; and its arrangement has as much effect on social interaction in the rooms, as the interiors of the rooms" (p. 628). Circulation paths are not roads; they are places where people can pause and interact with others selectively as well as with the environment. To facilitate this, circulation patterns should be generous and well lit. They should be adjacent to common areas so that people will always pass the space but can choose whether or not to stop.

Meaning is enhanced by Alexander's et al. (1977) pattern "Circulation Realms," the sequence of buildings and spaces that make up a building complex: "Lay out very large

Figure 3.8 Spatial depth is achieved by progressing from less to more private areas as one moves through a space.

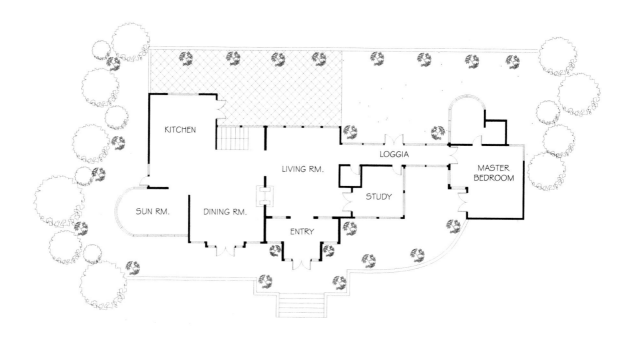

buildings and collections of small buildings so that each one reaches a given point inside by passing through a sequence of realms, each marked by a gateway, to the next. Choose the realms so that each one can be easily named, so that you can tell a person where to go simply by telling him which realms to go through" (p. 484). This process adds coherence to environments, one of the four preferred characteristics identified by the Kaplans (1989). As we move through circulation realms, we can explore and gain understanding about our environment. Mystery is also enhanced as "realms" are revealed, especially if they connect visually or actually to the natural environment.

Sociofugal and Sociopetal Spaces

The spacing that we tend to place naturally between ourselves and others, called personal space zones, can be enhanced by certain design strategies that encourage or discourage communication and interaction. For example, environments such as railway waiting stations with their rows of fixed, side-by-side seating tends to keep people apart. This type of design creates sociofugal spaces. **Sociofugal spaces** are designed to discourage interaction and communication with others. However, some designs such as the placement of tables at a French sidewalk café tend to bring people together to the extent of mingling the restaurant patrons with the passersby. This type of design creates sociopetal spaces. **Sociopetal spaces** are designed to encourage interaction and communication with others (Sommer 1969). (See **Figure 3.9**).

Sociofugal seating arrangements should place people outside of intimate personal space zones at least eighteen inches apart. However, larger distances are recommended in settings that have high environmental loads and high social density. Ideally, sociofugal seating should be arranged so that direct eye contact can be avoided. Sociofugal seating can be used to support needs for *solitude* in a setting that does not allow one to retreat to an enclosed space or for *anonymity* in a high-density setting. Cultural norms and practices in many cultures respect

Figure 3.9 Sociofugal arrangements can be used to discourage interaction and support privacy in crowded settings. Sociopetal arrangements can encourage positive interactions while allowing individuals to exert a degree of control over those interactions.

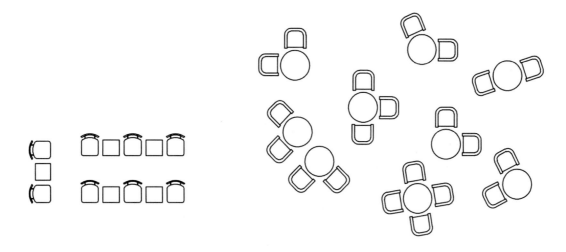

Sociofugal Seating Arrangement   Sociopetal Seating Arrangement

the desired privacy message communicated by those who chose to occupy sociofugal areas.

Sociopetal seating arrangements can be used to support needs for intimacy. Closer personal space distances (9 to 18 inches apart) facilitate ease of verbal and nonverbal (body language) communication. Seating placed at right angles to one another, instead of directly across from one another, have been shown to be more effective to facilitate this level of communication (Hall 1969).

Thresholds

We move from one space into another through barriers both implied and literal. Each time we move from one space to another, we cross a threshold, a place of transition. Doorways, bridges, arches, level changes, draped beds, and alcoves are all examples of real or implied thresholds.

The ancient Greek saying, "A threshold is a sacred thing," speaks to the strong symbolism associated with crossing barriers from one space to another. Thresholds symbolize the leaving of one state of being and the entrance into another. Throughout history, designers of religious structures have used thresholds masterfully to symbolize the journey of the soul toward heaven, leaving the worries and problems of the world behind. From the moment we pass beneath the arched doorway of one of the great cathedrals of Europe or mosques of the Middle East, we feel as if we have entered a different world, separate and distinct from what lies outside that doorway.

Thresholds are powerful symbols of territory. When used subtly, they connect. When used boldly, they distinguish. The ancient Romans understood the power of thresholds to define territory, using the triumphant arch to signify entrance into Rome. Whether that entrance was in Britain, France, or Italy, passing beneath the arch meant that one had entered Rome.

When used as part of a spatial hierarchy and combined with spatial depth, thresholds are used to reinforce the sequence of spaces from less to more private. The shape and size of the threshold is also important. Large thresholds imply public access. Alexander's et al. (1977) pattern "Low Doorway" addresses the implications of smaller thresholds: "High doorways are simple and convenient. But a lower doorway is more profound . . . make at least some of your doorways low enough so that the act of going through the door is a deliberate thoughtful passage from one place to another. Especially at the entrance of a house, at the entrance to a private room, or a fire corner—make the doorway lower than usual" (pp. 1057–1058). (See **Figure 3.10**).

Stimulus Shelters

Places where we can pause and get away from situations that demand too much directed attention are often restorative. Stimulus shelters create a buffer between ourselves and the overstimulation of some environments "by providing a temporary respite; a time out from prolonged or high levels of environmental demands or stressors" (Evans & McCoy 1998, p. 91). An example of this kind of stimulus shelter is the alcove. Alcoves are also a pattern that responds to our dual privacy needs to both interact and to restrict interaction. According to Alexander, et al. (1977), "people want to be together; but at the same time they want the opportunity for some small amount of privacy, without giving up community" (p. 831). These rooms within rooms allow us to have a degree of privacy while still feeling connected to others.

Alcoves are as effective in public spaces as they are in homes. In both cases they provide spaces where one person can retreat or a small group can interact comfortably within the larger environment.

Another effective stimulus shelter is the window seat. Window seats provide a place to withdraw temporarily from a larger space, and

LINK

How did Frank Lloyd Wright use alcoves to create intimate spaces in his homes? See Chapter 4, page 87.

Figure 3.10 Thresholds are effective ways to differentiate territories because they are symbolic of leaving one territory and entering another.

Thresholds

they also provide involuntary attention because they place us nearer to nature. Historically, window seats were used as places of retreat and prospect and refuge. Oriel windows that protruded from the exterior walls of castles and medieval homes provided an excellent vantage point from a position of safety and security. They also were effective rooms within rooms into which people could retreat for contemplation and for detailed work. Natural light, often streaming in from multiple directions, provided a pleasant retreat in an environment that was otherwise dark and void of private places.

Window seats are sometimes considered a luxury today. Alexander et al. (1977), however, discussing them as part of the pattern "Window Places" considers them a necessity. He explains, "These kinds of windows which create 'places' next to them are not simply luxuries; they are necessary. A room which does not have a place like this seldom allows you to feel fully comfortable or perfectly at ease" (p. 834).

Light

We need natural light to be healthy physically and emotionally. Our early ancestors understood this; our more recent ancestors seem to have forgotten it; now modern medicine confirms it. Because modern humans spend 90 percent of our time indoors and often in high-density environments, the opportunity to experience the restorative changing patterns, intensity, and color that natural light brings to our lives is often lost. Discussing the pattern "Wings of Light," Alexander et al. (1977) asserts, "It is much more pleasant to be in a building lit by daylight than in one which is not. But the trouble is that many of the buildings which are built without daylight are built that way because of density. They are built compact, in the belief that it is necessary to sacrifice daylight in order to reach high densities" (p. 527).

Human beings, like most species, are naturally attracted to light. We move and orient ourselves toward it. The places where we interact with others publicly as well as our private places are defined by light. The relentless, uniform, artificial light that most large scale contemporary buildings impose upon us, however, is unhealthy and not conducive to privacy. In nature, light does not merely illuminate a space; it reveals it. If we observe carefully, we see that light surrounds us in nature, coming from many directions. It is always changing, never uniform, with variations of brightness and contrast of shadows. This quality of natural light helps to create involuntary attention. It provides qualities of mystery, fascination, and connection.

To maximize the restorative potential of a private place, it should be designed to receive natural light from at least two different directions. Because people are attracted to the brightest spots in an environment, private areas should have lower light levels to define the area from other spaces and avoid drawing people to the private places.

Color

As all artists and designers learn in color theory classes, colors can be divided into two general categories: those that are warm (the red, orange, yellow groups) and those that are cool (the green, blue, purple groups). These color groups represent the two ends of the visible light spectrum, and most color theorists agree that they also represent differences in our physical and psychological reactions to color. According to color theorist and art historian Faber Birren (1969), we are naturally attracted to warm colors more than to cool colors. Warm colors speed up our metabolism, increasing our heart rate and breathing. Warm colors promote activity and interaction. Cool colors tend to calm us physically and emotionally. However, this information alone does not mean that warm surroundings are best for introverted people or that cool colors help excitable people calm

down. Solutions to psychological problems are much more complex than prescribing colors.

It does mean that, when combined with different light levels, color may affect whether we approach or avoid environments as well as how we direct our attention and focus. According to Birren (1969), "with high levels of illumination, warm and luminous colors in the surroundings (yellow, peach, pink), the body tends to direct its attention outward. There is increased activation in general alertness, outward orientation. Such an environment is conducive to muscular effort, action, and cheerful spirit" (p. 31). It may not, however, be conducive to all types of privacy. Conversely, Birren asserts that color and light may be used to direct attention away from the environment and toward the individual: "With softer surroundings, cooler hues (gray, blue, green, turquoise), and lower brightness, there is less distraction and a person is better able to concentrate on difficult visual and mental tasks. Good inward orientation is furthered" (p. 31). These conditions, says Birren, are better for activities that require concentration and detailed work.

However, Alexander's et al. (1977) pattern "Warm Colors" suggests that because our responses to color are tied inextricably to the quality of the light, all designs should provide "warm light in the rooms" (p. 1156). "The greens and greys of hospitals and office corridors are depressing and cold. Natural wood, sunlight, bright colors are warm. In some way, the warmth of the colors in a room makes a great deal of difference between comfort and discomfort" (p. 1153). However, nature's cool colors: green grass, purple flowers, blue sky are certainly not depressing. Birren's suggestion that cool hues and low brightness are less distracting, together

Figure 3.11 The cloister has been used for thousands of years to provide a visual, physical, and spiritual connection between natural and built environments. By creating the experience of prospect and refuge, they enhance the experience of solitude and of intimacy. Paulo Magalhaes/Getty Images.

with Alexander's et al. suggestion that the light should be warm, reflects nature's aesthetically pleasing use of cool colors and warm light. Some private environments—those that we require for concentration and detailed work—may also benefit from the use of nature's cooler colors with warm light.

Prospect and Refuge

We must consider degrees of enclosure and exposure when applying prospect and refuge to the built environment. Not all places afford the ability to create high places or total seclusion. The concept, however, of having a protected vantage point from which to view our surroundings can be translated into the built environment in a number of effective ways.

One powerful example used by architects and designers since ancient times to foster privacy using prospect and refuge is the cloister. Part porch, part arcade, neither inside nor outside, cloisters are the result of a combination of patterns identified by Alexander et al. (1977). They are the "Sheltering Roof" (p. 570) and "Arcades" (p. 581), usually used at

the "Building Edge" (p. 755). The sheltering roof is a prime symbol of refuge. Arcades, covered walkways attached to the edges of buildings, connect us with the outdoors while providing refuge. Alexander et al. advises, "Make sure that you treat the edge of the building as a 'thing,' a 'place,' a zone with volume to it, not a line or interface which has no thickness. Crenellate the top[s] of buildings with places that invite people to stop. Make places that have depth and a covering, places to sit, lean, and walk, especially at those points along the perimeter which look onto interesting outdoor life" (p. 755).

Greek and Roman courtyards and atriums used the concept of the cloister to create buildings in which the interior and exterior flowed together as one. Frank Lloyd Wright used the concept of the cloister to create loggias along the edges of his homes. For Wright, a loggia tied views of nature to the structure and provided a place where people could move from space to space while never losing sight of nature.

A cloister provides several choices for privacy. We can sit deep within its sheltering roof and observe the prospect of nature before us, walk

Figure 3.12 Physical characteristics that create the opportunity for prospect and refuge can provide for a variety of privacy experiences in interior environments.

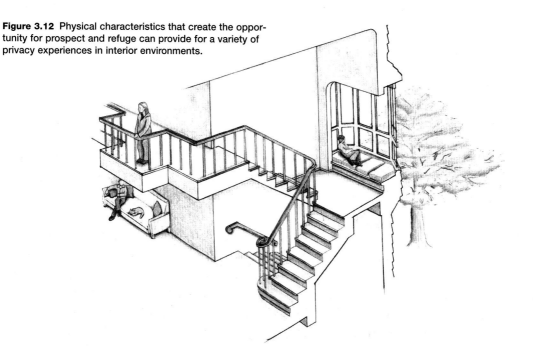

along its path and observe the changing scene, or leave the refuge and venture into the areas of prospect with the assurance that we are not fully exposed. In all cases we can experience involuntary attention and a sense of connectedness. Many cloisters also provide mystery and fascination by the arrangement of vantage points to the prospect. (See **Figure 3.11**).

The window seat is another important application of prospect and refuge. It is an alcove with a view, a stimulus shelter as discussed previously. Window seats project us into the view and provide a vantage point that enables us to better survey our surroundings. Depending upon their design, window seats can be dramatic spots or secret spaces. They can take us to another place or take us inside ourselves. (See **Figure 3.12**).

FINAL THOUGHTS ON THE PHYSICAL CHARACTERISTICS OF ENVIRONMENTS THAT PROMOTE PRIVACY

Privacy theorist Irwin Altman (1975) tells us that the dynamic relationship between people and environments means that there exists a mutual and dual impact between the two. The environment acts on people and people act on the environment. Although designers strive to create environments that meet human needs, we know that those needs are not static, and environments should not be static either. Rarely should we design for a fixed, unalterable "need." Our personal space zones expand and contract, territories shift and relocate, stress levels vary from time to time and place to place. This is why it is important to consider the three variables when designing for privacy: individual needs, environmental opportunities, and the interactions between the two. The patterns are the expression of the dynamic relationship between individual needs and environmental opportunities. As designers, we put together the "ingredients" that make the patterns live so that environments respond to and affect people while people respond to and affect their environments.

Designing for privacy needs requires that we view the physical characteristics of the built environment as flexible changing forms that can be manipulated, altered, and shaped to our needs. A great deal can be learned about this viewpoint by studying our needs to experience and affiliate with nature. Privacy and nature share a common quality. Both have the ability to provide restoration from stress and mental fatigue. Nature is never static. The constantly changing quality of nature is one reason it serves as an effective positive distraction. When designers integrate nature into private places, it is reasonable to suggest that the restorative experience truly may be enhanced.

In the next four chapters we will look at how the physical characteristics—both natural and human-made—that promote privacy may be applied to the design of the built environment. We will examine privacy needs, environmental opportunities, and the interactions between the two for four specific types of environments: residential, office, healthcare, and hospitality.

KEY CONCEPTS

1. A common thread running through the concepts and theories discussed in Chapters 1 and 2 is the assertion that the experience of desired privacy is restorative.

2. Privacy is effective in providing both physical and psychological restoration for three reasons: 1) It is an expression of both choice and control, essential factors in the development and maintenance of a healthy self-identity. 2) It can promote recovery from stress and mental fatigue by providing the

opportunity and resources that foster rest, recovery, and contemplation. 3) Through providing for desired levels of intimacy, privacy facilitates positive social interaction with those from whom we need social support.

3. Our reactions to environments fall into one of two broad categories that Mehrabian terms *approach* and *avoidance*. Approach behavior is a positive response to an environment involving our desire to be in that environment, to explore it, to interact with it and with other people. Avoidance behavior is a negative response to an environment that we perceive as unsupportive of our needs and performance of activities.

4. Environmental evaluation and subsequently whether we tend to approach or avoid certain environments depends on the environmental load; the ratio of novelty to familiarity; our individual ability to screen stimuli; our attitudes, expectations, memories and motivations; our feelings of affiliation with others in the environment; and our perception of the environment's ability to support our performance of necessary activities.

5. Preferences for environmental characteristics that promote privacy are those that are perceived to provide control by allowing us to establish desired visual, acoustical, and physical territories and personal space, and that provide the opportunity to redirect our attention away from stress-producing stimuli.

6. Characteristics of preferred environments include complexity, coherence, legibility, and mystery.

7. Private interactions with nature, such as the experience of wilderness solitude, provides some of the most effective restorative benefits to our health and well-being.

8. Designing for privacy requires an understanding of the relationship between three variables: individual needs, environmental opportunities, and the interactions between the two.

9. Using the "patterns" of Christopher Alexander and his colleagues, we can explore the ways that we respond, based upon privacy needs, to certain physical qualities of the environment.

10. Design elements and architectural dimensions linked to privacy include spatial hierarchy, spatial depth, circulation paths, sociofugal and sociopetal spaces, thresholds, stimulus shelters, light, color, and prospect and refuge.

ASSIGNMENT
IDENTIFYING PRIVACY PATTERNS

Learning Objectives:
• To create a list and sketchbook of physical characteristics that promote privacy from personal observation
• To identify the interactions (patterns) between privacy needs and environmental opportunities

Learning Outcomes:
• Development of observational abilities
• Development of analysis abilities
• Development of quick sketching skills
• Increased understanding of the relationship between human beings and the environment

Description:
Choose a place you prefer to go to when you need privacy. It may be an interior space or a natural outdoor environment. Take the time to settle in and observe the physical characteristics that support privacy for you. It may be the

degree of enclosure, the extent of the view, its remoteness, its familiarity, the amount of control you have over access to the space, the opportunity for prospect and refuge, or any of the many other characteristics described in this chapter that support your privacy needs.

Now look for patterns. What can you learn about the relationship between your privacy needs and the ways in which the physical characteristics of your private place support or promote the experience of privacy? Does the relationship make you want to explore (mystery)? Does it make you feel safe and secure (basic needs)? Does it connect you with something larger and more important than yourself (positive distractions)? Does it make you feel as if you have greater power over your environment (choice and control)? Does it change your visual and psychological perspective (prospect and refuge)? Does it shelter you from the outside world (stimulus shelter)? What other patterns can you identify that link your privacy needs to the characteristics of the physical environment that create your private place? How do these characteristics promote these responses?

Describe and sketch these patterns. Then save them and review them when you return again to your preferred private place. Or compare them against other private places you find over the next few months. Use your privacy sketchbook as reference to provide ideas and inspiration that will help you design for privacy in your projects and assignments.

REFERENCES

Alexander, C. (1979). *The timeless way of building*. New York: Oxford University Press.

Alexander, C. A.; Ishikawa, S.; Silverstein, M.; Jacobson, M.; Fiksdahl-King, I.; & Angel, S. (1977). *A pattern language*. New York: Oxford University Press.

Altman, I. (1975). *The environment and social behavior: Privacy, personal space, territory, crowding*. Monterey, CA: Brooks Cole Publishers.

Appleton, J. (1996). *The experience of landscape*. London: Wiley.

Birren, F. (1969). *Light, color and environment*. New York: Van Nostrand Reinhold.

Evans, G. W.; Lepore, S. J.; & Schroeder, A. (1996). "The role of interior design elements in human responses to crowding." *Journal of Personality and Social Psychology*, 70, 41–46.

Evans, G. W. & McCoy, J. M. (1998). "When buildings don't work: The role of architecture in human health." *Journal of Environmental Psychology*, 18, 85–94.

Hall, Edward T. (1969). *The hidden dimension*. New York: Anchor, Doubleday.

Hammit, W. (1982). "Cognitive dimensions of wilderness solitude." *Environment and Behavior*, 14, 478–493.

Hammit, W. and Brown, Jr., G. (1984). "Functions of privacy in wilderness environments." *Leisure Sciences* 6, 151–166.

Heerwagen, J. & Orians, G. H. (1993). "Humans, habitats, and aesthetics." In S. Kellert and E. O. Wilson (Eds.), *The Biophilia Hypothesis*, 138–172. Washington: Island Press.

Hollenhurst, S.; Frank III, E.; & Watson, A. (1994). "The capacity to be alone: Wilderness solitude and growth of the self." In J. C. Hendee, C. Martin, & G. Vance (Eds.), *International Wilderness Allocation, Management, and Research*. Ft. Collins, CO: International Wilderness Leadership Foundation, 234–239.

Hollenhorst, S. J. & Jones, C. D. (2001). *USDA Forest Service Proceedings*, RMRS-P-20.

Kaplan, R. (1984). Dominant and variant values in environmental preference. In A. S. Devlin & S. L. Taylor (Eds.), *Environmental Preference and Landscape Management*. New London: Connecticut College.

Kaplan, R. & Kaplan, S. (1989). *The experience of nature: A psychological perspective*. Cambridge: Cambridge University Press.

Kaplan, S. (1979). "Where cognition and affect meet: A theoretical analysis of preference." In J. L. Nasar (Ed.). *Environmental Aesthetics: Theory, Research, & Applications*, 56–63. New York: Cambridge University Press.

Kaplan, S. (1992). "The restorative environment: Nature and human experience." In D. Relf (Ed.), *The Role of Horticulture in Human Well-Being and Social Development: A National Symposium* [Proceedings of Conference Held 19–21 April 1990, Arlington, VA], 134–142. Portland, OR: Timber Press.

Kellert, S. (1993). "The biological basis for human values of nature." In S. Kellert & E. O. Wilson (Eds.) *The Biophilia Hypothesis*, 42–72. Washington, DC: Island Press.

Kellert, S. (1996). *The value of life*. Washington, DC: Island Press.

Koch, P. (1994). *Solitude: A philosophical encounter*. Chicago: Open Court Press.

Korpela, K., and Hartig, T. (1996). "Restorative qualities of favorite places." *Journal of Environmental Psychology*, 16, 221–233.

LaBastille, A. (1992). "The park of sacred spaces." *The Conservationist*, 46, 4–7.

Lyons, E. (1983). "Democratic correlates of landscape preference." *Environment and Behavior*. 15, 487–511.

Maslow, A. H. (1968). *Toward a psychology of being*. New York: Nan Nostrand Reinhold.

Mehrabian, A. (1976). *Public places and private spaces*. New York: Basic Books, Inc.

Nabhan, G. P. & St. Antoine, S. (1993). "The loss of flora and fauna story: The extinction of experience." In S. Kellert and E. O. Wilson (Eds.), *The Biophilia Hypothesis*, 229–250. Washington, DC: Island Press.

Newell, P. (1998). "A cross-cultural comparison of privacy definitions and functions: A systems approach." *Journal of Environmental Psychology*, 18, 357–371.

Orr, D. W. (1993). "Love it or lose it: The coming biophilia revolution." In S. Kellert and E. O. Wilson (Eds.), *The Biophilia Hypothesis*, 381–414. Washington, DC: Island Press.

Pedersen, D. M. (1997). "Psychological functions of privacy." *Journal of Environmental Psychology*, 17, 147–156.

Sommer, R. (1969). *Personal space*. Englewood Cliffs, NJ: Prentice Hall.

Storr, A. (1988). *Solitude: A return to the self*. New York: Ballantine Books.

Tuan, Y. (1974). *Toptphilia: A study of environmental perception, value, and attitudes*. Englewood Cliffs, NJ: Prentice Hall.

Ulrich, R. (2000). "Effects of healthcare environmental design on medical outcomes." In Dilani, (Ed.), *Design and Health: Proceedings of the Second International Conference on Health and Design.* Stockholm, Sweden: Svensk Byggtjanst.

Ulrich, R. (1995). "Effects of healthcare design on wellness: Theory, and recent scientific research." In S. O. Marberry (Ed.), *Innovations in Healthcare Design.* New York: Van Nostrand Reinhold, 88–104.

Ulrich, R. S. (1993). "Biophilia, biophobia, and natural landscapes." In S. Kellert and E. O. Wilson (Eds.), *The Biophilia Hypothesis,* 73–137. Washington, DC: Island Press.

Ulrich, R. S. (1983). "Aesthetics and affective responses to natural environments." In I. Altman & J. E. Wohlwill (Eds.), *Human Behavior and Environment,* 6, 85–125. New York: Plenum Press.

Veitch, R. & Arkkelin, D. (1995). *Environmental psychology: An interdisciplinary perspective.* Upper Saddle River, NJ: Prentice Hall.

Westin, A. F. (1967). *Privacy and freedom.* New York: Antheneum.

Williams, K., & Harvey, D. (2001). "Transcendent experience in forest environments." *Journal of Environmental Psychology,* 21, (3), 249–260.

Wilson, E. O. (1993). Biophilia and the conservation ethics. In S. Kellert and E. O. Wilson (Eds.) *The Biophilia Hypothesis.* Washington, DC: Island Press.

Wilson, E. O. (1984). *Biophilia: The human bond with other species.* Cambridge: Harvard University Press.

Wilson, E. O., & Kellert, S. (Eds.), (1993). *The biophilia hypothesis.* Washington, DC: Island Press.

Wohlwill, J. F. (1983). "The concept of nature: A psychologist's view." In I. Altman & J. F. Wohlwill (Eds.), *Human Behavior and Environment:* 6, 5–38. New York: Plenum Press.

CHAPTER 4

Privacy and Related Needs in Residential Design

HOME AS THE ULTIMATE PRIMARY TERRITORY

Home is both a physical setting and a psychological and social process. For all of us, the home is our ultimate primary territory that allows us a degree of control not often found in other locations. Privacy regulation enhances family functioning because as individuals we have control over interpersonal boundaries and social interactions. As we discussed in Chapter 1, the regulation of privacy contributes to our sense of well-being and self-identity.

Our homes provide opportunities for restoration, energy renewal, and regeneration (Tognoli 1987)—all facets of privacy. Home provides us with strong feelings of place attachment—the emotional bond with our immediate environment—and the privacy mechanism of territoriality that often manifests itself as feelings of ownership. At its best, home embodies feelings of safety and security.

Concepts about residential privacy have evolved and changed over time. Chapter 4 explores this development as well as privacy theories and related concepts that apply to residential design. Design application in this chapter includes information and recommendations for public spaces, private areas, and special use rooms. This chapter also explores a negative aspect of privacy—crowding—as shown in residential institutional living. Two case studies are provided in this chapter. The first case study, the failure of Pruitt-Igoe, dramatically demonstrates the results of privacy denied. The second case study, examples of Frank Lloyd Wright's work, demonstrates the effective use of the privacy theories and related concepts provided earlier in the chapter.

THE EVOLUTION OF RESIDENTIAL PRIVACY

Let's look first at the causes that precipitated a changed view of the desirability and need for privacy in the home. The concept of residential privacy evolved because of significant changes in architecture, interior design, and the human condition. Prior to these changes, many people had little experience of privacy, intimacy, or the comforts of domestic life. While single-family homes with some type of privacy have existed for hundreds of years, in medieval times the European rural population often lived in tiny homes that were little more than shelters for sleeping. For town dwellers of 14th-century Europe who were enjoying greater financial prosperity, many homes were filled with multiple generations of people living together in fairly public space. The design of a typical house (for an affluent family) featured a grand hall that continually operated for cooking, eating, entertaining, business, and sleeping. Often, there were no hallways, and one walked through rooms to get to other spaces. As late as the 16th century, there was little privacy for the individual, and domestic life changed slowly (Rybczynski 1986).

With the advent of the Industrial Revolution (*c.* 1760–1830), many businesses moved out of the home, leaving rooms unassigned. The most significant changes to privacy in residential architecture and design began at this time in the 18th century with the trend toward specialized, separate rooms in the home. Dining rooms came into common use—separate rooms with tables and chairs set up permanently for one designated function. A new room appeared in contemporary 18th-century interiors—the *chambre*—a private room intended exclusively for sleeping. The greater desire for privacy also introduced sleeping rooms that separated the masters from the servants. Often the children slept with the servants in bedrooms physically removed from their parents (Rybczynski 1986).

With these changes, the parents could have privacy and begin to think of themselves as a couple. As the house became a more private place, family life began to take on a more individual rather than communal character. Rybczynski (1986), writing about the home,

sums up this profound shift from public to private living: "Before the idea of the home as the seat of family life could enter the human consciousness, it required the experience of both privacy and intimacy, neither of which had been possible in the medieval hall" (p. 48).

As appreciation for the concept of residential privacy evolved, scholars from varied disciplines began to address privacy needs and related human needs, assembling a body of theoretical work that we know now is relevant for residential interior design and application.

PRIVACY THEORIES AND RELATED CONCEPTS THAT APPLY TO RESIDENTIAL DESIGN

Privacy in the home cannot operate within a void. Rather, privacy and privacy mechanisms (personal space and territorial behavior) mesh with related human needs that we all have. These needs include choice and control and self-identity and well-being.

Choice and Control

The needs for choice and control to achieve desired levels of privacy within the home are important key concepts. As a primary territory, the home should provide the ability for us to make choices about who has access to us and when as well as how much interaction we have within the home. Because primary territories are under the relatively exclusive control of the inhabitants, homes should provide the necessary controllability to alter the physical environment to meet our needs for privacy.

Self-Identity and Well-Being

Home is also central to the development and maintenance of our self-identity. If, as a primary territory, the home provides ample opportunity for choice and control, it will allow us the space and autonomy for contemplation, self-observation, and self-evaluation. We often look to the home to provide a respite from the high load environments that typically characterize much of modern society. When correctly designed, private places within the home can help to facilitate restoration from the mental fatigue and stress associated with high load environments and thus contribute to our sense of physical and psychological well-being.

Types of Privacy

The types of privacy most often required in our homes are solitude and intimacy. As we learned in Chapter 2, solitude contributes to creativity, contemplation, rejuvenation, and feelings of autonomy. Intimacy contributes to rejuvenation and recovery by providing a sense of refuge and relaxation (Pederson 1997). Other related concepts that we and others (Appleton 1996, Evans et al. 2001, Heerwagen 1990, Hildebrand 1991, Scott 1993) have linked to privacy include prospect and refuge, complexity, order, and mystery.

INTERIOR DESIGN APPLICATION FOR RESIDENTIAL PRIVACY

Any residential interior design project must begin with a comprehensive understanding of the client's needs. A thorough interview conducted by the designer will reveal privacy needs as well as the client's lifestyle, and preferences. A sample form Designer's Interview of the Client that includes privacy considerations used in programming for the entire house is included at the end of this chapter.

Privacy Considerations and Criteria for Residences

We know that profound changes in family life have occurred over a period of years. Today, more than half of the women in the United States are employed outside of the home. The family structure has radically changed as well. Many couples are childless by choice or other determinants. High divorce rates in recent years (51 percent, National Center for Health Statistics 2002) have reshaped the historical pattern of two parents living with the children in one home. Divorced parents today often share family responsibilities, and children may divide their time between two homes. Other families have blended, creating new families who may sometimes have even more challenging needs for privacy.

Design Elements that May Compromise Privacy Needs

Several factors in our contemporary interiors can sometimes compromise privacy needs. We know that spaces that are open make areas look larger and provide flexibility for activities. The down side of this is that in large open areas, privacy can sometimes become compromised if all members of the family universally claim the space. Ideally, space planning delineates a space as public or private, but because houses are most often designed for families, many spaces have to accommodate both public and private activities. Electronic equipment such as stereo systems, larger televisions, and talking computers bombard us with noise. The use of double volume spaces with high ceilings as well as hard surface flooring further increases the sound level. Even leaving home is not the answer, for we have eliminated privacy in our cars as well. We have video plug-ins and car phones, and even having a conversation with one's child in the car is not always possible. We live our lives in an increasingly noisy and intrusive world.

None of us wants spaces that are relentlessly public, and many of us typically do not desire the kind of privacy found in remote areas isolated from the main core of the plan. Traffic patterns that link spaces within the residence should be carefully planned to direct the major traffic flow away from or around the most private areas. The design can also communicate visual cues as to whether a space is public or private. Changing ceiling heights can send a subtle message because high ceilings usually indicate public areas while low ceilings signify intimate private spaces. Changes in lighting levels reinforce the message as well with high levels of ambient light indicating public spaces and lower levels of ambient light as well as portable lighting indicating a private space.

> **FYI** A good home balances private and communal space throughout. It offers magnetic and lively centers, reinforced by light and ceiling shape, with circulation at the edges; and it provides claimable private areas for everyone, even if the spaces are tiny (private niches, desks, window seats, and alcoves). Some spaces are exclusively common; some exclusively private; but most often good rooms are a subtle mixture of the two.
>
> **(Jacobson, Silverstein, & Winslow 2002, p. 14)**

Separate rooms as well as open areas require clarification by the intended use. Is it public with all of the family members utilizing a space? Does the particular space need to support a mix of public and private activities? Or is the room completely private, an "away" room where a person can retreat? The clarification of an area as public or private depends upon the intended function, but the lifestyle of the family can contribute to the designation as well. For example, kitchens can reflect a public or private orientation depending upon family habits. Does one person cook or do several people share in the process? Does the family entertain and encourage guests to congregate in the kitchen, or does the host/cook prefer to have privacy and be undisturbed? These types of preferences emerge from a thorough client interview.

Square Footage Needs and Implications for Privacy

Programming for a residential project often begins with an assessment of square footage needs required for either new home construction or the retrofitting of an existing residence.

> **FYI** Places conducive to solitude are stable and orderly. Sounds are muted and drawn the mind toward quietness. Textures are soft and smooth. Light and colors are quiet and harmonious. Fragrances are soothing and fresh. Seating is comfortable but encourages alertness . . . .
>
> **(Lawlor 1997, p. 155)**

Considerations of square footage include the needs of the client, the size of the family, lifestyle choices, and privacy. Historically, privacy has often not been a concern of the client. The client may express concern for other needs based upon functional requirements such as the number of bedrooms required. Or they may state requirements such as special need rooms and large-sized rooms. On occasion, concerns with size can represent status-based needs for a certain image. The problem with designing and building to appeal to a client's desire for grandeur is that while there may be a transient satisfaction with a house that projects an upscale image, the occupants soon learn that the house may not support their human needs. For example, houses need to be scaled to human size (Susanka 1998), and imposing structures often are not. In addition, a house built as a temple to indicate high success often lacks the cozy private areas that we all need in our homes.

Whether privacy preferences are expressed or not, designers need to recognize that privacy is a legitimate need that must be addressed in residential interiors. A good client interview can establish square footage needs based upon activities that the family pursues, both public and private, and the rooms or areas required, including the concept borrowed from eastern cultures that rooms can support multiple activities, including privacy. Architect Sarah Susanka (1998) comments on the ideal family room: "Think about what happens in the family room: There's a place to watch TV, a place to enjoy the fireplace, a place to do homework, a place to pay bills, a place to play Scrabble. When we think of the family room in this way, it's no longer merely a space bounded by four walls and a ceiling. It can be defined another way altogether: as a series of alcoves, each offering shelter around an activity and surrounding a central sitting area. When this kind of thinking is extended to the entire house, a new definition emerges. A house is a sequence of places for all the different activities that happen there" (pp. 33–34). (See **Figure 4.1**).

Prime Privacy Areas—Bedrooms and Bathrooms

Real privacy, also known as architectural privacy, is the physical privacy usually provided by doors, walls, locks, and other restrictive devices.

Some activities in the home always require real privacy such as the bathroom, rooms for sleeping and sexual intimacy, and certain types of work. Bedrooms are almost always an example of real privacy because privacy is typically the ultimate goal.

CREATING AREAS OF PRIVACY WITHIN THE HOME

• Place rooms along a privacy gradient, with the most public spaces near the entry and the most private more remote.

• Borrow space from the edges of the more public rooms to create passages that enliven the space but don't disrupt the activities taking place within.

• Create an intimacy gradient by using changing ceiling heights across the house. High ceilings usually define public areas and low ceilings can define intimate spaces.

(Jacobson, Silverstein, & Winslow 2002, p. 181)

Figure 4.1 Sequence of place, public and private areas.

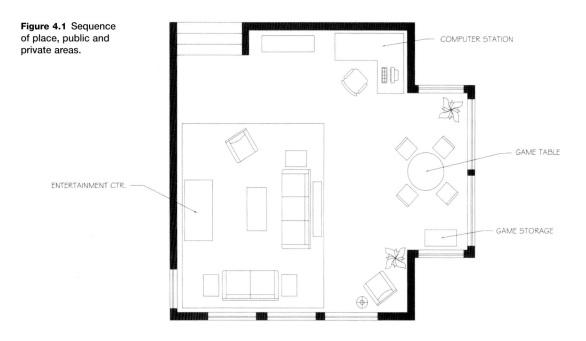

COMPUTER STATION

GAME TABLE

GAME STORAGE

ENTERTAINMENT CTR.

If at all possible, a master bedroom should function as more than a sleeping room. Alexander et al. (1977) designated a pattern called "Couple's Realm," which illustrates the importance of creating private areas for adults apart from the public and children's areas: "Make a special part of the house distinct from the common areas and all the children's rooms, where the man and woman of the house can be together in private. Give this place a quick path to the children's rooms, but at all costs, make it a distinctly separate realm" (p. 650).

Design application can enhance the feeling of being in a private realm. Heavy-duty insulation inside the walls and/or the use of fabric textiles on the wall will buffer the space from unwanted acoustical intrusions. This special place should be planned for a number of activities. It should be a place to sit and talk privately; a place for solitary contemplation; and a place for redirected attention by providing the opportunity to read, watch television, or listen to music in private. To further enhance the need for choice and controllability necessary for privacy, Alexander suggests that this area should have a transition space such as an anteroom or at least a distinctive threshold that separates it

!APPLICATION!

Provide spaces for parents and children to be alone as well as together. Bedrooms should not become primary spaces for family interactions.

(Maxwell 1996)

from the other areas. He also suggests that the bed be tucked away into an alcove with its own window, that the space have a fireplace and a balcony or door of its own to the outdoors, both of which provide redirected attention and therefore can enhance restorative experiences.

Perhaps no room epitomizes primary territory more than the bathroom. In some homes, bathrooms are the only private spaces, but even the smallest most modest home usually furnishes the minimal privacy of four walls and a lockable door. In some situations, the bathroom is the only truly private space in the home. Bathrooms furnish privacy and sometimes, if space and budget permit, allow for restorative experiences. The space planning of a bathroom contributes to the possibility of restorative experiences. For example, a large whirlpool tub located by a window with a protected view to the outdoors encourages leisurely bathing and relaxing in an atmosphere of privacy. Planning toilet facilities in another lockable room within the space creates an even more private refuge. If possible, the use of natural light in the bathroom area at least part of the time can enhance feelings of relaxation and well-being.

LINK
For a definition and an illustration of an inglenook fireplace, see p. 87 and p. 88, this chapter.

Creating Private Residential Spaces

While one of the rewarding experiences of family life is the ability to interact with those around us, we also need opportunities for privacy experiences that restore and rejuvenate us in our homes. In this primary territory, we need the kind of time that refreshes us so we can reenter the outside world, and these qualities are often found in privacy experiences. Sometimes, as we learned in Chapter 3, fascination is part of the experience with its ability to provide us with nondirected attention. Or it may be the mood of a space with intimations of peace and solitude.

Prospect, Refuge, and Nature Opportunities

Prospect and refuge needs dating back to antiquity are timeless. One of the most satisfying experiences of residential privacy is the feeling of safety, of being in and looking out. Children understand this experience intuitively when they make hiding places in tree houses or cardboard boxes. As Sarah Susanka (1998) comments, "The alcove is the adult's equivalent of the cardboard box," and it contributes to the experience of prospect and refuge. Many tucked-up places in a home can serve as refuge: inglenook fireplaces, landings, window seats, porches, corners, and any kind of partially concealed and raised advantage.

Prospect and Refuge

Think about perches, playhouses, alcoves, and window seats: solid backs and open fronts. In all cases, the core of the experience is being able to observe the outer world comfortably from a position of relative security. Usually, the refuge is at a higher position and is enclosed and dark—the outlook is normally below, unenclosed, and light. At its simplest, we are inside looking out.

(Jacobson, Silverstein, & Winslow 2002, p. 16)

Prospect enhances visual privacy at the same time that it serves our need for a connection to nature, particularly if our design application maximizes prospect opportunities. One way of accomplishing this is to expand the views. Designing large open spaces rather than boxes of rooms separated by passageways or hallways is effective. In addition, if the footprint of a home is oriented so that one can look along the diagonal from one corner to the opposite corner, the space will appear larger, and the view of the exterior will seem larger also. Additionally, the use of corner windows will "dissolve the corner" and carry the eye in an unbroken line to the outside world. (See **Figure 4.2**).

Alcoves and Corners

We can find ourselves in environmentally overwhelming situations in many of our environments, including our homes. In Chapter 3 we learned that stimulus shelters are places where we can find respite and restoration, leaving behind situations that demand too much directed attention and often cause fatigue. A residential alcove is an example of a stimulus

Figure 4.2 Diagonal planning to maximize prospect and enhance views of nature. © Karen Melvin Photography for Sara Susanka Architect and Eric Odon, Sala Architects.

shelter that provides for our dual privacy needs to both interact and to restrict interaction. The alcove is a physical extrusion from a core space, and while it is completely connected to the larger space, it can serve a separate function such as a reading area or a private writing area. (See **Figure 4.3**). In a residential alcove, we are in a public space where we may interact with others, but the alcove has a feeling of privacy and removal from the rest of the space.

FYI Corners and angles in a house are symbols of solitude for the imagination, providing opportunities for secluded space in which to hide or withdraw.

(Bachelard 1969)

Unlike alcove areas that are grafted upon the core, corners are part of the common space. Every public area of a residence has corners that can be utilized for privacy. For example, window seats work well in corners to create a sense of privacy. Window seats are another type of

stimulus shelter, and as we learned in Chapter 3, they provide prospect and refuge opportunities as well as allow for involuntary attention because they place us closer to nature.

Windows

Windows are the visual link between the interior of the residence and the outdoor world. In any built environment, we want windows and the view to the outside (Heerwagen et al. 1986, Heerwagen 1990). At the same time, we want privacy in the primary territory of our homes. Placement of the windows has implications for residential privacy. On the first level, placement relative to the floor is important. Most of us want to see the ground outside as well as the horizon and the sky.

FYI Tall vertical windows help capture the full spectrum of daylight because it comes from more sources from the sky all the way to the ground.

(Tolpin 1998)

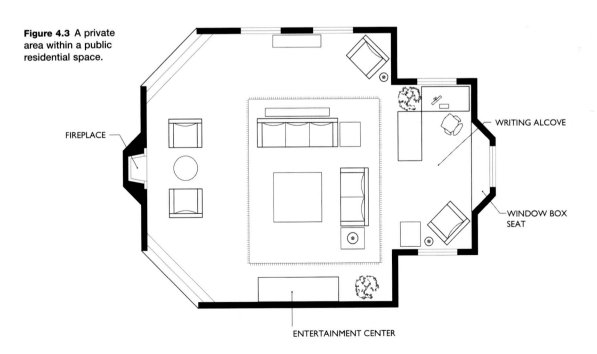

Figure 4.3 A private area within a public residential space.

FIREPLACE

WRITING ALCOVE

WINDOW BOX SEAT

ENTERTAINMENT CENTER

A recommended height for first floor windows is 16 inches from the floor. However, low windows also allow people to see into the house, so depending upon the window treatment, 16 inches is not always practical. On the second floor, low-placed windows are preferred also so that viewers can see more than just the sky (Tolpin 1998).

In some situations, we can leave windows in untreated, pristine condition to maximize a beautiful view and to enhance our connection to the outdoor world. There are, however, variables such as the unstable nature of natural daylight, changing weather conditions, and our needs for privacy. Treatment of the window glass to eliminate glare or to protect privacy may be sufficient and will eliminate the need for additional window treatments. If this is not practical, design application should include consideration of privacy needs relative to the type and level of light desired (Tolpin 1998). The types of window treatments that are desirable for privacy are treatments that offer options between open and closed. Besides the standard adjustable window treatments that we use, examples of other treatments include shades that work from the bottom up or translucent fabrics that allow light to come through but obscure details within the home.

FYI Unfiltered light coming through a window can feel harsh and create unpleasant contrasts of light and dark. Filtered light full of dancing shadows (from a treated window) creates a cheerful ambiance.

(Tolpin 1998)

Lighting

An abundance of natural light streaming through windows provides a strong connection with the daily and seasonal changes of the natural world. Private residential spaces that

!APPLICATION!

• Shape the house so that light can enter every important room from at least two sides to create a balance.

• Plan the placement of rooms so that each space receives light at a suitable time of day for the activities that occur there.

• When light from a second side is not possible, allow for light from above through skylights or clerestory windows.

(Jacobson, Silverstein, & Winslow 2002)

include natural light from multiple directions create the opportunity for redirected attention that may enhance the restorative potential of these private spaces.

Artificial lighting is a powerful tool in design application for visual privacy in residential interiors. Lighting, perhaps more than any other element of design, determines the mood of a space. Designing an environment conducive to privacy requires contrast in lighting levels and types. If every area is lit uniformly, the house will feel static, bland, and public. Contrasts in lighting levels furnish cues as to an area's public or private function. A pool of bright ambient light over a space sends a visual cue of public use, while adjacent areas with lower levels of lighting have connotations of privacy or intimacy.

FYI Light is always interrelated with shadow. With balanced lighting, pools of bright light draw us in because they highlight an area. Shadowy corners or edges lend mystery to a well lit interior. It is the play of light and shadow that brings life to our environment.

(Jacobson, Silverstein, & Winslow 2002)

Choosing the type of lighting to enhance privacy for a residence requires consideration of the intended activity. We know that privacy is not always about solitude. It is also about the types of interaction that we desire with others. Private activities require lighting that is interesting, intimate, and may contain an element of mystery. Luminaires that work well for privacy needs include

- *Table and floor lamps (especially those that direct the light upward or diffuse the light through softly textured colored shades)*
- *Accent lighting (to highlight artwork, plants, or focal points)*
- *Lighting integrated into furniture and cabinetry*
- *Wall sconces*

Dimmable switches that can be incorporated into any of these luminaries are desirable because they can change the mood and the privacy level of a space. Ideally, a lighting control system should be installed throughout the home to enhance the changing individual needs for privacy.

Ceiling Heights and Changes in Floor Levels
A space that has high ceilings, no changes in floor level, and a high degree of homogenous

lighting usually indicates a public area. A residential space that is very open, that has more than one ceiling height or floor level, and that contains contrast in lighting will usually appear as a space with both public and private options. (See **Figure 4.4**). In residential interiors, if there are different ceiling heights, typically the core or public spaces have the higher ceilings. A dropped ceiling within a space identifies an area such as an alcove or a dining room as a more intimate space. A change in floor level reinforces the perception that the area is different, either more or less private, from the rest of the space.

Ceiling treatments also contribute to the perception of privacy in the residence. If a room receives a flat, smooth, unadorned ceiling in a light color such as in an entry hall, it will feel taller and indicate more public use. If the ceiling treatment is dark, textured, or treated with coffers or beams such as a study or den, it will appear lower and heavier. The visual weight of that treatment will bring down the height of the space, often suggesting an area for private use, because low ceilings intensify the intimacy of a room (Susanka 2001).

All of these variables influence the quantity and quality of sound traveling through a space. In general, if the space is large, open, and has a high ceiling, the potential for the loss of acoustical privacy is high. To enhance acoustical

Figure 4.4 Change the ceiling height and the lighting levels to indicate a public or private area.

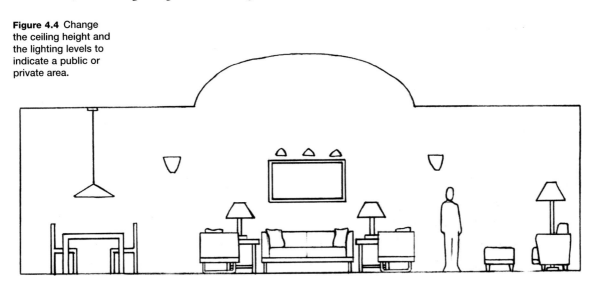

privacy in this type of public residential space, seating areas should be planned in sociopetal arrangements and within social distance zones as described in Chapters 2 and 3. Excess noise in these larger public residential spaces can also be compensated for by the use of sound absorbing materials on walls, floors, and upholstery.

Floor and Wall Treatments

Floor and wall treatments can significantly contribute, either positively or negatively, to the experience of acoustical privacy. Both impact sounds and airborne sounds must be considered when specifying flooring for private areas. In these areas designated as private, good choices for acoustical privacy in flooring include carpeting and resilient flooring. Cork and linoleum are excellent natural resilient flooring choices and good alternatives to vinyl and rubber, which are petroleum based products and therefore contribute to poor indoor air quality in enclosed private spaces. These treatments work well because they are "soft" and have a low incidence of noise reflectance. The designer must evaluate the noise level of the specified floor before specifying wall treatments. If the flooring is noisy, then the designer can compensate by specifying a wall treatment that provides additional acoustical privacy.

Smooth finished painted walls will bounce more of the sound waves back. Heavily textured painted walls will yield less sound. Walls treated with sound-absorbing wall coverings or textiles will absorb more sound. Sometimes we must compromise for the sake of a more private ambience. For example, if a hard surface flooring is desired or necessary, stone or wood while still considered acoustically lively, will generate less noise reflectance than ceramic tile.

Areas that combine public and private activities usually make up the majority of the square footage of a residence. Flooring treatments can provide visual cues about the combined use of these blended spaces. For example, marble or wood floors often suggest public use. If a private activity area is nearby, we might specify a wood floor accompanied by a large area rug. If we want maximum acoustical privacy, we can specify deep pile carpeting over a dense pad.

Special Use Rooms

Contemporary residential interiors often include special use rooms because Americans have typically believed in spaces (as large as possible) designated for a sole activity. In addition, with our increased technology, the lines between work and home are becoming increasingly blurred.

Home Offices

Many people today work at home on a full-time and sometimes exclusive basis. When an office is brought into the home, it creates a serious privacy challenge: a potential conflict between the accepted notions of work privacy and home sociability. In addition, problems may arise if the work involves clients and employees coming to the residence and intruding into the sanctuary of the home. Before examining specific types of design applications for home offices, the designer should understand the needs that research studies have determined are critical for the optimal experience of privacy in home offices. (See **Figure 4.5**).

Design and Privacy Considerations for Home Offices
Magee (2000) examined how people can integrate work spaces within the home to achieve two important goals: to reinforce the social structure of the family while also providing the privacy of limited and protected communication that work experiences demand. Magee's survey of home owners indicates that they placed "significant emphasis on fundamental behavioral concerns such as privacy and mental well-being over factors such as aesthetics and physical features" (p. 39). (See **Table 4.1**). Magee's study indicates that while home owners first selected the location of their office spaces

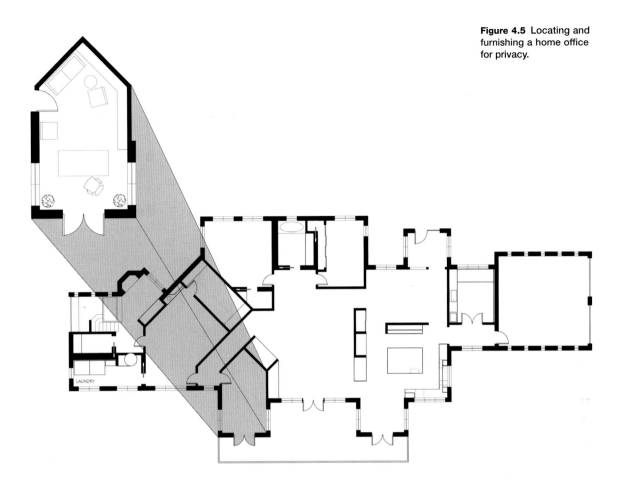

Figure 4.5 Locating and furnishing a home office for privacy.

based upon availability (90 percent), the second most important reason expressed was the seclusion of the work spaces and their separation from busy areas (84 percent).

The same survey revealed that whenever possible the homeowners set up their offices in a space defined by permanent walls (94 percent). In addition, 47 percent of the workers kept their office spaces completely devoted to work activities. The designated work spaces rarely allowed nonoffice activities to occur in the spaces. Offices became private work retreats away from family activities, but home workers moved outside of the offices and back into public areas to fulfill needs for interaction with family members. Magee concluded that the spatial overlap between home and work ran in one direction only. While work could overflow into the home environment, home activities could not enter the work space.

Respondents working at home who participated in an earlier survey (Ahrentzen 1989) were questioned about their feelings after bringing their work into the home for a period of time. In general, most of the people who worked at home still regarded the home as a haven and even more of a refuge than before. Respondents mentioned the relief of being removed from the stresses of corporate life and the necessity of commuting. Others, however, revealed that the sense of refuge had evolved into feelings of isolation and entrapment with a few extreme agoraphobic reactions. For those reporting negative feelings, the home felt like less of a refuge, particularly when "invaded" by clients. Exposure of family members and private areas of the home to clients reduced the desired separation of public activities from domestic life. Some of the people who worked at home occasionally expressed feelings of isolation. They coped by leaving the residence

Table 4.1 Selecting a location for a home office.

Availability and privacy are the main reasons a certain space in the home is selected for work.

REASONS FOR SPATIAL SELECTION

Availability	90%	Close to entry	16%
Private and separate	84%	Close to family	15%
Size	40%	Appearance	6%
Views and light	27%	Other	5%

Magee, Jennifer L. (2000). **Home as an alternative workplace: negotiating the spatial and behavioral boundaries between home and work.** *Journal of Interior Design, 26, 1.*

!APPLICATION!

DESIGN APPLICATION TO ESTABLISH PRIVACY IN HOME OFFICES

• Include a lockable door, if possible, such as closed wood.

• If the door is more open, such as a French door with glass panes, and visual privacy is important, use window treatments on the open parts of the door.

• Specify acoustical treatment of walls to keep out unwanted noise.

• Use thresholds with different treatments on each side: one side to imply public use (the family) and one side to imply private use (the office).

• Use level changes whenever possible if you want to signal the transition from a public to a private space.

---

frequently, having lunch out, and making phone calls to friends. Ahrentzen's survey, bolstered by other studies within the corporate culture, determined that overall, working at home is a positive experience if it is handled in a way that respects the privacy needs of the worker while integrating the social needs of the family.

Determining Client Privacy Needs for Home Offices
When interviewing clients about their home office privacy needs, designers should pose three specific questions prior to any type of design application.

  • *What is the composition of the family at the present time?*
  • *What is the nature of the work?*
  • *What are the options and preferences for the location of the office?*

The answers to the first question will reveal the level of privacy required. Is it an all-adult environment, or are there children? How old are they? Does anyone else live with the family? This information is critical prior to undertaking the design of a home office.

Answers to the second question also determine levels of privacy needed. Some types of work require high degrees of directed attention with no outside interruptions. Other work is less intense, and the need for a high privacy level may not be so acute. The designer also needs to assess the personal needs of the person who works at home. While most workers require a fairly high degree of real privacy, there is the occasional person whose needs for communication and sociability outweigh privacy needs. This is best determined by frank interview questioning and observation.

The third question is the most complex. Choosing a location for the home office often involves compromise. Is a location chosen because it offers deep privacy, or is it chosen because it allows the home worker to keep an eye on the children? Is the space selected for outdoor views, proximity to the front door, large square footage? Is it the only space available (Magee 2000)? Ahrentzen (1989) presents what home workers feel are the desired locations for the home office. The responses show inconsistency, probably because answers are colored by factors such as the family mix, the need to have client meetings in the home, and the nature of the work itself. (See **Table 4.2**).

While Ahrentzen found consensus difficult, in general there are areas of mutual agreement. The following areas are preferred to be kept far away from work areas: bedrooms, TV rooms, the private living areas of the home, the den, and the rooms with views outdoors. However, people who work at home often expressed a desire to see into such spaces as the outdoors, corridors, or living rooms. This probably indicates a need for a sense of prospect with these spaces to allow visual distancing without making contact with people. An example is the desire of a home worker to watch children playing outside. The rooms they desire to be distant from are usually the rooms that generate noise: TV room, den, and kitchen, but also rooms where noise from the work space, such as printing, could disturb other people who are sleeping.

In Ahrentzen's study, 86 percent of home workers wanted a separate room, but only six and a half percent wanted a separate, detached structure. Over 69 percent expressed a strong desire for a work place that could be shut off from noise. When others are present in the household, home workers stated that they prefer their work space to be visually inaccessible to others. Home workers who had business meetings at home wanted physical characteristics that maintained separateness of the work space from other parts of the house: direct outside entrance to work space, separate conference room, and no visual accessibility for the family.

Ahrentzen found strong feelings of territoriality among home workers. Respondents indicated that they did not like household members or friends to go into their offices. Interestingly, the same home workers mentioned that because they worked almost exclusively at home, other

Table 4.2 Preferences for home offices.

Percentage of Respondents Who Mention Desired Location of Rooms in Relation to Work Space.

ROOMS CLOSE TO WORK SPACE	ROOMS AWAY FROM WORK SPACE	ROOMS VISIBLE FROM WORK SPACE
62.5% Bathroom	35.6% Bedroom(s)	10.6% Outdoors, yard, balcony
33.7% Kitchen	31.7% Kitchen	5.8% Living room
12.5% Front entry	20.2% Living room	2.9% Corridor
8.7% Living room	17.3% Den, rec room, TV room	2.9% Kitchen
6.7% Den, rec room, TV room	11.5% "Living" areas of home	
5.8% Bathrooms	8.7% TV room	

Magee, Jennifer L. (2000). Home as an alternative workplace: negotiating the spatial and behavioral boundaries between home and work. *Journal of Interior Design, 26, 1.*

parts of the home had become the refuge from the work spaces.

Design Application to Provide Privacy for Home Offices

The best solution for privacy in a home office is to locate the space appropriately. We know from Chapter 3 that using Alexander's Intimacy Gradient pattern of locating more private areas deeper within the space enables people to be able to make better choices between interaction with others and privacy.

We also need to provide the ability to control visual and auditory privacy. Glass doors solve many needs. They provide a visual connection to the home and to the family, while at the same time providing auditory privacy. If a greater degree of visual privacy is desired, screening devices such as shades and blinds are used. Visual separation is important for another more subtle privacy reason. Leaving a closed private area and returning to the family areas at night establishes the needed feeling of separation between work and home.

Home offices require design application geared to residential type solutions. One reason that home workers need residential type applications is to balance the "high tech" with "high touch" that John Naisbitt recommends, as discussed in chapter 3. Many of the needs of modern offices are at odds with residential interior design. Electronic equipment alone presents the designer with a sea of plastic. Using softly textured, sound-absorbing textiles in residential type patterns on upholstered furniture can help soften the high tech characteristics of the equipment. A view to the outdoors will furnish the needed connection to nature and help to provide nondirected attention. Live plants and artwork depicting scenes of the natural world can contribute to making time spent in the home office a pleasant experience of privacy as well as interaction on some level with nature.

In spite of many changes in lifestyle, when we are at home we want the emotional support of well-being, rejuvenation, and affiliation with family members. A home office must not only support these needs but also must function as a professional environment equal to that provided by an office away from the home. Research studies (Becker 1993) indicate that if home offices are perceived as inferior to a traditional office away from the home, home workers can sometimes suffer feelings of inadequacy and lowered self-esteem.

Homes have changed with the introduction of work practices into our primary territories, but professional work within the home is not a negative experience. As humans, we are adaptable. Our homes can accommodate new needs and remain strong havens if we are sensitive to deeply embedded needs such as privacy.

Children's Spaces and Bedrooms

Children experience home differently than adults. According to Alexander et al. (1977), ". . . in general the child's world is not some single space or room—it is a continuum of spaces" (p. 653). Places inside the home that adults take for granted can become places of fascination, enchantment, and wonder for children, usually through the use of imagination. The dining room table with its long draped cloth can become a fort or a hiding place. A space under the stairs can become a secret place, another home, or a grocery store. Alexander (1977) refers to these places as Child Caves, places that offer a child sized alternative to "adult spaces." He suggests that these places have very low ceiling heights of two feet six inches to four feet and that the entrances be even smaller.

Research studies have documented the preference that children have for small, enclosed places. Enclosure satisfies strong needs for privacy, represents protection from the outside world, and furnishes the feeling of belonging (place attachment) to a specific place. In addition, small, enclosed spaces support strong needs during childhood for seclusion, exploration, and imagination (Boschetti 1987).

Children's Experience of Privacy

Children experience privacy differently than adults. For a child, residential privacy is power in a microenvironment controlled by adults. The shelter of a child's bedroom provides feelings of aloneness within the familiar confines of the home. Here a child can fantasize, develop self-identity, and most of all exercise some control over access to his or her world. Children beyond infancy need the experience of control within their own age-specific limitations. Control experienced long enough will typically lead to autonomy at a later stage of their development. Control for a child in his or her room is dependent upon interior design application as well as the cooperation of the parent. Obviously a lockable door signifies control, but may not be an option, depending upon the age of the child. Allowing the child to participate in some of the design decisions in the bedroom can provide control. For example, the design concept can represent some interest or passion of the child rather than merely a selection made by the designer and the parent. Colors are important to children, and within reasonable limitations, a child should assist in the selection of a color scheme. Other control enhancing options include getting the child's opinion on the location for treasured possessions and allowing the child to personalize the space to represent his or her own interests.

Other factors, however, may threaten the experience of privacy in the bedroom. Sharing a room with a sibling often poses a frustration to a child's sense of autonomy and control. In shared rooms, crowding can become a real issue, either because of constrained spaces or the perception of lack of territorial privacy. Research studies (Maxwell 1996) have shown that children do not seem able to adapt successfully to crowding.

Children have a sharply defined sense of territoriality based on the immaturity of their own needs. Everything is "mine." Where more subtle expressions of territorial behavior may work for adults, children require physical boundaries to clarify "mine" from "yours." Space planning should minimize things that have to be shared such as desks. "Separate but equal" works best in children's bedrooms. Even a blatant line painted down the middle of the space to separate the "property" can be effective, particularly with siblings who squabble.

LINK
Want to know more about children and crowding? See Chapter 8, page 201.

Design Application to Provide Privacy for Children's Rooms

The first step is to recognize and acknowledge a child's need for privacy. In some cases such as blended families, the need for privacy may be even stronger if feelings of affiliation for the other members of the family have not yet been established. In any family, ideally each child must have a place of his or her own for retreat and refuge (Susanka 1998). The next step in planning any child's bedroom is to consider the age. A young child has privacy needs, and so does a fifteen-year-old adolescent, but their age-specific needs are different. Even if a child has sole "ownership" of the room, others will occasionally enter the space. What areas of the room must be open to other's inspection, and what areas need to be reserved for magical or private things?

Zoning

In a shared bedroom, territorial privacy is critical because each occupant needs to feel ownership of the space. Zoning the room through space planning for each child helps clarify shared areas from private areas. Design applications such as furniture layouts and personalization can present clear and unambiguous ownership of the space. (See **Figure 4.6**).

Sleeping Areas

Children have great flexibility in their sleeping habits because they can usually fall asleep easily

Figure 4.6 Zoning for privacy in shared children's bedrooms.

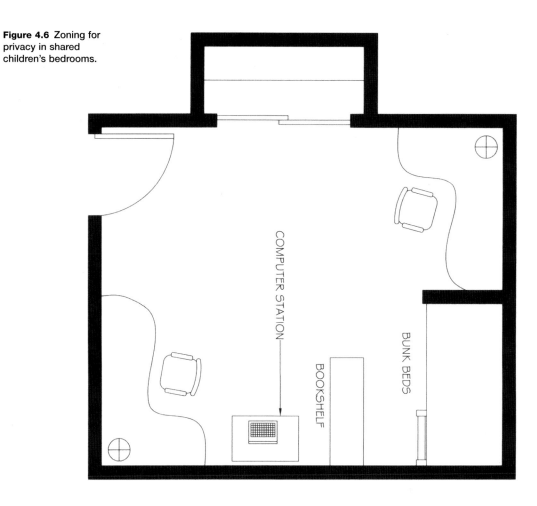

COMPUTER STATION

BOOKSHELF

BUNK BEDS

and often in places that adults might consider undesirable (on the floor or in the back seat of the family car). The designer of the child's bedroom will want to balance sleeping needs with privacy and the other needs that research studies and writers from different disciplines tell us are crucial for a child's development. For example, children need places that are scaled to their size and places that offer opportunity for play and invention (Susanka 1998). Imaginative play experiences for a child are similar to an adult's restorative experiences of privacy.

Most young children love bunk beds for their cozy quality of privacy and their feelings of safety and protection. Using privacy as a priority in design planning, single beds set out individually that might have occupied the major part of a space can be reconfigured, possibly as bunk

beds. Perhaps the beds can be set into an alcove with a ship's ladder for accessing the upper bunk. Now the sleeping space has an "away" feel and becomes a refuge within a refuge. The use of bunk beds in their own alcove or "away" space also frees up additional square footage that can now be used to separate the shared space from the private space in the room. (See **Figure 4.7**).

Activity Areas and Workstations

Territorial privacy is achieved when each child can perform selected activities independently and somewhat separately. Private activities include sleeping, working at a desk, working on a computer, and reading. The spaces that

Figure 4.7 Private alcove for bunk beds. Courtesy of Associates III, Denver, Colorado.

support these separate activities should be located as distantly as possible within the confines of a shared room. For example, the corners of rooms are often wasted space. Stimulus shelters in the form of window seats work well in corners and provide a feeling of privacy. Vertical space is sometimes underutilized. A hammock hung above eye level in a bedroom and near a window can provide an agile child with a space for daydreaming and experiencing nature.

Work performed at a desk, even for a young child, often requires concentration, and many children become easily distracted. Work surfaces should be laid out in a way that prevents eye contact with a sibling.

Lighting

A shared, ambient, overhead light fixture usually signals a public space. For privacy, additional lighting in shared children's bedrooms should be separate and independently operated. Task lighting focused on a work surface provides control and an aura of privacy, particularly if the light level is brighter than the surrounding space. Bedside lighting, individually switched, also enhances privacy and feelings of control.

Personalization

Personalization is the process of expressing one's values, preferences, identity, or territory through modification of the physical environment. Personalizing a space enhances feelings of privacy in the home because it reinforces ownership of primary territory. Personalization in children's bedrooms makes the spaces their own. The act of personalizing can include design applications such as nameplates over private areas, artwork that expresses individual interests, and bulletin boards. If ownership of anything in the room is shared such as a computer, a permission pad with reservation times can lessen conflict and bolster territorial privacy needs.

Modern life has introduced new complexity into all aspects of the built environment, including children's rooms. Because children have privacy needs somewhat specific to their ages, design application demands fresh ideas and innovative approaches within a sometimes small and shared space.

Away Rooms

Sometimes we might dream of places that provide high levels of privacy because they are completely removed from our homes, such as a second home in the mountains or at the shore. If we don't have that option, many of us want an "away room" in our primary residence. An **away room** is an escape room and is typically not intended for work. Escape needs range from separation from noisy entertainment and other acoustical interferences to needs for solitude, reading, or meditation.

If an away room is to be used for private experiences, acoustical intrusion from other areas is unwanted. Design applications might include additional insulation within the walls or the use of a sound-absorbing textile wall covering. Flooring should be quiet as well. Cork can work well as can a floating wood floor with area rugs that help absorb sound as well as define territories and activity areas.

The away room must be furnished for the appropriate activity and preferably should have some flexibility for diverse activities. For example, a window seat, furnished with a soft seat pad and with a wall-mounted reading lamp, can become a cozy area for reading for one person. A small work surface can provide a private area for writing letters or using a notebook computer. There are also times when privacy but not solitude is desired, for example, when two people need to speak privately. Comfortable lounge chairs, placed at right angles in a sociopetal arrangement will create an intimate setting for those types of situations.

CROWDING

Until now we have been discussing privacy needs in single family residential homes. We now turn to a discussion of the psychological state of crowding. Crowding, as we discussed in Chapter 2, is a negative and subjective aspect of privacy that always results in negative feelings (Gove, Hughes, & Galle 1979, cited by Tognoli 1987).

> **FYI** Residents of crowded homes with greater architectural depth, i.e., the number of spaces you must pass through to get from one room to another, are less likely to withdraw socially or to be psychologically distressed than residents who live in crowded homes with relatively low architectural depth.
>
> **(Evans, Lepore, & Schroeder 1996)**

Recent studies (Evans, Lepore, & Schroeder 1996) have confirmed that "overall, individuals living in more crowded homes have higher levels of psychological distress" (p. 43). These responses are consistent whether they emerge from studies of single family homes or other environments. Our discussion of crowding will focus on institutional living and low income housing.

CROWDING AND INSTITUTIONAL LIVING

When we leave home to begin some other lifestyle, such as apartment living or living in a campus dormitory at school, our privacy needs go with us, and there are new challenges to privacy that are not always encountered in the family home. Institutional living environments on college and university campuses present the potential for a number of crowding issues.

While early research studies indicated that high population density alone does not always result in perceptions of crowding and negative social experiences (McCarthy & Saegert 1979), if we find ourselves in environments that are difficult to understand and visually organize and that expose us to unpredictable and uncontrollable social interactions, we often respond in negative and socially alienated ways. McCarthy and Saegert comment:

> High densities contribute to social and cognitive overload by increasing the number of other people with whom an individual may have to deal and by putting those people in close enough proximity that some experience of them is difficult for the individual to avoid (p. 56).

Research studies tell us that anytime students are housed in a greater population density than was originally designed for the plan (such as tripled dormitory rooms intended for two people), the students report that their rooms feel cluttered, public rather than private, and chaotic. Students who experience perceptions of crowding in their dormitories are less satisfied with the residential experience and express negative feelings about the dormitory and about their neighbors (Hopstock, Aiello, & Baum 1979).

> **FYI** Dormitory rooms with more natural light are perceived as less crowded than same sized rooms 85 less natural light.
>
> **(Evans, Lepore, & Schroeder 1996)**
>
> College and university students who report using a wider variety of (successful) privacy regulation mechanisms to avoid unwanted contact with their fellow residents are less likely to drop out of school by the end of the second year.
>
> **(Harris, Brown, & Werner 1996)**

When interior designers can subdivide spaces, delineate spaces as public or private, identify spaces as "belonging" to a specified occupant or used for a particular function, and provide prospect and refuge opportunities, they can enhance feelings of privacy and mitigate the negative experience of crowding.

!APPLICATION!

In college dormitories, provide a common area such as a sitting room between the public corridor and the entry point into the bedrooms instead of providing direct entry from the corridor into the bedrooms. This transitional space can reduce environmental stress and additionally, enhances visual privacy.

(Evans, Lepore, & Schroeder 1996)

CASE STUDIES

Crowding, in any setting, is sometimes the result of actual conditions of population density. The presence of crowding along with insensitivity to privacy needs can have disastrous results. At these times, design fails on a grand scale to meet human needs for privacy and related concepts. Our first case study is a poignant recounting of the failure of privacy.

Case Study #1—Low Income Housing:
Privacy Denied

The most spectacular failure in the neglect of territorial privacy needs on a large scale was the Pruitt-Igoe low income housing project in St. Louis, Missouri, built in 1956 and demolished in 1972. Hailed as an architectural milestone, the project received an award from the American Institute of Architects in 1951. (See **Figure 4.8**).

The original design decisions made by the architect and his firm reflect a clear understanding of territorial privacy needs, i.e., feelings of ownership in multi-family residential environments. Unfortunately, between the time of the design plans and the completion of construction, decisions made by the city in response to the U.S. Supreme Court's decision to strike down segregation greatly restricted the funds available to construct the project. Over the architect's protests, the city forced the design team to double the density, eliminate the low-rise buildings, and severely curtail expenditures for landscaping and services such as gyms, playgrounds, a proposed grocery, and even public restrooms (Sÿpkes 2001).

From the beginning, the revised design of Pruitt-Igoe demonstrated problems. Corridors, lobbies, elevators, and stairs became covered in graffiti and littered with garbage and human waste (Newman 1973). As its reputation for crime and vandalism grew, the population of Pruitt-Igoe declined. In 1972 after spending more than five million dollars attempting to cure the problems of Pruitt-Igoe, the St. Louis Housing Authority demolished three of the high-rise buildings. A year later, aided by the U.S. Department of Housing and Urban Development, the city declared Pruitt-Igoe unsalvageable and razed the rest of the buildings (von Hoffman, online).

The fatal flaw in Pruitt-Igoe was the failure to address human needs, including privacy, specifically territorial privacy, in the finished project. We know that territorial privacy needs concern behavior and how people feel about a space, in this case their primary territory of the home. In Pruitt-Igoe, residents had little or no opportunities for territorial privacy. Consequently, no one had the opportunity to feel a sense of ownership. If we do not own something or feel that we own it, we may or may not take care of it. In Pruitt-Igoe, the latter scenario occurred. The costs for Pruitt-Igoe are not recoverable, but the learning experience is

Figure 4.8 The failure of territorial privacy. © Bettmann/CORBIS.

profound, and the message is clear—in the end, human needs must prevail over financial constraints or current styles in architecture and interior design. Human needs predominate whether we live at home with a family, in an apartment alone or shared, or in some type of communal living arrangement.

Case Study #2—A Celebration of Privacy and Related Needs: Frank Lloyd Wright

Many people have contributed to the body of knowledge on privacy (Altman 1975, Evans et al. 2001, Hall 1969, Newell 1998, Pederson 1997, Sommer 1969). For a number of years there was no formalized link of theory and application to residential privacy. We did have, however, practitioners with vision who intuitively understood the need for privacy. While many architects and designers, academicians and practitioners alike, have contributed to the body of knowledge about residential privacy and related human needs, the person who embodied an understanding throughout his life and career of the many facets of privacy and closely related human needs was Frank Lloyd Wright. Wright had an intuitive knowledge of humankind's most sacred needs, speaking often of "his belief in the organic,

his sympathy with nature, the art and craft of the machine, the concept of shelter, and the destruction of the box" (Hildebrand 1991, p. 27). Wright believed that humans preconditioned by nature will seek out those places that afford them safety and privacy, unthreatening views of nature, and a certain level of complexity and order tempered by elements of hazard and mystery.

The Home as Haven

Beginning with the design of the early Prairie Houses, Frank Lloyd Wright created the home as a haven with strong emphasis on refuge and privacy. The heart of the home was always the fireplace, frequently an **inglenook** design with seats built in along the wall just large enough for a few people to gather (See **Figure 4.9**). To increase the sense of intimacy and privacy, Wright often lowered the ceiling height over the fireplace, making the fireplace area an additional refuge zone within the room that is already a haven. Lowering the ceiling height was a communicative device that Wright used to imply intimacy, and he frequently used the same technique over dining tables (Hildebrand 1991).

Wright's interiors, at least during his early years, were fairly dark. He had little interest at

Figure 4.9 The Home as a haven: Frank Lloyd Wright's inglenook fireplace.

this time in bringing natural light into the space because he envisioned the house as a haven. Consequently, he restricted natural light levels and used artificial light sparingly. He did, however, use brighter levels of lighting in areas that conveyed prospect.

Prospect and Refuge

Wright is often credited with inventing the open plan in residential design, moving away from segmented rooms that cut themselves off from the exterior and from one another physically and visually (Tolpin 1998). This openness allowed him to shape areas into contrasts of prospect and refuge. Quiet corners, frequently with lowered ceiling heights, provided refuge areas, and the open plan heightened the sense of prospect by allowing a vision of the whole space, "analogous to looking past the trees at the edge of the forest to view the meadow beyond" (Hildebrand 1991, p. 36). Many Wrightian residential interiors convey the sense that spaces lie beyond spaces. Spaciousness enhances prospect by giving the users a better view of the surrounding environment while providing a private zoned area to let the users survey within the security of partial concealment (Scott 1993).

FYI   The typical window is a flat surface that defines only one direction. The use of corner windows (two windows that come together in a corner) extends the diagonal views to the horizon, presenting no boundaries to the view.

(Susanka 1998)

Complexity, Order, and Mystery

The residential work of Frank Lloyd Wright is strong in both complexity and order. From his design of the Prairie Homes until the end of his career, Wright respected the need for aesthetic experiences, most often involving privacy, which in turn requires high levels of complexity and order. Complexity and order designed into an environment provide safety, security, and coherence (Hildebrand 1991). A sense of mystery often appears in Wright's residential architecture. Mystery enhances the experience of privacy because mystery contributes to restorative experiences by redirecting attention with its promise of more information.

As early as 1904 with the design of the Cheney house, Wright began a pattern that persisted throughout his domestic career—the design of hidden entry doors. In the Cheney house, there is no clearly defined or centrally located door. The house "protects its actual access through ambiguity (the dual walkways), masking (the screening of view to the door from the street), and convolution" (Hildebrand 1991, p. 38). Finding the door involves a complicated asymmetrical route with level changes that ends ultimately at a private door under the eaves. In the design of the Cheney house, this effective symbol of privacy uses mystery to promise more information rather than revealing the entrance in a straightforward manner. (See **Figure 4.10**).

The sensitivity that Wright often showed for privacy and related needs is revealed even more vividly in what many consider to be his masterpiece, the Kaufman residence, more commonly known as Fallingwater. Designed in 1936, Fallingwater was a giant monolithic slab of a house to be cantilevered over water. The house presented Wright with the challenge to produce a design that by its nature could dramatically demonstrate his convictions about human needs for privacy, complexity, order, mystery, and prospect and refuge. At the same time, Wright had an unparalleled opportunity to envision and design a structure superimposed

Paths and Mystery

In scenes of low mystery, paths imply great distance from the viewer and the promised information. In general, the low mystery paths are straight and often terminate in a closed door or solid wall. In scenes of high mystery, paths are typically shorter and turned out of view or terminate with a partial view of the destination.

(Scott 1993)

Figure 4.10 Frank Lloyd Wright's Cheney House: mystery in residential design. Frank Lloyd Wright (b. 1867–d. 1959), architect. Edwin H. Cheney Residence, Oak Park, Illinois, 1903. Collections of Frank Lloyd Wright Preservation Trust, H&S H677.

upon the natural environment and subdued ultimately within the grandeur of the natural world (Hildebrand 1991). (See **Figure 4.11**).

Although the plan of Fallingwater is open and flowing, it nevertheless meets Wright's criterion for privacy needs because of the other elements it addresses. The house includes prospect and refuge areas that contribute to feelings of safety and security. Fallingwater is also strong in complexity and order, crucial to the design of a large structure. The juxtaposition of the house in its natural setting introduces the element of mystery: can a house cantilevered over rushing water maintain itself, and is it designed in harmony with nature, or in defiance of nature? Hildebrand (1991) describes what to him is Wright's triumph:

> For the house as built does not simply overlook nature's drama, it participates in it, and can only do so located as it is. And this helps us to understand the impor-

tance of the trays cantilevered into space over the water, for they are the essential elements on which this architectural participation depends.... (Hildebrand 1991, p. 104). (See **Figure 4.12**).

Design, like many other disciplines, has the power to fail dismally, as it did in the case of Pruitt-Igoe. However, when design succeeds, there are a multitude of reasons, but at least one of them is because human needs have been addressed with sensitivity and within the context of the entire solution. Our most personal and meaningful experiences often occur in the privacy of our homes or in our homes away from home. Design theory and design application that recognize the importance of privacy needs and related human needs can bolster our image of home as the archetypal human experience. In the end, our homes, no matter what size, are our private castles.

Figure 4.11 Frank Lloyd Wright's Kaufmann Residence: prospect and refuge, complexity and order, mystery, hazard, and harmony with nature. Photographs of Fallingwater courtesy of the Western Pennsylvania Conservancy.

FALLINGWATER

MAIN FLOOR PLAN

Figure 4.12 Floor plan, Kaufmann residence, "Fallingwater" floor plan drawings provided by Astorino, Pittsburgh, PA.

FINAL THOUGHTS ON RESIDENTIAL PRIVACY

Privacy in residential interiors is the ultimate restorative experience. Here we can savor the richness of solitude, enjoy the experience of intimacy, and participate in the experiences of family life. As designers, we are invited in, entrusted with secrets on some occasions, and charged with the task of breathing order, serenity, and privacy into the sacred space that everyone calls home. It is a privilege to be invited.

KEY CONCEPTS

1. Home is the ultimate human territory. As such, it is both a physical setting and a psychological and social process involving both choice and control.

2. The characteristics of the physical environment that can be used to promote residential privacy include prospect and refuge, complexity, order, and mystery. These characteristics are linked to privacy because they contribute to the rejuvenating effects of privacy as well as to refocusing our attention.

3. The types of privacy most often required in our homes are solitude and intimacy.

4. In general, people living in more crowded homes have higher levels of psychological distress.

ASSIGNMENT

USING THE CLIENT INTERVIEW TO DETERMINE AND DESIGN FOR PRIVACY NEEDS

Objectives:
• To use the interviewing process to reveal personal needs for privacy

- To consider cross-cultural similarities and differences in design
- To formulate and apply design solutions that support the client's privacy needs as well as other needs

Learning Outcomes:
- Increased understanding of the designer's ability to affect people and the environment
- Development of active listening skills, and critical, analytical, and strategic thinking leading to effective interpretation of client's needs
- Increased understanding of human privacy needs and their relationships to other needs
- Development of skills in problem identification, problem solving, and concept development
- Increased understanding and appreciation of alternate points of view (age, culture)

Description:

Using the Client Interview form, choose a friend or classmate of a different age or cultural background that you are to interview for the purpose of designing a personal private space. The space can be a bedroom, home office, or other *individual primary territory* within the *larger primary territory* of the home. Sketch the existing space in $\frac{1}{4}''$ scale and include all windows, doors, and architectural features. Make notations of how the space relates to adjacent spaces (hallways, other rooms, patios, etc.).

Analysis:
Using the information in Chapters 2, 3, and 4, analyze your "client's" needs according to the following criteria:

- Types of privacy to be accommodated and why: Most common are solitude and intimacy. Isolation (extreme condition of privacy) is rarely required in residential environments.

- The cultural patterns of accepted behavior (Chapter 2) within the home will define how much privacy is desired, how much privacy is respected or afforded, and what physical elements are commonly recognized within the home as privacy markers.
- The existing physical characteristics of the space and their relationship to adjacent spaces identify the characteristics that will support and those that will compromise the types of privacy required. Look for such privacy enhancing characteristics as spatial hierarchy, spatial depth, placement and types of thresholds areas of prospect and refuge, and connections with nature.

Solution:

1. Provide a design concept statement for the space that illustrates your understanding of the client's privacy needs and how you have designed the space to support those needs.

2. Provide a list of privacy considerations and solutions for the space including color, material, and lighting choices. Include your rationale for the choices in this list.

3. Prepare sketches illustrating the development of your design ideas to enhance privacy in the room.

4. Prepare a detailed and annotated space plan for the room that utilized the physical characteristics of environments that support privacy.

DESIGNER'S INTERVIEW OF THE CLIENT
The following client interview sample form, while intended to assess privacy needs, is also useful for clarification of general client needs. The interview has three parts: basic information, lifestyle choices, and preferences for privacy.

Basic Information

How many persons live in the home, full- or part-time, and what are their ages?

How often is the whole family in the home together and for how long?

Is there extended family, such as an older relative, living in the home?

Does anyone in the home have a disability or special needs? What are those needs?

Lifestyle Choices

What is everyone's occupation?

What are the schedules of the residents (conventional business hours, night work, stay-at-home caretaker, or working parent)?

What are the levels of stress connected with the family members' occupations?

What are the hobbies and interests of the family members?

How often does the family entertain? Is it usually done as a family or by the parents for adult friends?

Does anyone work from home on a full- or part-time basis? What type of work is conducted from the home on a regular basis?

What are the special needs for the work conducted at home (intense concentration, solitude and quiet, power tools)?

Are there special pressures associated with the work conducted at home, such as deadlines or general time urgency?

What special interests do family members pursue at home? Examples might include cooking, gardening, listening to music, watching football games, exploring family genealogy, or arts and crafts projects.

Privacy Preferences

How many separate and different activities are typically occurring in the home during the day and night?

What activities require privacy? Each family member should consider this question from their personal perspective.

Where do family members prefer to go when they need privacy at home?

What sort of physical characteristics (furnishings, equipment, views, etc.) do they need in these private spaces to support their privacy needs?

Does the family pursue activities together in the home? What is the noise level of the activity? Do all members participate? What type of space is required for the activities? Are the activities compatible or incompatible? For example, is someone developing film in a darkroom, requiring privacy and darkness? Is someone playing drums? Is another person engaged in meditation?

Is there a need for a home office?

For a family member working at home, how important is acoustical privacy?

REFERENCES

Ahrentzen, Sherry. (1989). A place of peace, prospect, and . . . a p.c.: The home as office. *The Journal of Architectural and Planning Research*, 6:4, 271–288.

Alexander, C. A.; Ishikawa, S.; Silverstein, M.; Jacobson, M.; Fiksdahl-King, I.; & Angel, S. (1977). *A pattern language.* New York: Oxford University Press.

Appleton, J. (1996). "The experience of landscape." London: Wiley.

Altman, Irwin. (1975). *The environment and social behavior.* Belmont, CA: Wadsworth Publishing Co.

Bachelard, Gaston. (1969). *The poetics of space.* New York: Orion Press.

Becker, Franklin. (1993). The ecology of new ways of working: Non-territorial offices. *Site Selection, Industrial Development Section,* 162, 1.

Boschetti, Margaret A. (1987). Memories of childhood homes: Some contributions of environmental autobiography to interior design education and research. *Journal of Interior Design Education and Research,* 13(2), 27–36.

Evans, G.; Lepore, S.; & Schroeder, Alex. (1996). The role of interior design elements in human responses to crowding. *Journal of Personality and Social Psychology,* 70, 1, 41–46.

Evans, G.; Saegert, S.; & Harris, R. (2001). Residential density and psychological health among children in lower income families. *Environment and Behavior,* 33, 2, 165–180.

Gove, W. R.; Hughes, M.; & Galle, O. R. (1979). Overcrowding in the home. *American Sociology Review* 44 (1), 59–80.

Hall, Edward T. (1969). *The hidden dimension.* New York: Anchor, Doubleday.

Harris, P.; Brown, B. B.; & Werner, C. M. (1996). Privacy regulation and place attachment: Predicting attachments to a student family housing facility. *Journal of Environmental Psychology,* 16, 287–301.

Heerwagen, Judith H. & Orians, Gordon H. (1986). Adaptations to windowlessness, a study of the use of visual décor in windowed and windowless offices. *Environment and Behavior,* 18, 5, 623–639.

Heerwagen, Judith H. (1990). *Windows, windowlessness and simulated view; Psychological aspects of windows and window design.* Symposium conducted by the Polytechnic Institute of New York, Brooklyn. Copyright 1990 by Environmental Design Research Association.

Hildebrand, Grant. (1991). *The Wright space.* Washington: The University of Washington Press.

Hoffman, Alexander von. Why they built the Pruitt-Igoe project, online, path is *http://www.soc.iasstate.edu/soc415a/PruittIgoe.html.*

Hopstock, P. J.; Aiello, J. R.; & Baum, A. (1979). Residential crowding research. In John R. Aiello & Andrew Baum (Eds.) *Residential Crowding and Design.* New York: Plenum Press.

Jacobson, Max; Silverstein, Murray; Winslow, Barbara. (2002). *Patterns of home.* Newtown, CT: The Taunton Press.

Lawlor, A. (1997). "A home for the soul." New York: Clarkson Potter Publishers.

McCarthy, D. & Saegert, S. (1979). Residential density, social overload, and social withdrawal. In John R. Aiello & Andrew Baum (Eds.) *Residential crowding and design*. New York: Plenum Press.

Magee, Jennifer L. (2000). Home as an alternative workplace: Negotiating the spatial and behavioral boundaries between home and work. *Journal of Interior Design*, 26, 1, 35–47.

Maxwell, Lorraine E. (1996). Multiple effects of home and day care crowding. *Environment and Behavior*, 28, 4, 494–511.

Naisbitt, J. (1999). *High tech high touch: Technology and our search for meaning*. New York: Broadway Books.

National Center for Health Statistics. (2002). "National vital statistics reports." Hyattsville, MD: U.S. Department of Health and Human Services.

Newell, P. B. (1998). A cross-cultural comparison of privacy definitions and functions: A systems approach. *Journal of Environmental Psychology*, 18, 4, 357–371.

Newman, O. "Defensible space: Crime prevention through urban design." New York. MacMillan, 1972.

Pedersen, D. M. (1997). Psychological functions of privacy. *Journal of Environmental Psychology*. 17, 147–156.

Rybczynski, Witold. (1986). *Home*. New York: Viking Penguin Inc.

Scott, Suzanne. (1993). Complexity and mystery as predictors of interior preferences. *Journal of Interior Design*, 19 (1): 25–33.

Sÿpkes, Pieter. *http://www.arch.mcgill.ca/prof/sijpkes/arch528/fall2001/lecture13/pruitt-igoe.html*

Sixsmith, A. J. & Sixsmith, J. A. (1991). Transitions in home experiences in later life. *Journal of Architectural and Planning Research*, 8, 181–189.

Sommer, R. (1969). "Personal space." Englewood Cliffs, NJ: Prentice-Hall, Inc.

Susanka, Sarah. (1998). *The not so big house*. Newtown, CT: The Taunton Press, Inc.

Susanka, Sarah. (2001). *Creating the not so big house*. Newtown, CT: The Taunton Press, Inc.

Tognoli, J. (1987). Residential environments. In D. Stokols & Irwin Altman (Eds.) *Handbook of environmental psychology 1*, New York: John Wiley & Sons.

Tolpin, Jim. (1998). *The new cottage home*. Newtown, CT: The Taunton Press.

Hoffman, Alexander von, online path is *http://www.soc.iastate.edu/soc415a/PruittIgoe.html*

CHAPTER 5

. . . In work settings an environment must not only make it possible to carry out important tasks in an efficient way, it also must provide a sense of pleasure, promote feelings of rootedness and belonging, provide sensory variability and change, allow for self expression and personalization, and allow persons to regulate their behaviors to meet changing needs for social interaction and privacy.

JUDITH HEERWAGEN ET AL. 1995

Privacy and Related Needs in Work Environments

THE ROLE OF PRIVACY IN WORK ENVIRONMENTS

The nature of work has changed radically, and a new work paradigm has reconfigured the built environment. The relationship of person to environment has shifted as well. Today, workers often utilize a work process of creative thinking and problem solving. Knowledge work is result-oriented, which allows a fairly high degree of autonomy, a benefit of privacy. This heady freedom comes with a price. We have more openness in the built work environment than ever before, and we don't separate from others as often. The openness of office layouts and our communication devices allow us to stay connected with one another almost constantly. In that process we may sometimes find that it is more difficult to experience privacy.

In this chapter we will examine the events and developments that reinvented the contemporary work environment and the subsequent evolution of privacy and related human needs. Privacy theories and related concepts that apply to office design will be explored within the context of the past and the present. Interior design application recommended for meeting privacy needs will address specific types of privacy

relevant to the work environment: acoustical privacy, visual privacy, territorial privacy, and informational privacy. This chapter also addresses work environments that require enclosed offices for privacy as well as nonterritorial offices and their privacy issues. The benefits of functions of privacy and related human needs are discussed throughout the chapter.

THE EVOLUTION OF PRIVACY NEEDS IN THE WORK ENVIRONMENT

In the design of the typical office of the mid and late 1800s, typically, the head of the firm and other executives occupied individual enclosed offices. Secretaries as gatekeepers sat just outside of their doors to assure their privacy. The rest of the staff occupied individual desks in large rooms with open spaces (Yee 1983).

Figure 5.1 The hierarchal structure: communication through a chain of command. Photographed by Charles J. Hibbard, Minnesota Historical Society.

Management was clearly elevated from the lower echelon of workers. Communication was possible only through a chain of command, but communication was not a priority at that time. (See **Figure 5.1**).

At that time, privacy existed only for people with enough status in the hierarchy to have a private office (Yee & Gustafson 1983). This linkage of status to privacy flourished under the hierarchical system and to some extent persists today. Design application at that time reinforced the prevailing philosophy of the workplace: spatial separation of management and labor; communication hindered by space planning between the layers of the organization; and clear delineation of status based on enclosed walls, rigid allocation of square footage, amenities, and outdoor views.

THE ADVENT OF MODERNISM IN OFFICES

In the latter part of the 19th century, new technology with the invention of the elevator and advances in building construction permitted the erection of skyscrapers, and the "modern" office had arrived. The introduction of international style architecture (see **Figure 5.2**) in the 1950s with its grid system of consistent and regular placement of interior columns provides a

Figure 5.2 International style architecture in mid-20th-century America, an architectural way to allocate size and status. © Bettmann/CORBIS.

striking example of the influence of the physical environment to achieve or not achieve privacy. The strong hierarchical system still prevailed, and offices based on the grid and columns could be assigned in sizes that reflected employees' rank. Highly valued people received large offices on the highest floors with the best views. The remaining workers occupied small windowless offices or worked in open, unprotected arrangements (Yee & Gustafson 1983). Acoustical, visual, and territorial privacy were not present in this environment.

In the 1950s radical changes in workplace philosophy reinvented the design and the privacy experiences of the European and the American work environment.

Office Landscape (Europe)

In Germany in the 1950s, the Quickborner team, a management consulting group, concluded that enclosed offices hindered the productivity of work. They reasoned that employees should be grouped not on the basis of status but on the basis of proximity for communication and collaborative work. Teaming up with a space planning group, they eliminated partitions, all enclosed offices, and the geometric grid. The new space plan, **Burolandschaft (office landscape)** provided open desks in completely open areas for managers and staff, configured in asymmetrical clusters separated by large plants. The resulting curving pathways contributed to the feeling of an interior landscape (Yee and Gustafson 1983).

Office Landscape (United States)

In the United States, office landscape presented a radical departure from the conventional organizational structure that isolated top management and separated middle managers from the people working under them (Yee & Gustafson 1983). The openness of office landscape promised new patterns of collaborative work and enhanced communication, but the design created new problems for the privacy needs of workers, as privacy needs sometimes became subordinate to the needs for interactive work and communication (Smith & Kearny 1994).

Office landscaping premiered in the United States in 1967 with the design of the du Pont facility in Wilmington, Delaware (Smith 1987). The most threatening feature of office landscaping to Americans was the lack of privacy, and the complete openness of office landscaping received a dubious and tepid reception by American workers (Yee & Gustafson 1983).

Open Office Planning (United States)

Pure office landscaping never became widely accepted in America because of the excessive openness of the plan. In 1960 Robert Probst, working for the Herman Miller Company, developed the Action Office—a system of office components with the capability to stand on legs or to be attached to panels. (See **Figure 5.3**). The Action Office System (still in production today) solved several problems and overcame some of the Americans' objections, primarily because the panels of different heights could provide varying degrees of visual privacy (Smith

Figure 5.3 Action Office System—The American adaptation of office landscape. The panel system provides architectural privacy and flexibility. Courtesy of Herman Miller, Inc.

1987). The modified version of office landscape with the use of panels came to be known in the United States as open office planning, with workstations often dubbed "cubicles." The trend toward cubicles has flourished and continued with many variations available today.

CHANGES IN THE AMERICAN WORK ENVIRONMENT

The introduction of open office planning in America with its emphasis on collaborative work reconfigured the physical environment. With the subsequent changes in technology that occurred in the mid 1980s, the American workplace began a new era. Huge strides in information technology coupled with global economic pressures for improved communications generated profound changes in the work process. During this time many companies began to realize that the old ways of working did not work anymore because America had steadily moved away from a product economy to an information society (Cutler 1993).

The new work deals with information. Workers today require a high degree of autonomy to do their work effectively and to maintain their self-identity. These new workers, sometimes called "knowledge workers" by business futurists, are the embodiment of choice and control, and they often work in collaboration with one another.

Before moving onto examining the specific privacy issues of workers and knowledge workers, let's look at our general needs for privacy in the work environment, which we have learned are outgrowths of privacy theories.

PRIVACY THEORIES AND RELATED CONCEPTS THAT APPLY TO OFFICE DESIGN

The optimum work environment experience requires opportunities to experience privacy. The workplace has never been more open, noisier, and more oriented to group rather than individual work. Over the years, theories of privacy that are relevant to different areas of interior design have emerged from the literature. In the work environment, we can address theory, benefits of privacy, and related concepts that are operating today.

Choice, Control, and Territorial Behavior

In an information society, learning and disseminating information demands empowered creative workers. **Empowerment** for the worker is the practice of using creative strategies for problem solving and exercising relative autonomy in the process. These types of workers need settings that facilitate their needs, and two of their bedrock needs are choice and control (Conger & Kanungo 1988, Thorlakson & Murray 1996). In today's work environment, it is typically not possible to find opportunities for true privacy without having choice and control because the orientation of many offices today is skewed in the direction of open and collaborative work experiences. In Chapter 1 we learned that choice and control are ways in which we can achieve privacy. Choice lets us decide how much interaction we want with others in the environment, and control lets us regulate that exposure. Choice and control are the prerequisites to exercising territorial behavior at work. Territorial behavior reinforces our right to be there, our sense of ownership about our space, and our feelings of self-evaluation. Without the freedom of territorial behavior, it is usually not possible to experience the other functions and benefits of privacy such as well-being, self-identity, and self-evaluation. This is a convoluted arrangement because without a sense of well-being, self-identity, and self-evaluation, workers will not experience the empowerment that the new type of work demands. Without empowerment, choice and control become more difficult to achieve, and privacy opportunities can become compromised.

Environmental Load and Environmental Stress

Currently, the environmental load, i.e., the total amount of information—audio and visual—in the contemporary work environment, is higher than ever because of the stimulation of our electronic technology. The immediacy of our technological capacities increases the two major contributors to environmental stress: lack of control and constant, rapid change within the environment (O'Neill & Carayon 1993). We also have incessant acoustical intrusions because much of our technological equipment is buzzing and humming throughout the day. This is in addition to the events that have always raised the environmental load in the workplace such as overheard conversations or arrivals and departures of workers.

Environmental stress is also high today. We have increasing time pressures because we have the technological capability to communicate with one another instantly on a global basis (Heerwagen 1996). It is not always possible to experience privacy opportunities for rejuvenation and recovery because some of us have obliterated the lines between work and home. Our communication devices are often with us as we move from one area of life to another, saturating others and ourselves with information. In this emerging new lifestyle, there is often little downtime in which restorative privacy experiences might occur.

Crowding and Density

Another experience that today's workers may sometimes face is the psychological and negative condition of crowding. This particular type of workplace crowding has been precipitated by the increasing spatial density of workstations and the decreasing square footage of the interiors of workstations. Workstations are much closer together than in former years, and many of the suggestions and recommendations for acoustical privacy do not work today because of the workstations' proximity to one another. The loss of square footage in workstations poses another challenge not only to functions of work but also to feelings of territorial privacy. In some work environments, the currently recommended one-size-fits-all interior measurement of eight inches by eight inches (64 square feet) is the same recommended dimension for a prison cell. (See **Figure 5.4**).

The openness of collaborative working experiences may also affect worker perceptions of crowding. The majority of open spaces for collaborative work are planned to allow for comfortable interactions with peers, but if they are located in busy high traffic areas or around a circulation point such as a water cooler, the perception of crowding may be unavoidable (Steelcase 2004).

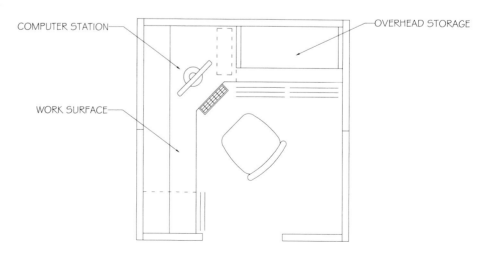

Figure 5.4 Shrinking workstations and the challenges to privacy needs.

COMPUTER STATION

OVERHEAD STORAGE

WORK SURFACE

INTERIOR DESIGN APPLICATION FOR WORK ENVIRONMENT PRIVACY

Lack of privacy is often an issue, whether it is in an enclosed or open office. Design application for privacy in the open office plan is presented here first, followed by a short discussion of privacy issues in enclosed offices. In the open office plan, workers overwhelmingly express the strongest need for acoustical privacy followed by visual privacy, territorial privacy, and informational privacy (Herman Miller staff 1987, Steelcase 1997, ASID 1997, Harris 1991).

Acoustical Privacy

Acoustical privacy is defined in two ways as: 1) the ability to protect information as it is being transmitted in face-to-face conversation or via telecommunications and 2) the freedom from unwanted acoustical intrusions such as conversations. In a recent survey, 70 percent of workers said that their productivity would increase if their offices were less noisy. A number of studies have also shown a strong connection between lack of acoustical privacy and work-related stress. The greatest offender to acoustical privacy, while not the loudest, is overheard conversations because of their intelligible nature (Steelcase 2004). In addition, the trend to locate workstations closer and closer to one another worsens acoustical conditions for workers who perform individual tasks.

Acoustical privacy is a balancing act between extremes. Just as too much noise disturbs a worker's privacy, too much quiet can interfere with a worker's ability to focus (Steelcase 1997). Prior to beginning the design of any open office plan, the designer must have an understanding of how sound travels.

Blocking the Paths of Sound in Open Offices

In a furnished environment, the first step in our design of an acoustically comfortable environment in the open office is to interrupt the paths of sound. Design applications with acoustical panels use one or more of the following methods for sound control: sound absorption, sound blocking, or sound masking. (See **Figures 5.5a** and **5.5b**).

Figure 5.5a Sound is buried to diminish audibility.

Definitions:

Sound Absorption   **Sound absorption**—Sound is trapped or buried so that audibility is diminished. Sound absorption materials are light and porous, such as fiberglass, and they reduce overall noise levels in a space.

"It's a Matter of Balance: New Understanding of Open Plan Acoustics," **Herman Miller 2002**

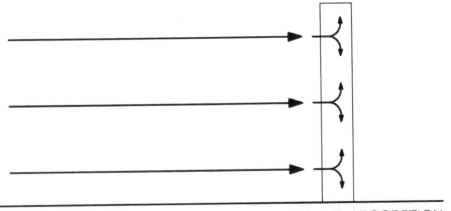

SOUND ABSORPTION

Figure 5.5b Sound is bounced off a surface. Sound blocking is more effective than sound absorption.

Sound Blocking	**Sound blocking**—sound is reflected or bounced off a surface. Sound blocking materials are hard and dense, such as masonite or solid metal, and they are an effective way to control the transmission of sound from one side of a surface to another.
Sound Masking	**Sound masking**—A contoured, consistent, broadband, low-level background sound that masks conversational distraction and unwanted noise. Sound masking devices are integrated into the plenum of the ceiling or into individual workstations. By creating a background sound artificially, other sounds and conversations become harder to hear.

"It's a Matter of Balance: New Understanding of Open Plan Acoustics," **Herman Miller 2002**

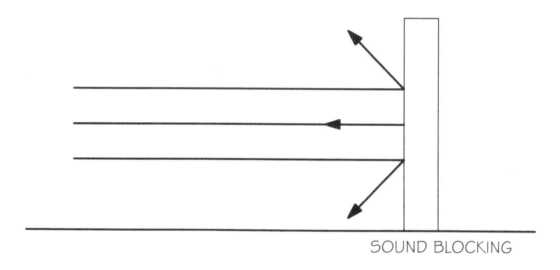

SOUND BLOCKING

An Integrated Solution to Acoustical Privacy

Meeting acoustical privacy needs requires an integrated solution that addresses the four interior building environment elements of ceilings, panels, floors, and sound masking (See Steelcase, Inc., Integrated Solution). Each element contributes to reducing workplace noise and distraction. Combining them strategically increases the effectiveness of the solution.

Ceilings and Luminaires

The choice of a ceiling system becomes the most important decision in planning the acoustical environment because the ceiling is

the largest sized sound-reflective element (Kleeman et al. 1991). Specifications for ceiling tiles should reflect our awareness of the need for high absorption so that the sound reaching the ceiling is trapped before it bounces back and reaches adjoining workstations (Harris 1991, Young 1999).

Placement of luminaires in the ceiling will enhance or diminish acoustical privacy (Herman Miller 1987, Young 1999). Improperly placed fixtures cause high sound reflection into adjacent workstations. Luminaires should not be positioned directly over panels between workstations, but located in a more central position over the workstation

AN INTEGRATIVE SOLUTION TO ACOUSTICAL PRIVACY

CEILING SYSTEMS primarily serve to absorb sound. There are standard absorption criteria for critical human speech frequencies that might be considered noise distraction.

SPEECH SOUND FREQUENCIES	ABSORPTION COEFFICIENT (PERCENTAGE OF SOUND ABSORPTION)
500 hertz	.65 minimum
1,000 hertz	.85 minimum
2,000 hertz	.85 minimum
4,000 hertz	.85 minimum

In addition, the articulation class rating of ceiling material affects the amount of sound that is absorbed at specific angles. A rating of 180 to 200 seems to be an industry standard.

PANELS are one of the main furniture components that can control noise in the workplace, based on both their composition and their height. Furniture panels should have a Sound Transmission Class (STC) performance rating of 18 or greater. Panel heights lower than 53 inches are largely ineffective in reducing noise. In addition, panels can absorb sound based on their Noise Reduction Coefficient (NRC). An NRC of at least .60 is recommended. Finally, the configuration of a workspace can contribute to its capacity to reduce noise.

SOUND MASKING SYSTEMS create background sound to mask conversational distractions and unwanted noise. They consist of electronic devices mounted above the ceiling plenum that generate a sound signal. The systems are typically set at a sound level of NC 40, which corresponds to 48 decibels (dBA) +/- 2db.

CARPET SYSTEMS absorb airborne sound, reduce surface noise (often called "footfall noise"), and help block sound transmission from above floors. The chart below indicates the Noise Reduction Coefficient and Impact Insulation Class (IIC) ratings recommended for carpet systems.

FLOORING TYPE	NRC RATING
Bare concrete only	0.015
Jute (28 oz/yd^2 carpet face)	0.20
Polyurethane cushion	0.25
(28 oz/yd^2 carpet face)	0.25

FLOORING TYPE	IIC RATING
Bare concrete only	34
Jute (28 oz/yd^2 carpet face)	60
Polyurethane cushion (28 oz/yd^2 carpet face)	62

Reprinted with permission from Steelcase Inc., *Workplace Acoustics,* 1997a

(Herman Miller 2002). (See **Figures 5.6a** and **5.6b**). Unfortunately, we know that the placement of luminaires in a ceiling panel based on an existing layout of the workstations is usually not a permanent installation. With the frequency of changes and workers moving in the workplace today, reconfiguration of the cubicle workstations will also require reconfiguration of the lighting plan, and that is not always a practical option.

Panel Systems

Panels are demountable partitions, acoustically treated and used as "walls" to enclose open workstations. They are the second component of the integrated solution. In the early years of open office planning, acoustically treated panels were often considered the most important element in the delivery of acoustical privacy. We know now that panels are actually the weakest part of the integrated solution (Herman Miller 2002). While panels contribute to the attractiveness of the open office plan as well as provide us with options to use hang-on components and tackable

pinup items (both of which diminish the acoustical properties of the panel), all of the other elements of the integrated solution—ceilings, sound masking, and flooring—contribute more significantly to acoustical privacy (Harris 1991, Young 1999).

**Sound Blocking
and Sound Absorption**

Acoustically treated panels have both sound absorption and sound blocking qualities, but the sound *blocking* ability of panels is the more effective of the two because of the increasing trend of locating workers in more compact and dense workstations.

(Herman Miller 2002)

The height of the panel influences privacy. Over the years, panels have ranged from low (42") to medium (60") to high (82"). Typically

Figure 5.6a Correct lighting over workstations.

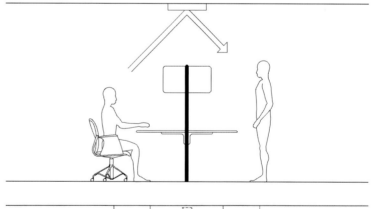

Figure 5.6b Incorrect lighting over workstations.

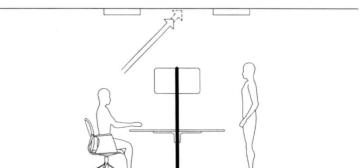

*"It's a Matter of Balance:
New Understanding of Open Plan
Acoustics,"* **Herman Miller 2002**

we specify optimal panel heights by balancing the needs for access and the needs for privacy as well as the type of work to be performed. Shorter panel heights (less than 45") provide easy communication for group work. Slightly higher panels (about 56") provide privacy when employees are seated, but allow a clear line of sight when they are standing. (See **Figure 5.7**). The American Society for Testing Materials is an agency that reviews the testing standards of materials. In a 1993 review of ASTM E-33, their committee on open plan spaces has determined that any panel lower than 60" is not effective as a sound barrier. They report that for effectiveness higher panels (82" or floor-to-ceiling designs) significantly reduce auditory and visual distractions and provide greater privacy.

FYI

Panel Heights

Panels should be high enough (60 inches) to protect the privacy of workers at both seated and standing heights and to discourage "prairie dogging," the practice of workers conversing over the tops of the panels.

(Herman Miller 1987)

Floor Coverings (Carpet)

Carpet and carpet tiles absorb airborne sound, reduce footfall noise, and help block sound transmission from the floors above and below (Kleeman et al. 1991, Steelcase 1997, Young 1999). Thick pile carpet that is laid over a dense pad can lessen ambient sound by as much as 70 percent. Carpet and pad can reduce impact noise and vibration noise as well. Carpet over pad, however, is not practical in areas with systems furniture because of the furnishings, including caster chairs and roller-type equipment. For that reason, we will typically specify carpet or carpet tiles in a direct glue-down installation (no pad). This application will deliver the same amount of noise reduction and enhance acoustical privacy (Steelcase 1997).

Sound Masking Systems

Sound masking systems are the final addition to the integrated solution for acoustical privacy needs. Sound masking is the addition of background noise at a decibel level higher than that of the ambient sounds in the open office. After we have addressed the interior building environment elements of ceilings, panels, and flooring, we use sound masking devices to handle any remaining sound (Steelcase 1997).

Figure 5.7 Desirable heights for panel systems for visual privacy are 60" or higher.

Sound masking is delivered in two ways. The first method is to locate a series of speakers approximately every 16 feet in the plenum above the ceiling. The second application, considered the more desirable solution, is to locate the sound masking system in the cubicle workstation (see **Figure 5.8**) with the speakers mounted three feet above the floor. Individual controls allow the user to adjust the decibel level in response to changing ambient noise in the workplace. The second method, while more expensive, is preferred because of the level of control available to the worker (Young 1999). While sound masking is not a perfect solution, nevertheless it does make it a little harder for us to understand other people's private conversations.

Protocols for Acoustical Privacy

While problems of acoustical privacy are generally solved with specification of products that

• Channel most foot traffic and noise away from areas where workers need to concentrate.

• Position office equipment, such as fax machines and printers, so the noise does not adversely affect those who work nearby.

• Limit the amount of tackable materials that workers can use to personalize their workspace, as these items often reduce the quality of sound absorption of surface materials.

• Build in private spaces for people to retreat to when acoustical privacy is needed.

"Workplace Privacy: A Changing Equation"
Steelcase 2004

Figure 5.8 Drawing of a sound masking system installed in a workstation.

modify the built environment, products alone cannot always assure acoustical privacy. As walls and doors have come down, protocols have replaced them. **Protocols** are rules or guidelines that enhance the nature and level of privacy desired in the work environment. They are standards established around the specific business needs, the worker needs, and the communication needs. Once established, protocols become cultural patterns of accepted behavior, which Altman (1975) identified as a privacy mechanism that we use to achieve desired privacy.

Privacy, as we have suggested in earlier chapters, is a regulatory device that restores mental equilibrium, reduces stress, and enhances creativity. Reducing the intensity of acoustical intrusions and using protocols enhances opportunities for privacy and makes a significant contribution to the work experience.

Visual Privacy

Visual privacy occurs when workers either "have" or "feel" that they have privacy, i.e., that they are unobserved by others and able to work undistracted by sudden movements and other unexpected sights. Closing a door or the option to close a door provides a mechanism of control for the owner of an enclosed office. Workers housed in cubicle workstations, however, do not have the option for this specific control mechanism of privacy and are more at risk of being seen and of being interrupted.

The ability to regulate visual privacy through closure of horizontal blinds or draperies enhances feelings of control. However, studies of high degrees of enclosure within cubicles indicate that total enclosure is often not a successful design solution (Arachea 1977). When workers are completely enclosed, they have high visual privacy, but they lack feelings of control because they cannot see outside of their space, and consequently are unprepared and startled by sudden, unanticipated sounds. If

we place workers behind glass walls where they can see everything that is happening all of the time, and they also can be seen from outside, they may feel that they are in a fishbowl and have feelings of increased vulnerability (Heerwagen 1990). Designers often specify an acoustical panel that has been treated with a combination of glass panels and opaque fabric tiles. In this way we can balance the needs of privacy with accessibility.

Artificial Lighting and Visual Privacy

Lighting is a component of visual privacy because lighting provides us with visual cues about whether a space is public or private. We know that low levels of illumination contribute to feelings of intimacy and/or privacy, and that type of visual cue will also encourage the appropriate type of behavior in a private space for passersby. High levels of illumination imply open public spaces (Herman Miller 1993), and such visual cues communicate that this is a more public area and that a higher level of noise is acceptable. We see again that the ability to achieve privacy is dependent upon the physical environment and the cues that our design application sends.

Research studies have shown that employees prefer lower light levels, and manufacturers have responded with lighting that is integrated into the furniture. Furniture-integrated lighting produces a softer, more intimate level of light. This type of reduced light level (fewer foot candles) also works well for work that is more and more computer screen–based rather than paper-based. A number of work environment specialists have consistently recommended that employees be provided with individually controlled task lighting (Bennet, Atkinson, & Loftness 2000; Herman Miller 1993; Steelcase 2004). Individually operated task lighting enhances the experience of visual privacy because it gives choice and control to the worker with the simple act of turning on a light at the beginning of a workday and turning it off at the end of the workday.

Natural Lighting and Windows in the Delivery of Visual Privacy

Natural light comes from many sources and many directions. The quality of natural light surrounds us; it is always changing, never uniform, and has variations of brightness and contrast of shadows. This quality of natural light helps create involuntary attention as it provides qualities of mystery, fascination, and connection. Our bodies need natural light to be physically and emotionally healthy, but because we typically spend 90 percent of our time indoors and often in high-density environments, the opportunity to experience the restorative changing patterns, intensity, and color that natural light brings to our lives is often lost. The relentless, uniform, artificial light that most large scale contemporary buildings impose upon us is unhealthy and is not conducive to privacy.

Some innovative architectural projects (William McDonough + Partners for Herman

Figure 5.9 Using natural light in interior environments, Herman Miller Spa Facility, William McDonough and Partners, Architects. © William McDonough + Partners: Photo by Tim Hursley.

BENEFITS OF WINDOWS

* access to environmental information—what's going on

* access to sensory changes—weather, time of day

* a feeling of connection to the world outside

* respite, restoration, and recovery

Windows, Windowlessness, and Simulated Views, Heerwagen 1990

Miller SQA 1997 and Oberlin College 1996) have explored the use of natural lighting as a major source of illumination in office and other interiors. (See **Figure 5.9**). While this appears promising for the future, specialists in illumination design for the office remind us that in general, natural light should be used only as a pleasant addition to artificial lighting because natural lighting is neither stable nor predictable (Leslie 1998).

Effects of Windows on Visual Privacy

The use of cubicle workstations often lessens the possibility of looking out a window, yet surveys, such as the one shown on Table 5.1, overwhelmingly reveal that people have strong preferences for windows (Biner, Butler, & Winsted 1991; Butler & Biner 1989; Heerwagen 1990; Siekman 1997). (See **Table 5.1**). The research work of Judith Heerwagen et al. (1990) tells us that rather than preferring natural light as an end in itself, what workers want is the view to the outside afforded by the windows.

An outside window is a window with a direct view to the outdoors. An inside window is a window that is open to the interior environment. However, some inside windows look

Percent of Occupants Preferring Daylight or Electric Light for Different Psychological or Physical Needs

NEEDS PSYCHOLOGICAL OR PHYSICAL NEED	DAYLIGHT BETTER	ELECTRIC BETTER	BOTH EQUAL	NO OPINION
For psychological comfort	88%	3%	3%	6%
For office appearance and pleasantness	79%	0%	18%	3%
For general health	73%	3%	15%	8%
For visual health	73%	9%	9%	9%
For color appearance of people and furnishings	70%	9%	9%	12%
For work performance	49%	21%	27%	3%
For jobs requiring fine observation	46%	30%	18%	6%

Lighting & Psychological Comfort, *Lighting Design & Application*, April, 1986, Judith H. Heerwagen and Dean R. Heerwagen

Table 5.1 "Survey-Preferences for Natural Light" by Judith H. Heerwagen and Dean R. Heerwagen

into other workstations that have views to the outdoor environment. (See **Figure 5.10**). These windows use borrowed views. There are significant differences in visual privacy effects between the two types of windows. The outside window provides relief from the task at hand, providing redirected attention, fascination, and access to nature. The inside window, while it may access the outdoor environment through the borrowed view of someone else's outside window, looks inward primarily. Inside windows can work in a positive manner, however, providing a view of other people in the work environment and enhancing visual communication needs. Outside windows do not allow this communication. However, the openness of an interior window also permits outsiders, as well as supervisors and coworkers, the option to look into the person's space. The experience of visual privacy may be compromised, depending upon who is able to look into the office. Having no

window at all is probably better than having a window that allows unwanted intrusions because a pleasant view of the outside world loses its psychological benefits if it is accomplished at the expense of desired privacy (Heerwagen 1990).

In general, however, exterior windows enhance privacy, and interior windows reduce visual privacy (Biner, Butler, & Winsted 1991).

Protocols for Visual Privacy

Formal protocols or guidelines for visual privacy can include previously agreed upon signals that communicate no interruptions except for emergencies. Less formal protocols include do-not-disturb signs, closed doors, or wearing headphones or earplugs. We sometimes will recommend other protocols that feature more extreme methods such as turning one's task chair to face the wall, burying oneself in a corner of the workspace, or positioning an easel outside

Figure 5.10 Use of interior windows: looking outdoors through a borrowed view.

of the cubicle's opening that blocks access into the workstation (Steelcase 2004).

Territorial Privacy

In the contemporary work environment, the most complex privacy need is territorial privacy.

Since there are fewer primary territories (private offices) in today's workplaces, workers often find themselves dealing with the unsure rules and less exclusive control associated with secondary territories. Unlike acoustical and visual privacy whose solutions are often product-

Figure 5.11 Space planning of activity areas to establish a sense of "neighborhood" can reinforce feelings of ownership and territorial privacy. Courtesy of Haworth Facility.

based, territorial privacy is behavior-based. Territorial privacy is strongly related to feelings. Knowledge workers, like many other office workers, need to feel that they belong, that they "own" a designated space, and that the space is theirs alone. They need to know that they will not be disturbed and that they are not in anyone else's way. They need "a space to personalize, and they often need to retreat and re-fuel" (Cornell & Baloga 1994 & 2004). Territorial privacy is a major factor as well in collaborative work endeavors.

Collaborative Work Privacy Needs and Territorial Privacy

Workers on team projects also have territorial privacy needs at the "neighborhood" scale resulting in the increased use of the concept of neighborhoods and villages as activity settings for collaborative work. (See **Figure 5.11**). The thinking behind this space planning concept is that people in smaller work areas linked by "streets" have more of a feeling of ownership and affiliation and can also work better collaboratively. Small well-marked areas with distinctive markers of territoriality and group identity reinforce the concept. The microenvironment is linked to the rest of the office via wide interior streets, at times winding in a manner reminiscent of Burolandschaft. Such features as wide streets, piazzas, gardens, coffee stands, and other elements help bring people together to socialize and to communicate (Duffy 1997, Nussbaum 1997).

Recommendations and Protocols for Territorial Privacy Needs

A designer must approach any project with a clearly defined understanding of the company itself, the work of the company, and the workers' needs to achieve privacy. The goal for interior designers is to create a sense of ownership and control for workers through design application. Here are recommendations as suggested by Steelcase Inc.

- *Isolate workers from main traffic patterns, and locate team members near one another.*
- *Establish clear boundaries between work spaces.*
- *Use existing architectural elements such as walls (if available) to create corner spaces that facilitate enclosure.*
- *Orient workstations so that individuals do not face main aisles.*
- *Provide different desk heights with seated or standing option.*
- *Give choices on office accessories.*
- *Create opportunities to personalize the workstation such as tackable surfaces for photos.*
- *Supply privacy enhancing furnishings such as easels, rolling files, and screens.*

Workplace Privacy: A Changing Equation
Steelcase Inc. 2004

Using office protocols can also enhance feelings of territorial privacy. Some protocols include

- *Determining who may use different work spaces and what may be off limits to visitors.*
- *Establishing a reservation system for using unassigned, shared space.*
- *Setting time limits for occupying unassigned space.*
- *Cleaning a shared room when finished so it's ready for the next user.*
- *Giving keys to teams with assigned rooms, so they can lock the door for security.*

Workplace Privacy: A Changing Equation
Steelcase Inc. 2004

Informational Privacy (Confidentiality)

The last type of privacy in the work environment to be discussed is informational privacy or confidentiality, a direct outgrowth of the conditions of the contemporary workplace. The definition of **informational privacy** is the assurance to workers that confidential information cannot be overheard, that private meetings will not be interrupted by the unwanted presence of others, and that sensitive or confidential documents in the work space cannot be read by others (Steelcase 2004).

People have rights to privacy by federally mandated law. In the work environment today, there are many reasons to protect information, and interior designers have a responsibility to help clients ensure that sensitive, classified, or simply private information is not available to the wrong people. Informational privacy provides convenience as well as security for workers or teams. With proper planning such as positioning work surfaces so that people can't read over someone's shoulder and providing lockable drawers for quick stowage of confidential documents, informational privacy needs are accommodated easily (Steelcase 2004).

Before we can begin to help our clients with their confidentiality needs, we must first address their needs for acoustical privacy and visual privacy. The current literature reinforces this by noting that all of the sensory stimuli that intrude on a space such as people talking or moving and equipment humming must be addressed early to assure the needs of informational privacy.

After those prerequisites are satisfied, we move onto an analysis to meet the needs for informational privacy. This analysis is contingent upon an assessment of the physical environment, the needs of knowledge workers, and the nature of specific work activities (Smith & Kearney 1994, Zelinsky 1998).

The new work paradigm that has shifted emphasis from tangible product to information service makes informational privacy needs critical in the contemporary fixed work environment. Informational privacy, unlike territorial privacy, is objective. The goal is real privacy, security, and safety. While the language of informational privacy is often expressed subjectively as "feelings," i.e., that workers "feel" that

they are not being overheard, or that they are not being seen when they need privacy (O'Neill & Carayon 1993). Solutions for informational privacy are straightforward, based on design application and product recommendations.

ENVIRONMENTS THAT REQUIRE ENCLOSED OFFICES FOR PRIVACY

Despite the trend of increasing the number of open offices, there are still specific environments that require enclosed offices for privacy. Examples include physicians' and lawyers' private offices where sensitive medical or legal information is shared. In addition, some workers engage in work that requires high levels of concentration, and they *must* be distraction free. Interior designers are often involved in the planning process early, and we can make intelligent recommendations about open versus enclosed spaces.

Alexander (1977) describes the pattern Workspace Enclosure, which is neither an open office nor an enclosed office, but rather a combination of the two that includes several

!APPLICATION!

INFORMATIONAL PRIVACY

• Provide spaces with doors, where appropriate.

• Isolate workers from main traffic patterns.

• Use card key access.

• Use screensavers on computer monitors.

• Arrange guest chairs so that they are as far as possible from work surfaces containing confidential materials.

Workplace Privacy: A Changing Equation Steelcase 2004

PROTOCOLS TO ASSURE PRIVACY

• Assign passwords to screensavers.

• Keep confidential information out of view when the worker is not in the work space.

• Agree not to divulge any information that might get overheard in a team's work area.

Workplace Privacy: A Changing Equation
Steelcase 2004

physical characteristics of each. Ideally, according to Alexander, to facilitate the need to interact with others yet not be distracted by them, the office should be 50 to 75 percent enclosed by walls or windows. There must always be a wall behind and to one side of the worker, and the worker must have a "view out" into the larger work space. If other people are working nearby, the enclosure should be designed so that the worker "has a sense of connection to two or three others, but never put more than eight work spaces within view or earshot of another" (p. 851).

Considerations related to decisions about open office workstations versus enclosed offices include company size, budget, type of work performed, and image. To some degree the enclosed office will always present a viable design solution.

Specific Privacy Issues of Enclosed Offices: Noise and Distraction

On the surface, it would appear that a fully enclosed office provides the maximum in privacy. The enclosed office, however, poses different problems for interior design privacy, as the open ceiling plenum allows sound to carry from one office to another. In addition, elements such as electrical outlets leak sound, particularly if they are lined up symmetrically (Harris 1991, Herman Miller 1991). (See **Figure 5.12**).

Figure 5.12 Electrical outlets, lined up symmetrically on the demising walls between offices, carry sound into adjacent spaces. Locating outlets in a staggered configuration on these walls minimizes sound leakage and enhances acoustical privacy.

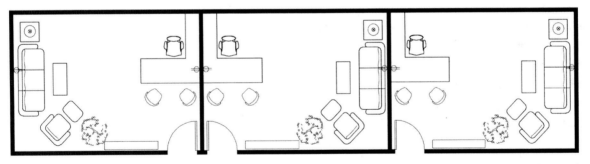

No

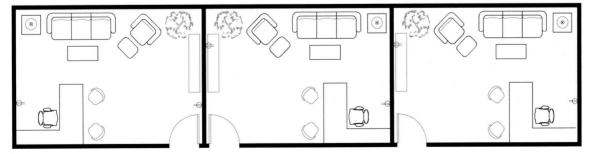

Yes

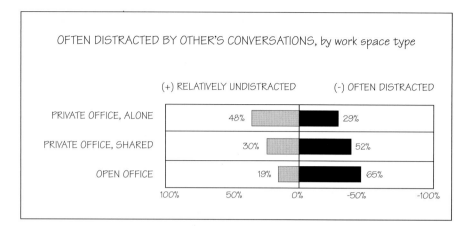

Figure 5.13 Trade-offs—Distractions in the workplace, open and private offices.

Research studies (Brill et al. 2001) indicate that the ability to do distraction-free solo work (privacy) is often cited by workers as their highest priority. However, the workers also consider informal interactions with coworkers, when desired, a top workplace design priority. The logical question to ask is: what type of office space—open or enclosed—best supports the priorities of the company, its types of work, and its workers? The graph above, furnished by **BOSTI** (see **Figure 5.13**), a research team of consultants for the design of offices, indicates that while 29 percent of workers in private offices are often distracted, the percentage shifts upward to 65 percent when workers are in open offices.

Work environment planners make a valid case that open offices are actually quieter than enclosed offices if an integrated solution of ceilings, panels, floors, and sound masking devices is used properly in the design of open offices. However, open offices are quieter only within an environment of normal levels of voiced communication. When voices are raised, speaker phones are in frequent use, and group discussions occur within the area of individual workstations, acoustical privacy is compromised (Brill et al. 2001).

Design Application for Acoustical Privacy in Enclosed Offices

Some interior spaces in closed office environments require high degrees of sound separation. These include conference rooms, private

offices, restrooms, and corridors. Closed offices also require that sound leaks are sealed. These include areas around and under doors, window glazing, cracks at junctions of walls and window mullions, and cracks at the junction of walls and floor. Luminaires in enclosed offices can also leak sound because they have holes or openings. Specification of large cell (four inches by four inches) parabolic lenses minimizes the problem, as well as using a solid box surrounding the back of the fixture (Harris 1991).

Resolving the ongoing debate of open offices versus enclosed offices is probably not possible. It is one of those issues with strong feelings on both sides, and there is no single-purpose one-style-fits-all resolution. There are options, however, to provide responsive environments that allow for the performance of both distraction-free solo work and for work in activity settings for collaborative experiences (Stone & Luchetti 1985). The "caves and commons" concept that was introduced a number of years ago in European architecture and is used often in the United States for collaborative work is an example of a responsive environment. (See **Figure 5.14**). The **caves and commons** spatial design emphasizes group work with shared equipment and meeting areas laid out in an open design (commons) ringed by individual private work areas (caves) for individual work. Often the private cubicles have integrated architectural, computer, and work process technology within the workstation (Cornell & Baloga 1994 & 2004).

Figure 5.14 Designing responsive environments for private and collaborative work.

PRIVACY IN NONTERRITORIAL OFFICES

Until now, we have confined the discussion of privacy issues in the contemporary work environment to physical spaces that are always located in a single environment or territory. As recently as the 1990s, most workers operated within an office-based orbit. Their equipment and/or tools remained on-site, and the work required the support presence of both administration and clerical staff. Today, the boundaries and roles of organizations have changed, and work can occur anywhere. The result has been a variety of alternative work practices. The term, **alternative officing**, is the practice of working away from the central office. With the continued improvement in computer and telecommunications technology, information work is virtually location-independent. Accordingly, we will look at privacy needs in this new arena, the alternative office. Our discussion will examine three types of alternative officing: teleworking, hoteling, and virtual officing.

Teleworking

Teleworking or as it is sometimes called, telecommuting is the practice of working from a remote location, i.e., other than the centralized office. Locations can include the home, a hotel room, or the beach. Typically, workers return to the office on a weekly basis, using some kind of shared, nonassigned workstation. The mantra for teleworking is that you can work anywhere because you always have your mind with you.

> **FYI**
> Work has become transportable and ubiquitous, almost a state of mind. Like a bubble of pure concentration that one can turn on and off with or without the help of tangible tools, work is where you are.
>
> **Paola Antonelli**

For some workers, teleworking is an attractive alternative to conventional work practices. The flexibility of teleworking integrates well with the new work style of working anywhere. Teleworking also gives back a precious resource to people who no longer have to commute, the gift of time regained—time for richer contact with family, leisure experiences, and even the experience of restorative privacy (Herman Miller 2001).

Privacy Issues in Teleworking: Advantages and Disadvantages

A study conducted by IFMA and Haworth (1995) revealed that from a privacy interaction standpoint, workers have feared social isolation from their peers, of being "out of the loop" when career advancement opportunities arise, and they have expected some family conflict with the increased privacy needs of working within the home.

The home office is a sometimes stark contrast to the coziness of the same people/same time/same place environment. Historically, offices have served as social meeting places with options for interactive exchanges as well as opportunities for selected privacy. Communication needs can be a challenge for the knowledge worker who telecommutes (Herman Miller 1998).

Design Considerations for Teleworking

Design consideration for teleworking requires that the quality of the remote office equate or replicate the conditions of the real office in the workplace. People who have worked at home in the past have often had makeshift conditions such as taking over the family dining table or using a corner of the family room. Research studies (Magee 2000, IFMA 1995) indicate that these conditions work adversely against the success of serious sustained teleworking. A makeshift nonprivate work space does not usually allow for personalization opportunities, and it certainly may erode any feelings of pride and ownership (territoriality). In addition, research studies have revealed that the worker in those conditions generally feels undervalued by the parent company (Magee 2000).

The designer's first task is to assist the worker in determining the preferred or optimal location for the home office within the home. Interviewing the worker, preferably in the home, will reveal information about the footprint of the home, square footage options, lifestyle, size of the family, and special needs (Ahrentzen 1989, Magee 2000). In general, work environment specialists agree that privacy is a high priority in the selection of the space.

LINK
If you want to know more about preferred privacy locations for home offices, see Chapter 4, page 76.

Hoteling

Hoteling is an on-site space allocation program that does not permanently assign desks or workstations to specific individuals. Different persons or teams use nonassigned workstations throughout the course of a day, a month, or occasionally longer. Nonterritorial offices fill a need because most telecommuting experiences are still organized around connection to the central office, usually on a weekly basis.

Other persons, such as outside sales workers, often have little need for assigned fixed office space. Using space on a shared rotation basis by different workers and even by different teams is cost effective and helps offset the costs of outfitting the telecommuter's home office. What, however, is the impact on privacy needs in hoteling?

The type of privacy need most at risk in hoteling is that of territorial privacy. Historically, in the same time/same place work setting, offices became the places not only to work together but also to interact and socialize. How does a worker who "owns" nothing in the fixed office retain a sense of place, self-identity, control, status, and territoriality?

Our interior design application must focus on options and choices that reinforce the parts of territorial privacy—ownership, identity, and control. Mobile carts for workers in nonassigned workstations can help meet some of these needs. The carts contain workers' records, files, and other needed or personal equipment, making it a portable primary territory. (See **Figure 5.15**). In many hoteling experiences, workstations are on a reservation basis, and when the worker arrives, the person's name is on the assigned cubicle, and the mobile cart with the worker's professional belongings is in place (Herman Miller 1999).

The Virtual Office

The third type of alternative to the fixed work space, the virtual office, is the most extreme.

Figure 5.15 Reinforcing territorial privacy for nonassigned workers in hoteling: Herman Miller's pedestal. Courtesy of Herman Miller, Inc.

The term **virtual office** refers to the practice of having a central office only in cyberspace with workers working from a variety of nontraditional places, such as in the client's office, in airline clubs, or on airplanes. The "road warriors" operate outside of the central office and replace it with their personal communication devices of portable computers, portable printers, modems, fax machines, and cell phones. The "you can work anywhere" concept finds full expression in the concept of the virtual office.

PRIVACY NEEDS AND WORKER SATISFACTION IN NONTRADITIONAL OFFICES

The concept of the virtual office is too new to have conclusive data on privacy needs. A major study conducted by LaSalle Partners and IFMA in 1998, however, has implications for privacy. This study revealed that different types of nontraditional work experiences (teleworking, hoteling, and virtual officing) brought out different feelings of satisfaction and dissatisfaction from the workers involved. Table 5.2 demonstrates the overall satisfaction with AWS (alternative workplace strategies).

Of the respondents, 65 percent reported an increase in morale associated with telecommuting.

NONASSIGNED WORKSTATIONS

• Provide mobile tables, files, and screens that easily accommodate individual needs for privacy, storage, and work staging.

• Provide work surfaces that are adjustable by the users themselves to accommodate people of different physical sizes and abilities.

• Provide adjustable keyboard trays or stands.

• Provide fully adjustable task chairs to ensure that any size user can get proper lower back support while performing a wide range of office tasks.

A Growing Alternative Work Style
Herman Miller 1999

Overall, satisfaction scores were highest for the virtual office and lowest for the nonterritorial on-site office. This is consistent with other studies indicating that, in general, telecommuters enjoy their work experience (ASID 2000). In the second alternative work experience, hoteling, both territorial privacy and the need

Table 5.2 "Worker's satisfaction in nonterritorial officing" workers were most satisfied with the virtual office.

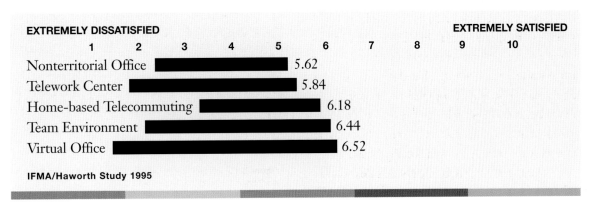

IFMA/Haworth Study 1995

for personalization become difficult to express in a system where no one "owns" anything. Choice and control, the ability to develop and maintain self-identity, as well as the privacy mechanism of territoriality may not be possible in hoteling and similar experiences. This could explain the decline in morale associated with nonterritorial offices, but validated research is not available at this time.

The third type of alternative work experience, the virtual office, scored highest in satisfaction, possibly because it is a logical expression of the new work paradigm. There is no reporting in for duty; there is no supervision, and often there are few progress reports. Instead, the knowledge worker invents a new environment. The worker serves simultaneously as gatekeeper and CEO. The work process is autonomous and flexible, reflecting the nature of the knowledge worker's preferences.

Alternative work practices liberate workers from conventional work experiences while at the same time creating new opportunities and challenges to privacy. The privacy issues are a significant part of the experience, and only time will determine if alternative work practices become part of the mainstream American work experience.

FINAL THOUGHTS ON PRIVACY IN THE WORK ENVIRONMENT

While our technology often races ahead of our human needs, it is indisputable that we need privacy, and as individuals working in environments that shift and change daily we need different levels of privacy. The type of work makes a difference and so does the age of the worker. Some workers can work in cubicle workstations and feel that they have their desired level of privacy. Other workers, again depending on the variables in the environment, may feel that they need a degree of architectural enclosure for privacy. Both kinds of workers

need individual spaces for territorial needs and private work as well as the ability to regulate social interactions and solitude by moving between places. Workers need quiet spaces, soft lighting, and low sensory stimulation to allow for privacy experiences of restoration and recovery. People yearn for a connection with nature in an increasingly technological and sometimes sterile environment. We need interesting visual and sensory experiences such as access to daylight and sunlight and indoor and outdoor stimuli.

LINK
If you want to know more about age-specific preferences in work environments, see Chapter 8, page 199.

Cyberspace has liberated us from the need to be together at the same time and in the same place. Now some of us can experience new work practices that reflect the fluidity of contemporary human life. In the past, our socializing experiences were tied to the places where we interacted with others and to those places where we retreated for privacy. Today, some of us have the freedom to work anywhere, going to the office every day, once a week, once a month, or even once a year.

There is no magic place or nonplace that satisfies all needs for all types of privacy and that works for everyone. The question is not where to work, but how to live and how to work, and that is an individual journey. Our responsibilities as designers must include awareness of these needs so that we may integrate them into the solutions that we design.

KEY CONCEPTS

1. The rapid advance of technological innovations in the last part of the 20th century changed the work environment profoundly.

2. A new work paradigm has emerged based on information rather than a product. The new paradigm emphasizes results rather than process, and consequently the hierar-

chical structure of the work environment has yielded to the flattened hierarchy.

3. This new egalitarian structure has required new workers who can work creatively, relatively free of supervision, and often collaboratively on teams.

4. The growing importance of collaborative work requires large open spaces, while also providing spaces for private work. Designers must become familiar with and implement solutions based on privacy theories and related concepts that apply to office design.

5. The combination of technological developments and the new work paradigm has freed us from the need to work in a same time/same place setting. We have alternative places and alternative work styles available to us. The practice of alternative working may change the work environment further.

ASSIGNMENT
DESIGNING FOR PRIVACY: OPEN OFFICE PLANNING OR ENCLOSED PRIVATE OFFICES

Learning Objectives:
- To analyze privacy needs in the work environment and compare the possible ways to meet these needs through space planning
- To formulate and apply design solutions that support the client's privacy needs as well as other needs

Learning Outcomes:
- Development of skills in problem identification, identification of client/user needs, analysis, and problem solving
- Development of space planning skills to accommodate specific, identifiable needs
- Increased understanding of the relationship between human behavior and the built environment
- Development of critical thinking skills through contrasting and comparison of possible solutions

Description:
Your client is a partner in a small law firm with fifteen total employees including two partners. All members of the firm (with the exception of two partners) currently have modestly equipped open office systems in a large central area. They all share the use of two private conference rooms for meetings with their clients. The partners are planning to remodel their offices and ask you, as their interior designer, if they should add more private offices or modify their current open office systems. The other lawyers and their assistants are split on whether they prefer the open offices, which some of them feel helps to facilitate communication between one another (typically three to four people work together on any given case), and private enclosed offices, which some of them feel are important for their clients' perception of confidentiality. All agree that either the enclosed offices or the workstations must support visual and acoustical privacy.

You have observed that the areas outside of the office cubicles are often used for informal conversations about clients and their cases. Those people who are working in their cubicles often ask that the conversations be moved to another location. The level of noise in the general area of the open offices is high, and you observe that this appears to distract and disturb some workers but not others.

Currently the size of the typical open office in the firm is 70 square feet and contains the following equipment and furniture:

work surface for paper-based tasks
work surface for screen-based tasks: net-
worked computer, small printer, and telephone
open shelves above one work surface; tack
board above the other work surface
two-drawer lateral file (all hard copies of
client files and information are kept in a
central, lockable area)
small table (36-inch diameter) with two sled
type guest chairs

Design Criteria:
Using the information from this chapter and
chapters 1, 2, and 3, prepare a privacy comparison by creating plans for two versions of a typical office for the members of the firm, one open
plan and one enclosed (four walls and a door).

- The minimum and maximum dimensions for
each version are: Enclosed office—
Minimum 80 square feet (8'×10');
Maximum 100 square feet (10'×10');
Open plan—Minimum 64 square feet
(8'×8'); Maximum 80 square feet (9'×9')
- Each version must maximize options for
visual and acoustical privacy while allowing
the workers to be able to communicate
effectively with one another when necessary.

Analysis:
- The types of privacy to support and why,
including the levels of interaction
- The expected benefits of privacy for each
version (Chapters 1 and 2)
- The advantages and disadvantages of each
version's ability to provide appropriate privacy
- Considerations of personal space and
territoriality
- Considerations for the environmental load
and how workers are coping with the load
levels (Chapter 3)
- The appropriate physical characteristics to
use to promote desired levels of privacy
(Chapter 3)

- Considerations for natural and artificial
lighting and use of acoustical materials

Solution:
1. Provide a statement that describes your
analysis of the privacy needs for the offices
and how you have designed the offices to
support those needs.

2. Prepare a detailed and annotated space
plan for each version that utilizes the physical characteristics of environments that support privacy.

3. Prepare two annotated interior elevations
for each version illustrating the use of
appropriate physical characteristics to
support privacy needs.

4. Based upon your analysis and the solutions
detailed by your drawings, present
recommendations to your client. Do you
recommend open or enclosed offices, or a
combination? Why? Use your drawings to
help explain your recommendations.

REFERENCES
Alexander, C. A.; Ishikawa, S.; Silverstein, M.;
Jacobson, M.; Fiksdahl-King, I.; & Angel, S.
(1977). *A pattern language*. New York: Oxford
University Press.

Ahrentzen, S. (1989). "A place of peace,
prospect, and . . . a p.c.: The home as office."
*The Journal of Architectural and Planning
Research*, 6:4, 271–288.

ASTM Committee E-33 on environmental
acoustics, standard guide for open office
acoustics and applicable ASTM standards.
(1993). *American Society for Testing Materials.*

Altman, I. (1975). The environment and social behavior. Belmont, CA: Wadsworth Publishing Co.

Arachea, J. (1977). "The place of architectural factors in behavioral theories of privacy." *Journal of Social Issues*, 33, 116–137.

ASID. (1997). *Sound solutions: Increasing office productivity through integrated acoustic planning and noise reduction strategies.* Washington, DC: American Society of Interior Designers, Armstrong, Dynasound, Milliken, and Steelcase.

ASID. (2000). *Workplace values, how employees want to work.* Washington, DC: American Society of Interior Designers, Ecophon Certain-Teed, Inc., Haworth, Inc., Vista Window Film.

Bennett, L. E.; Atkinson, M. B.; & Loftness, V. (2000). "The adaptable workplace lab." Paper presented at Neocon, Chicago.

Biner, P. M., Butler, D. L. & Winsted, III, D. E. (1991, May). "Inside windows: An alternative to conventional windows in offices and other settings." *Environment and Behavior*, 23, 3, 359–382.

Brill, M., Weidemann, S., & the BOSTI Associates. (2001). *Disproving widespread myths about workplace design.* Jasper, IN: Kimball International.

Butler, D. L. & Biner, P. M. (1989). "Effects of setting on window preferences and factors associated with those preferences." *Environment and Behavior*, 12, 1, 17–31.

Conger, J. A. & Kanungo, R. N. (1988). "The empowerment process: Integrating theory and practice." *Academy of Management Review*, 13, 3, 471–482.

Cornell, P. & Baloga, M. (1994 & 2004). *Work evolution and the new "office."* Michigan: Steelcase Inc.

Cutler, L. M. (1993). "Changing the paradigm: Is it workplace or work environment of the future?" Paper presented at the International Facility Management Association, Denver, CO.

Duffy, F. (1997). *The new office.* London: Conran Octopus Limited.

Harris, D. A. (1991). "Acoustic ergonomics." *Facility Management Journal*, 32–38.

Heerwagen, J. H.; Heubach, J. G.; Montgomery, J.; & Weimer, W. C. (1995). "Environmental design, work, and well-being managing occupational stress through changes in the workplace environment." *AAOHN JOURNAL*, 43, 9, 458–468.

Heerwagen, J. H. (1996). "Naturalizing the workplace of the future: Technology, ecology, and place." Paper presented at the International Facilities Management Seminar on the workplace of the future, Seattle, WA.

Heerwagen, J. H. (1990). "Windows, windowlessness and simulated view: Psychological aspects of windows and window design." Symposium conducted by the Polytechnic Institute of New York, Brooklyn. Copyright 1990 by Environmental Design Research Association.

Herman Miller, Inc. (1987). *"Acoustics and the action office system, how to control sound."* A research summary from Herman Miller, Inc. Michigan: Herman Miller, Inc.

Herman Miller, Inc. (1999). *"A growing alternative work style."* A research summary from Herman Miller, Inc. Michigan: Herman Miller, Inc.

Herman Miller, Inc. (2002). "It's a matter of balance: New understanding of open-plan acoustics." A research summary from Herman Miller, Inc. Michigan: Herman Miller, Inc.

Herman Miller, Inc. (1993). "Lighting in the workplace, new priorities." A research summary from Herman Miller, Inc. Michigan: Herman Miller, Inc.

Herman Miller, Inc. (1998). *"Office environments, the new perspective."* A research summary from Herman Miller, Inc. Michigan: Herman Miller, Inc.

Herman Miller, Inc. (1991). "Tailoring the gray flannel room, why the enclosed office remains and how it is changing." A research summary from Herman Miller, Inc. Michigan: Herman Miller, Inc.

Herman Miller, Inc. (2001). *"Telecommuting: working off site."* A research summary from Herman Miller, Inc. Michigan: Herman Miller, Inc.

IFMA Foundation & Haworth. (1995). *Alternative officing research & workplace strategies.* Holland, Michigan

Kleeman, W. B. Jr.; Duffy, F.; Williams, K. P.; & Williams, M. K. (1991). *Interior design of the electronic office, the comfort and productivity payoff.* New York: Van Nostrand Reinhold.

LaSalle/IFMA Report. (1998). *Alternative workplace study.* Chicago, IL.

Leslie, Russell P. (1998). "Lighting for sustainable buildings: Changes in goals, practice, and process." Paper presented at Environ Design3, Monterrey, CA.

Magee, J. L. (2000). "Home as an alternative workplace: Negotiating the spatial and behavioral boundaries between home and work." *Journal of Interior Design*, 26, 1, 35–47.

McDonough, W. (1998). Oral presentation. Monterey, CA: Environ Design 2.

Nussbaum, B. (1997). "Blueprints for business." *BusinessWeek*, 116.

O'Neill, M. J. & Carayon, P. (1993). "The relationship between privacy, control and stress responses in office workers." Proceedings of the Human Factors and Ergonomics Society 37th Annual Meeting.

Siekman, P. (1997). "The new industrial architecture." *Fortune*, 148.

Smith, C. R. (1987). *Interior Design in 20th Century America: A History*. New York: Harper & Row, Publishers, Inc.

Smith, P. & Kearny, L. (1994). *Creating Workplaces where people can think.* San Francisco: Jossey-Bass Inc.

Steelcase Inc. (1997). *"Workplace acoustics: A discussion of sound, noise and effective work."* A knowledge paper from Steelcase Inc. Michigan: Steelcase Inc.

Steelcase Inc. (2004). "Workplace privacy: A changing equation." A knowledge paper from Steelcase Inc. Michigan: Steelcase Inc.

Stone, Philip J. & Luchetti, Robert. (1985). "Your office is where you are." *Harvard Business Review*, 63, 2, 102–117.

Thorlakson, A. J. H. & Murray, R. P. (1996). "An empirical study of empowerment in the workplace." *Group & Organization Management*, 21, 1, online.

Yee, Roger and Gustafson, Karen. (1983). *Corporate Design*. New York: Interior Design Books. First published in London in 1983 by Thames and Hudson, Ltd.

Young, Renee. (1999). "A sound business plan." *Building Design & Construction*, 40, i6, online; http://web4.infotrac.galegrooup.com...968373 &dyn=33!ar_fmt?sw_aep=denver.

Zelinsky, Marilyn. (1998). *New workplaces for new work styles*. New York: McGraw-Hill.

Ideally . . . patients must have sanctu-aries or private places, analogous to animal nests, where they can withdraw from social pressures and stimulation. But there must also be environments that are graduated in opportunity for interaction, so that patients can achieve a level of interaction appropriate to their condition and momentary needs.

IRWIN ALTMAN (1975)

CHAPTER 6

Privacy and Related Needs in Healthcare Environments

The relationship between privacy and healing involves both the physical and psychological health of the patient, as well as the effects of the physical environment upon the healing process. The restorative capacity of privacy is central to this relationship. Privacy has the ability to provide a refuge that has been shown to promote healing by

providing rest, recovery, and contemplation (Evans & McCoy 1998, Ulrich 1995). The key concepts of privacy—choice and control—are essential to our overall well-being in any setting, but are even more important for both patient and staff in the often stressful, sometimes chaotic environment of healthcare facilities.

The modern concept of a **healing environment** is described as ". . . a therapeutic environment that has a positive influence on the healing process and can be achieved by incorporating design elements that provide comfort, security, stimulation, opportunities for privacy and control, positive distractions and access to a patient's social support network" (Suite Dreams Project, online). This definition reflects the central role that privacy plays in creating supportive, healing environments. Until relatively

recently, healing has been viewed primarily as the responsibility of the medical staff, having little to do with patient responsibility. Therefore, previous models for healthcare design rarely addressed the concept of privacy or its therapeutic effects. However, the discovery that stress can suppress the immune system and affect recovery has created an interest in how privacy functions to reduce stress.

In this chapter we will discuss how the restorative qualities of privacy can be integrated in the design of healing environments. To understand the importance of privacy in healthcare settings, it is useful to understand how the concepts of wellness and healing have evolved. We begin with a brief examination of the evolution of healing environments from natural settings to stark institutions to physically

Figure 6.1 Privacy enhancing residential elements and positive distractions characterize today's healing environments as seen here in the lobby of the Sky Ridge Medical Center in Lone Tree, Colorado. © Rion Rizzo/Creative Sources Photography. Architect: Gresham Smith & Partners, Nashville, Tennessee.

and psychologically supportive environments. We will examine the privacy theories and related concepts that help designers understand the impact of the design of the physical environment upon patients' overall health and well-being. Finally, we will discuss interior design applications for designing for privacy in healthcare environments.

THE EVOLUTION OF HEALING ENVIRONMENTS

Wellness is a universally understood but historically mysterious concept. The mystery of the relationship between health and illness and ultimately between life and death has haunted human beings since our beginning. Healers and shamans from almost every civilization on the planet, claiming to possess the secrets of life, have historically controlled and healed their people with their mysterious knowledge of the relationship between the body, nature, and the spirit. Wellness of the body meant wellness of the spirit and a life lived in harmony with natural forces. Nature, infinite in its wisdom, was once believed to possess everything that we needed to

heal ourselves. All we had to do was listen to and follow the advice of those who could interpret it.

Until the Middle Ages, there were no structures devoted to physical healing. The churches and temples were the primary places for treating illness. Within their walls, the body and the soul were tended to as one, reflecting the deep belief that healing the soul could cure illnesses of the body.

The ancient belief that people's physical illness was related to their spiritual state of being changed dramatically during the 17th century, in part because of philosopher Rene Descartes's assertion that the body and the mind (or spirit) are separate and distinct from each other. According to this philosophy, which influenced significantly the development of modern medicine in western cultures, illness and healing had nothing to do with a person's mind. They were merely physical processes to be treated physically. This belief continued to dominate western medicine even as the development of the science of psychology during the 19th century introduced new theories about the relationship between the body and the mind. (See **Figure 6.2**).

Figure 6.2 Historically, privacy considerations were not a part of healthcare design. Courtesy of the AMC Cancer Research Center.

As technology and science began to replace the instincts and experience of physicians as the primary way to diagnose and treat illness, the healing connection between the mind and the body was even further dismissed by most of modern medicine. Healthcare design focused upon functional efficiency resulting primarily in sterile, stressful, institutional facilities that we now know are detrimental to the healing process (Ulrich 1995 & 1992). However, thousands of hospitals, clinics, nursing homes, and treatment centers built using this model are still in use today.

The larger questions concerning wellness remained. Where does healing actually come from? Does healing come from within the person or is it applied from outside? Do we rid ourselves of illness by casting it out of our bodies with surgery and drugs, or do we heal by improving the health of our bodies within which the illness resides? How do we know when or if we are cured?

Data collected from research over the last two decades in a variety of disciplines indicate that there is indeed a strong illness/healing connection between our minds and our bodies. Our psychological state can affect our immune system and our body's ability to heal itself, and the physical environment, in turn, can significantly affect our psychological state. The ancient mysteries surrounding wellness have been revealed by modern science and research as the relationships between our physical and psychological states and our physical environments.

and changes in medical technology and facility use, the increased work demands and stress upon healthcare staff have changed both patient and staff expectations. These changes also affect the way facilities function. "Institutions for medicine," based upon Victorian principles of social engineering that treated only the disease, have now become "healing environments" based upon principles of integrated healthcare that support the total patient.

The worldwide demand for patient-oriented healthcare facilities has generated considerable debate about the types of environments that are the most appropriate for healing, and this debate has caused a dramatic transformation in healthcare design. This shift in the healthcare design paradigm demands that designers look beyond the traditional, accepted design criteria for new information about the effects of environmental characteristics upon patient health outcomes. Environmental psychologist and director of the Center for Health Systems and Design, Roger S. Ulrich (2000) explains, "The new broader perspective in medicine requires that the psychological and social needs of patients be strongly emphasized along with traditional economic and biomedical concerns, including disease risk exposure and functional efficiency, in governing the care activities and design of healthcare buildings" (p. 49). This perspective includes a new definition of healing environments that help provide the positive emotional, physical, and cognitive effects upon patients that ultimately contribute to their overall health and recovery.

HEALTHCARE DESIGN IN THE NEW MILLENNIUM

Healthcare design today bears little resemblance to healthcare design of previous decades. In addition to the dramatic changes in our understanding of illness and the approach to healing, the economic imperatives driving healthcare management, the growing number of elderly,

PRIVACY THEORIES AND RELATED CONCEPTS THAT APPLY TO HEALTHCARE DESIGN

The challenge to provide appropriate and desired levels of privacy in healthcare design is greater than for most other environments. The privacy theories and related concepts discussed in this section address many of the challenges these environments present.

Healthcare facilities are used by a wide variety of people with different needs and with different sets of individual characteristics. Patients, medical staff, and visitors experience a variety of physical and emotional responses in these environments that can affect wellness and the healing process. Privacy is equated with patient dignity in healthcare facilities. Yet, the considerations typically given to providing privacy for one's body in any other environment are not given the same priority in many healthcare settings (Turnock & Kelleher 2001). The methods and procedures involved in delivering quality healthcare are often physically and psychologically invasive for the patient. While in the hospital, the patients' autonomy is often eroded by rules and regulations that restrict their freedom of movement and by the regimentation that pervades their lives both day and night.

Anxiety and stress can be higher for patients and families in healthcare environments than in most other settings, thus requiring a greater need for reassuring experiences such as privacy. Additionally, the physical, mental, and emotional demands of long hours, heavy responsibilities, and prolonged directed attention can produce high levels of mental fatigue and stress for the staff. For these reasons, providing patients, visitors, and staff the ability to achieve desired levels and appropriate types of privacy is a necessary part of creating a restorative healing environment.

Types of Privacy

Our needs for privacy in healthcare environments include *solitude* for contemplation, rejuvenation, and autonomy; *intimacy* between medical staff and patients, between patients and family and friends, and among medical staff members to provide crucial social support; and *reserve*, in this case a type of informational or confidential privacy, so that patients can protect information about themselves from being conveyed to strangers. *Anonymity* is a type of privacy that is rarely wanted but often experienced in healthcare settings when people feel helpless, powerless, and depersonalized—just another patient lost in the crowd of hundreds of others.

Environmental Load

The perceived environmental load of healthcare facilities can vary from extremely high to extremely low. For patients of all ages, almost everything in these environments is unfamiliar, complex, uncertain, and beyond their control, which contributes to the high load environment. We know from the discussion in Chapter 3 that high load environments create arousal and require more directed attention, which can result in mental fatigue and increased stress. The lack of privacy inherent in most healthcare facilities means that patients have few opportunities to control the environmental loads which they must deal with almost continuously.

> **LINK**
> For a full description of the types of privacy and their respective benefits, see Chapter 2, page 19.

The environmental load can be high for the medical staff as well, especially in areas such as emergency rooms, recovery rooms, and intensive care units (ICUs). The need for directed attention (the ability to focus and avoid distractions to effectively perform mental tasks) is so great in these situations that it becomes essential for staff to have access to environments designed to relieve mental fatigue so that they can restore their ability to access directed attention when necessary.

Social density (the number of people per unit of space) also varies in areas such as registration areas, emergency rooms, and waiting rooms. These environments experience periods of high social density in which people gather to register and to wait for treatment or

> **LINK**
> For more information on directed attention, see Chapter 3, page 44.

for loved ones who are being treated. The environmental load and the stress levels change with the changing social density creating times of high load followed by times of low load.

For people who must spend long periods of time in these environments, the lack of positive distractions, together with monotonous (albeit unfamiliar) visual and acoustical surroundings can produce boredom and sensory deprivation. Sensory deprivation is also a concern for patient rooms. Although the surroundings may have a high level of novelty (unfamiliar equipment and medical staff coming and going), the environment may still produce sensory deprivation and be experienced as boring if it lacks positive distractions. As we will learn in this chapter, positive distractions are important qualities of supportive healing environments.

Territoriality

Healthcare environments are a combination of public and secondary territories for patients, and a combination of secondary and primary

territories for staff. The benefits of having their own territory in which to restrict access and to control interactions are rarely available to patients. Territory for patients in healthcare environments is often reduced to a chair or a bedside table. Personal belongings and items of meaning and value that provide familiarity and reassurance for patients often cannot be accommodated in healthcare environments. If space has been allocated for these items, it is often inflexible. For example, the placement of flowers and gifts in a patient room may be restricted to a space that is out of the patient's reach or even out of their view. Exam and treatment rooms often do not provide designated spaces to accommodate a patient's personal belongings. (See **Figure 6.3**).

Although a private patient room is often the space where patients spend the majority of their time when hospitalized, it is far from a primary territory. Medical staff and other healthcare workers, most of them strangers, have access to the room and come and go without the patient's

Figure 6.3 Typical examination rooms provide few opportunities for patient privacy. Ryan McVay/Getty Images.

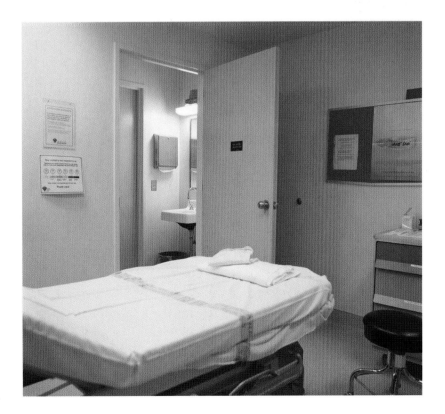

permission. Shared rooms provide even less opportunity to establish territory.

Waiting rooms, in which family members may spend up to several hours under high levels of stress, are often exposed areas with sociofugal seating arrangements that provide few, if any, places of privacy or opportunities for individuals or groups to establish temporary territories.

The medical staff members also need to be able to establish and control their territories. Secondary territories shared by the medical staff must provide space to protect access to information, for semi-private and private conversations, and for a degree of personalization. Private offices for physicians serve as primary territories and must be designed to accommodate the expectations and needs of this personal area. As discussed in Chapter 2, owners have relatively exclusive control over access to their primary territories, making these areas important regulators of interaction and sources of needed privacy.

LINK

Want to know more about privacy needs in personal offices? See Chapter 5, page 96.

Personal Space Needs

Although violation of personal space is an accepted and often necessary part of healthcare, it is no less traumatic in healthcare environments than in other environments. Perhaps it is even more so. Because of the stress and uncertainty surrounding most healthcare experiences, personal space zones are usually much larger than they would normally be when interacting with others. Patients may need to maintain greater distances to feel safe and secure. However, feelings of helplessness and intimidation may make it more difficult in healthcare environments to express the need for greater personal space using conventional methods of body language, verbal behavior, and control of the environment.

Environmental Stressors and Healing

Stress has been identified as a potential trigger for certain illnesses and as a major obstacle to healing (Evans 2001, Horsburgh 1995, Ulrich 1995). Patients experience stress related to the uncertainty and pain of illness and medical procedures, and they experience additional stress from healthcare environments themselves that produce noise, invade privacy, and create feelings of vulnerability, crowding, and lack of control.

We know that environmental stress occurs when the demands of the environment exceed our capacity to cope with or adapt to those demands. The two major contributors to environmental stress have been identified as 1) the lack of control over the levels and types of stimulus in the environment, and 2) constant, rapid change within the environment. Both of these environmental stressors are abundant in healthcare environments. Lack of control over our physical surroundings and access to ourselves is a serious problem that increases stress in these settings. There are many possible ways we respond psychologically to this stress. We may withdraw by turning inward and exhibiting the type of privacy known as *reserve* to limit the ability of others to gain information about us. We may also suppress a range of negative emotions from fear, rage, and hate, to depression, anxiety, and frustration. Research indicates that when we suppress negative emotions, especially if they become chronic, we will experience negative physical effects. The most significant of these negative physical effects is an impaired immune system (DeAngelis 2002). (See **Figure 6.4**).

It is also important to note that families, visitors, and particularly healthcare staff members experience stress in these environments as well. Workplace stress has been associated with low job satisfaction, poor job performance, high burnout rates, and high levels of absenteeism. While these results of stress are a problem in

Patient stress can manifest itself in a variety of ways that affect wellness.

- "Psychologically, stress is manifested [as] a sense of helplessness and such feelings as anxiety and depression."

- "Physiologically, stress involves changes in bodily systems, expressed by such measures as increased blood pressure or high levels of circulating stress hormones. A growing body of research has shown that physiological effects of stress can include reduced immune system functioning."

- "Behaviorally, stress is associated with a wide variety of reactions that adversely affect wellness, including verbal outbursts, social withdraw, sleeplessness, alcohol abuse, and noncompliance with medication" (Ulrich 1992, p. 89).

Figure 6.4 The physical and psychological stress on patients takes its toll.

any work situation, in healthcare situations they can be particularly problematic and potentially dangerous.

Two environmental stressors, crowding and noise, can be significantly reduced when environments are designed to support privacy needs. Both of these stressors are affected by the degree of control we have over the environment.

Crowding

Crowding has been identified as a primary environmental stressor (Evans 2001). In healthcare environments patients must often surrender control over access to their bodies resulting in more interaction with others than desired. This, together with the inability to control our surroundings, can result in feelings of crowding. The stress produced from crowding can cause the patient to withdraw psychologically and can produce psychological distress (Evans et al. 1999), which in turn can seriously hinder the healing process.

Noise

The effects of noise—defined as unwanted sound (Evans 2001)—on the healing process is another primary environmental stressor in

healthcare environments. The effects of noise are not as well researched and documented than the effects of crowding. However, noise annoyance or unwanted noise appears to vary with the individual depending upon personal and environmental factors (Byers & Smyth 1997). Studies suggest that as an environmental stressor, unwanted sounds can interfere with concentration and the performance of certain tasks, as well as cause frustration and irritation and reduce tolerance for pain (Grappell 1995). Some studies have shown that noise in healthcare environments can raise blood pressure and produce sleeplessness (Yinnon et al. 1992, Hilton 1985).

Noise levels are above recommended levels for comfort in operating rooms, recovery rooms, many treatment rooms, intensive care units, and often patient rooms. Studies have found that equipment and conversations between healthcare staff are the major sources of noise in these areas (Kam, Kam, & Thompson 1994). For example, the noise levels produced by the equipment in dialysis treatment facilities are typical of those found in machine shops. This high noise level affects the ability of patients to relax or sleep during their treatment as well as their ability to talk with one another or the healthcare staff (Bame & Wells 1995).

The stress associated with the pain and uncertainty of medical procedures can be heightened by environmental stressors. Designs that are sensitive to the causes of environmental stress can help to minimize the overall stress experienced by patients in healthcare environments. Roger Ulrich (1992) suggests, "To promote wellness, it is fundamentally important that healthcare facilities be designed to foster coping with stress. At the very least, facilities should not raise obstacles to coping with stress or contain features that are in themselves stressors, and thereby add to the total burden of illness. Further, environments should be designed to facilitate access or exposure to physical features and social situations that scientific studies suggest can have a therapeutic stress-reducing influence" (p. 21). Using the information and guidelines provided in this chapter to develop an understanding and sensitivity for privacy needs, designers can create environments that significantly reduce the environmental stress found in most healthcare facilities.

The Concept of High Tech/High Touch

When social forecaster John Naisbitt announced in 1982 that we were entering into an era of "high tech/high touch," he predicted a future more or less dominated by technology that we would seek to balance or escape through pursuits that connected us to one another and to things of lasting value and meaning. Naisbitt asserted, "Whenever new technology is introduced into society, there must be a counterbalancing human response—that is, *high touch*—or the technology is rejected" (p. 39). Over two decades later, we find ourselves surrounded by and dependent on technology for just about every aspect of our professional lives and for much of our personal lives as well. In accordance with Naisbitt's predictions, many high touch responses have occurred. Among these is the concept of the total healing environment.

Healthcare facilities must maintain a balance between the high tech of modern medical science and the high touch of patient centered care. High touch is associated with familiarity. Novelty dominates most healthcare experiences, but because that novelty is often tinged with fears,

Figure 6.5 High touch elements provide familiarity. © Rion Rizzo/Creative Sources Photography. Architect: Gould Turner Group, PC—Nashville, Tennessee. Project: HealthCenter Northwest—Kalispell, Montana.

it adds to the environmental load and stress for most patients. Technology surrounds patients with machines that monitor physical functions, provide food and medication, and literally keep them alive. The complexity and noise associated with high tech medical equipment and procedures requires a high touch balance to reassure and provide patients with a sense of control. Familiar, noninstitutional elements (artwork, music, residential quality furnishings, nature) provide a much needed high touch balance. The restorative benefits of privacy are also enhanced when familiar, comforting high touch elements are included in the design of private spaces. (See **Figure 6.5**).

THE REDISCOVERY OF THE BODY/MIND CONNECTION

Both scientists and healthcare professionals are now recognizing that who gets sick, who gets well, and why, are determined in part by our psychological state of mind. They are also recognizing that the physical environment has a strong effect upon our psychological state of mind and therefore upon our physical health and well-being. A great deal of this rediscovery of the body/mind connection to wellness and the relationship of the physical environment to healing is the result of two major influences: the new science of psychoneuroimmunology and Roger Ulrich's Theory of Supportive Design.

Psychoneuroimmunology

The term **psychoneuroimmunology** (PNI) describes the multidisciplinary study of the connection between the brain and the body's physical systems, particularly the immune system. PNI brings together knowledge from studies in endocrinology, immunology, psychology, neurology, and other fields. This new science was founded in 1975 by Dr. Robert Ader, director of behavioral and psychosocial medicine at the University of Rochester in New York.

According to PNI, psychological experiences such as stress and anxiety can influence the function of the immune system and in turn may affect the healing process. PNI research is also examining how psychosocial factors such as an optimistic frame of mind and social support can affect stress responses. According to healthcare expert Patrick Linton (1995), the multidisciplinary research is revealing that all of the body's systems, including the nervous system, endocrine system, the immune system, and the brain continuously interact with and influence one other. Linton explains, "The human being, even at a physical or psychological level, is a very holistic, interdynamic entity" (p. 125). This description reflects the complexity of the science of psychoneuroimmunology itself. Each of the multidisciplinary sciences that contribute to PNI is also highly complex, making it difficult to isolate and study any individual concept.

However, for the purposes of our inquiry into the universal need for privacy, we will examine design solutions involving the central premise of PNI: that environmental stress (resulting from lack of control over our surroundings) produces psychological responses that suppress the immune system and hinder the healing process. Knowledge concerning the link between our emotions (including stress), our body's regulatory systems (including the endocrine, immune, and central nervous systems), and physical health increasingly suggests that our physical environments can be designed to help reduce stress. As we have learned, environmental stress can be reduced by providing the ability to control how much sensory stimuli we must process and how much interaction we have with others. Psychoneuroimmunology's holistic view of how the body works and interacts with its own systems and with its environment provides important evidence-based data for designers to create the stress reducing, restorative quality of privacy in healthcare environments.

Roger Ulrich's Theory of Supportive Design helps to translate PNI theories into design criteria. Choice, control, positive distractions, and privacy are central concepts of Ulrich's supportive design theory.

The Theory of Supportive Design

Environmental psychologist Roger S. Ulrich introduced the Theory of Supportive Design in 1990, providing an important scientifically based guide for the design of healthcare facilities. The Theory of Supportive Design is unique in that it combines two major areas of research, healthcare facility design and human interactions with nature, with a focus on how our experiences with environments affect our physical and psychological health and well-being. This theory has been the basis for many changes in the ways interior designers, architects, and healthcare professionals look at the relationships between the natural and built environments and healing.

Since 1992, Ulrich has urged designers to realize the potential that our decisions have to either promote or hinder patients' psychological and physical health and well-being. He explains, "Certain design choices or strategies can work for or against the well-being of patients. Research has linked poor design to anxiety, delirium, elevated blood pressure, increased need for pain medication, and longer hospital stays following surgery. Conversely, research has shown that good design can reduce stress and anxiety, lower blood pressure, improve postoperative courses, reduce the need for pain medication, and shorten hospital stays" (p. 20).

In addition to the recognized design goals to create healthcare facilities that meet functional, economic, and code requirements, Ulrich (1995) asserts, "Another critically important goal of designers should be to promote wellness by creating physical surroundings that are 'psychologically supportive.' Supportive surroundings facilitate patients'

coping with the major stress accompanying illness" (p. 88).

Psychologically supportive healthcare environments reduce the environmental stress, and they support the patient's ability to deal with illness and surgery by fostering three important qualities.

1. A sense of control over physical/social surroundings and access to privacy
2. Access to social support from family and friends
3. Access to nature and other positive distractions in one's physical surroundings

We will now examine how these qualities of supportive healing environments can serve specifically as design considerations and criteria for privacy.

PRIVACY CONSIDERATIONS AND CRITERIA FOR HEALING ENVIRONMENTS

Each of the three qualities of supportive healing environments involves the concepts of privacy we have discussed in this text. The first quality relates to the need to control the environment, to regulate interaction, and to achieve desired levels of privacy. The second quality relates to the type of privacy defined as *intimacy*, the need to be alone with others such as friends, lovers, or family without interference from unwanted intrusions. The third quality involves an important benefit of privacy, the ability to take us away (physically and/or psychologically) from the sources of stress.

A Sense of Control and Access to Privacy

In Chapter 2 we learned that humans have a fundamental need to control access to ourselves and to at least some aspects of our physical environments to maintain autonomy and a healthy self-identity. This need becomes critical in the high load situations that typically occur in healthcare environments. Without some control over the environmental load in these settings, research shows that we can become depressed and passive, our blood pressure rises, our immune system is suppressed, and recovery is hindered. However, research also indicates that these negative effects can be greatly reduced or even eliminated if we have a sense of control over our physical environment (Evans & Cohen 1987). Designs can be created in patient rooms as well as in the more public areas to facilitate control through privacy in a variety of ways.

Adjustment of the Space to Provide Varying Degrees of Visual and Acoustical Privacy (See **Figure 6.6**).

* *Sequence spaces to create a spatial hierarchy in which to progress from less to more private spaces or areas within a space.*
* *Provide elements that can be adjusted to communicate one's desired level of privacy and to furnish varying degrees of enclosure (movable screens, dividers, curtains).*

Figure 6.6 As seen in this example of an assisted living unit, visual and acoustical privacy can be enhanced by a variety of space planning configurations that provide spatial hierarchy and prospect and refuge.

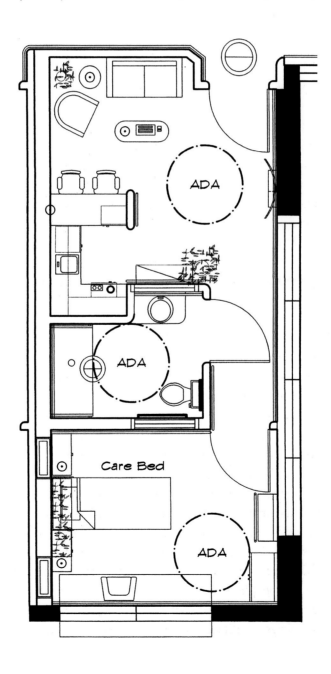

- *Provide easily movable comfortable furniture and a space plan that accommodates different arrangements as social density changes.*
- *Provide control of lighting.*
- *Provide control of television and music.*
- *Provide stimulus shelters (alcoves, window seats, use of room corners for intimate conversation).*

Adjustment of the Space to Accommodate Personal Space Zones and Territoriality to Provide a Sense of Safety and Security

- *Use implied or real thresholds (arches, columns, lowered ceilings, changes in flooring materials, variations in lighting levels) to differentiate territories and define spatial zones.*
- *Provide areas of prospect and refuge (orient toward views of nature or into other interior spaces while providing a degree of enclosure around the individual).*

Access to Social Support from Family and Friends

The benefits to patients from frequent or prolonged positive interaction with family, friends, and healthcare staff are significant. Patients who have strong social support experience less stress and achieve higher levels of overall wellness than those who have low or no support (Ulrich 1992). It is also important to foster social support between the family and friends of patients spending long periods of time waiting together. The staff members also benefit from social support between one another.

Privacy is an essential quality of these environments. Positive social support in healthcare settings requires choice and control over interactions. If we are unable to control the levels of interaction that we have in these environments, increased stress may result. Ulrich (1995) explains, "It should be emphasized that designs should be avoided that strongly promote social interaction to the point of denying access to

privacy. An interior arrangement that enforces social interaction but denies privacy will be stressful and work against wellness" (p. 94).

Supportive healthcare settings provide comfortable, controllable environments for positive social interaction between patients, caregivers, family, and friends. These environments should offer a variety of settings that support intimacy. Although individual needs for social support vary, designers should provide a variety of environmental opportunities for varying degrees of social interaction, including the following:

Areas of Visual and Acoustical Privacy for Intimate Conversations

- *Create areas of prospect and refuge that allow groups to see and experience their surroundings without being disturbed (level changes that comply with ADA, alcoves overlooking or open to gardens, or larger interior spaces).*
- *Provide adjustable, comfortable seating to allow people to create desired types of sociopetal or sociofugal arrangements (informal groupings of lightweight chairs with varying back heights, circular tables of different diameters).*
- *Use implied or real thresholds (arches, columns, lowered ceilings, changes in flooring materials, variations in lighting levels) to differentiate territories and define spatial zones.*

Shared Positive Distractions

- *Provide views of or access to nature via windows, sunrooms, atriums, or outdoor gardens that offer a sensory respite from the indoor environment and can be shared by patients, staff, and visitors.*
- *Create focal points and areas of interest to stimulate positive conversation.*
- *Provide elements of familiarity that can evoke positive memories and associations and*

can create the sense of a common social environment (residential-like furnishings, artwork depicting natural scenes).

- *Provide visual and physical access to a variety of settings within the facility that offer different views of the interior, different activities, and varying levels of interaction with others.*

Access to Nature and Other Positive Distractions in the Physical Surroundings

Positive distractions are qualities or features of the environment that have been shown to be effective in reducing patient stress and promoting wellness. Positive distractions have the ability to improve our moods and overall sense of well-being (Ulrich 2000). In Chapter 3 we discussed how positive distractions provide relief from directed attention, which in turn can reduce stress and mental fatigue. Healthcare environments often require a great deal of directed attention by the medical staff to concentrate on and perform certain critical tasks. The novelty, uncertainty, and lack of control that patients can experience in healthcare environments often require also that patients maintain directed attention, which can add to the mental fatigue and stress of their experience.

Of equal importance is the need to prevent sensory deprivation, particularly for patients. A great deal of the environmental stimuli in healthcare environments is repetitive, such as equipment sounds, uniformly high light levels, monotonous colors and materials, and lack of textural variations because of the need for sterile and easily cleanable surfaces. According to Ulrich (1995), "Some of the most striking scientific evidence regarding negative human consequences of poor design has emerged from studies of patients exposed to low stimulation or sensory deprivation in health facilities" (p. 94).

There are many elements and situations that can be experienced as positive distractions.

Almost anything that we personally consider fascinating or interesting can qualify. According to Ulrich, the most effective positive distractions are those elements or features that have been important to human beings throughout our evolutionary history.

1. Nature and natural elements such as trees, plants, and water
2. Happy, laughing, or caring human faces
3. Unthreatening animals, such as pets

Social support is an effective form of positive distraction. The smiling, caring, happy faces of family and friends can reassure us and take our minds off of the pain and stress that often accompanies the healthcare experience. The practice of introducing pets into healthcare facilities has grown more popular during the past several years as studies have shown that they elicit positive responses in patients, including relief from stress, lowered blood pressure, and greater overall well-being (Crawford, Pomerinke, & Smith 2003; Becker 2002). Nature, however, may be the most powerful positive distraction that we can use in the design of healing environments.

Nature as a Positive Distraction

The rediscovery of the mind/body connection to healing has once again raised awareness of the importance of nature to overall health.

Studies of how we use outdoor space in hospitals reveal that when asked the simple question, "Where do you choose to go when stressed?" Ninety-five percent of those interviewed responded that they experienced a significant change from feelings of depression, stress, and anxiety to a more calm and balanced mood after spending time outdoors. The elements of nature that caused this mood shift were trees, flowers, the changing of the seasons, colors, sounds of water and birds, and fresh fragrances (Marcus & Barnes 1999).

(See **Figure 6.7**). The ability to actually experience and affiliate with natural environments provides the highest level of distractions and restoration. The relationship of novelty to familiarity, sense of connectedness, symbolic meaning, mystery and fascination, as well as a heightened awareness of places, seasons, and time inherent in natural environments, are especially effective in promoting the involuntary attention that positively distracts us from the stress, pain, and uncertainty of illness and recovery.

An important relationship exists between the experience of nature and the ability to achieve restorative privacy. According to Ulrich (1992, 1995, 1999, 2000) and others (Kellert 1993, Heerwagen & Orians 1993), the therapeutic benefits of privacy can be enhanced by certain qualities of the natural environment that provide positive distractions. There are a variety of ways that nature can be integrated into the design of healthcare environments to provide positive distractions that contribute to the experience of privacy.

Figure 6.7 The use of natural elements inside can visually connect the viewer to natural elements outside creating positive distractions that enhance supportive social interaction in healing environments. © 1996 Richard Mandelkorn.

Windows with Views of Natural Elements

- *Provide windows with lowered sill heights (20 to 30 inches) in patient rooms so the view can be seen from a reclining position or a wheelchair.*
- *Provide at least a 20-foot distance between windows that look directly across an outdoor space or corridor from one another.*
- *Provide windows that overlook sunny areas versus dull or shaded areas.*
- *Provide windows that offer views with visual context (for example, a view of the sky is more effective as a distraction if it is framed by the branches of a tree, which also may serve as a habitat for birds).*
- *Provide windows that allow for natural ventilation when appropriate.*

Studies of longer-term exposure such as for patients recovering from surgery indicate that the view through the window can significantly affect healing. Ulrich (1984) found that patients recovering from gallbladder surgery benefited from views overlooking a natural setting with trees compared to patients with views of a brick wall. Tree-view patients had shorter post-operative stays, lower post-surgical complications such as headaches and nausea, and needed less medication for pain relief than wall-view patients. Additionally, nurses' notes contained fewer negative comments for tree-view patients, such as "patient is upset" than did comments for the wall-view patients.

Windows with views of nature offer many ways to provide the restorative quality of involuntary attention, including the ability to orient oneself to the time of day, the weather, and geographical location; observe changing patterns of light, color, and pattern; and focus on something that continues to appear and function normally outside of the confines of the healthcare environment.

Interior Green Spaces

- *Create interior spaces filled with diverse natural elements, including combinations of local seasonal and blooming plants and moving water to be enjoyed as a social environment or as a place of retreat and contemplation.*
- *Provide interior spaces with large scaled natural plantings as well as smaller plantings to create a sense of shelter and refuge.*
- *Create spaces that allow natural light to come from multiple directions.*
- *Create areas of enclosure or small "rooms" with planters and seating to provide visual privacy and allow more direct physical contact with the natural elements for contemplation and a sense of fascination.*

Interior green spaces can provide the experience of "nearby nature," which can significantly redirect our attention by allowing us to interact directly on a more human scale with natural elements. When designed with privacy in mind, interior green spaces provide shelter and a buffer from the often chaotic and unfamiliar surroundings of healthcare facilities. These spaces soften the severity of hard surface materials and unfamiliar equipment by creating pockets of color and texture, soothing sounds of water, and the warmth of natural light.

Gardens

- *Provide direct access to nature available to patients, visitors, and staff that encourage them to leave the indoors and interact on a personal basis with natural elements.*
- *Provide areas to participate actively in nature (tending plants, exploring, etc.) as well as to participate passively (observing, contemplating, and listening).*
- *Create cloisters (arcades with sheltering roofs) surrounding the garden at the building edge to allow for varying degrees of exposure and enclosure.*

Well designed gardens in healing environments should provide for movement and exercise, temporary escape, social support, and visual privacy (Ulrich 1999). In this way, gardens become very effective positive distractions. The concept of the healing garden, discussed later in this chapter, is an example of the growing recognition of the restorative power of nature for overall health and recovery.

Art Depicting Natural Scenes

* *Provide artwork rich in natural, serene, inspiring, symbolic content, including scenes with nonthreatening animals in their natural habitat (pastoral), scenes of sunrise or sunset, scenes of water, mountain and forest settings, and scenes in which natural light illuminates and reveals nonthreatening yet mysterious natural places.*
* *Use art depicting nature as a design element for fabrics, ceiling treatments, and lighting (see applications section for examples and descriptions).* (See **Figure 6.8**).

Research shows that not all art is perceived as positive, and some may even increase stress. Representational paintings in which nature or natural elements are the dominant subject tend to be preferred over abstract, challenging art. According to Ulrich (1992), "The great majority

of patients prefer representational art depicting serene, spatially open natural environments having scattered trees and/or nonturbulent water features—but consistently dislike abstract art" (p. 24). In 1984 Ulrich conducted studies to determine whether exposure to certain types of artwork in intensive care units reduced stress and had additional positive effects on recovery. Open heart surgery patients were randomly assigned a picture of nature dominated either by water or by trees or an abstract image. The control group had no pictures. Patients exposed to the pictures depicting water had less postoperative anxiety than did the patients with the other types of pictures or the control group. Additionally, the patients exposed to abstract pictures experienced higher anxiety levels than the patients from the control group. Considerations for these findings can help healthcare designers to choose and integrate art that enhances the restorative experience of private spaces.

FYI "The basic healing elements we will see throughout architectural history are water, sky, earth, weather, direction, and so forth. All these elements recur, if not in our buildings, at least in our minds."

(Kellman 1995, p. 42)

Figure 6.8 Photographs of soothing natural scenes may be used as ceiling tiles or mounted on the ceiling or walls in light boxes to provide positive distractions. © Catalina Curtain Co.

Music

Another positive distraction that can be used to enhance the restorative experience of privacy in healthcare environments is music. Music is being used more frequently as environmental design by healthcare facilities to help alleviate stress, fear, and anxiety, and to provide aesthetically supportive environments that promote the healing and recovery process. Like art, music with its cultural, historical, and personal meaning can evoke images and memories and can heighten or reduce stress levels (Mazer & Smith 1995). Therefore, if used sensitively and appropriately, music can become a valuable positive distraction. For the same reasons, it can also become a negative distraction.

Music can mask the unpleasant sounds of equipment and pain. Patient choice and control of music can provide a level of privacy by allowing patients to "screen" out unwanted, unpredictable noise intrusions and provide pleasant, positive distractions.

Age-Specific Privacy Consideration for Healing Environments

Although our needs for privacy in healthcare environments change continually as we age, two age groups in particular appear to be most vulnerable to the lack of privacy found in many healthcare facilities: adolescents and the elderly.

Adolescent Privacy Needs in Healthcare Settings

Although adolescents have urgent age-specific privacy needs in many settings, these needs become exacerbated in situations such as hospitalization. There is no mechanism in place to allow adolescents to control their environment or their social interaction. For the adolescent, autonomy and decision making are suspended temporarily in these environments. (James, Jenks, & Prout 1998).

For adolescents who undergo hospitalization as an isolated one-trip visit, the experience may be stressful, but it is short-lived. For adolescents suffering from trauma or chronic illnesses, the hospital experience can become a major part of their lives. How then do adolescents cope with what they perceive as a gross violation of their privacy?

Adolescents often perceive a loss of status within their peer group during hospitalization (Hutton 2002) undoubtedly because they are removed from their peer group and placed back under the control of their parents and other authority figures. Life for the hospitalized adolescent can be a series of painful experiences. Three events stand out in the literature regarding hospitalized adolescents.

- *Embarrassment and fear of scrutiny for bathroom experiences*
- *Lack of privacy on the telephone and time restrictions on usage*
- *Invasion of their bedrooms by hospital staff members*

Embarrassment and Fear of Scrutiny

Adolescents are universally embarrassed about their bodily functions. Studies conducted on hospitalized adolescents with chronic conditions, explored these concerns and the possible design solutions to ease some of the problems. Researchers (Hutton 2002, Hutton 1999, MacKenzie 1988, Slee 1996) found that adolescents are embarrassed to walk down a hospital corridor to use a toilet. They feel that they are advertising their intent to go to the toilet to the rest of the ward. If they must walk past other patient rooms and the nurses' station, they feel that they are being scrutinized. Another source of concern for the adolescent is communal showering. Common showers with open doors are found in many hospitals. Because most adolescents enjoy a certain degree of privacy in their bathrooms at home, they view lack of privacy in the hospital while showering, grooming, and using the toilet as violations to themselves (MacKenzie 1988).

Lack of Privacy on the Telephone

For adolescent patients, privacy is the only experience that allows them to capture briefly their feelings of independence. The vehicle used most often by hospitalized adolescents for both independence and privacy is the telephone. The telephone is crucial to maintain the line of communication with their peers and, in addition, telephones provide intimacy and opportunities for private conversations. If telephones are located at the nurses' station only, the adolescent endures an experience similar to going to communal toilets. They are unable to have auditory privacy with their peers if they know that others can overhear them, and there may be restrictions on time spent on the phone. There is no intimacy possible in this type of setting.

Sharing Rooms and Invasion by Hospital Staff

Adolescents view their bedrooms as primary territories, places to experience solitude, to unwind, to have some free time, to escape from the rest of the world, and to pursue quiet activities. Sometimes chronically ill adolescents feel a need to withdraw from social interaction and to deal with their emotions (Newman & Newman 1991, Gillies 1992). Because patient safety dictates hospital procedure, adolescents can never have the luxury of complete privacy in their hospital bedrooms. For design professionals, designing semi-private and private areas into other spaces such as a library or snack room may provide greater privacy for adolescents. Adolescents in hospital settings want the same things that nonhospitalized adolescents want: control and choices. Interior design can aid that process.

Designing for the Elderly:
Privacy and Communication

Facilities for the elderly are a special category of healthcare environments. Similar to other healthcare facilities, the design of residential care environments in which an individual can "age in place" (remain in one facility for the rest of their lives) are responding to the rediscovery of the relationship between wellness and the total person. Both physical and psychological needs play important roles in designing these environments, but the need for a high touch balance is perhaps more critical here than in any other type of healthcare facility.

In residential care facilities, we are designing for a population that is aging or ill and may have mobility problems and possible cognitive limitations. The need to provide them with privacy for autonomy is balanced by the need for social interaction to maintain physical and psychological health and well-being. In addition to providing opportunities for privacy, designers must also create sociable environments that draw the residents out of their rooms so that they may enjoy the social support necessary for wellness.

Physical Distances from Public to Private Spaces

To encourage social interaction it is important to consider the physical distances that residents must travel from private spaces to public or social spaces.

LINK
Want to know more about how to design environments that minimize isolation and encourage socialization for the elderly? See Chapter 8, page 216.

Over the years, a resident's social sphere may shrink since distance affects the probability of social contact. Additionally, long corridors are not compatible with residents who have difficulty walking (Noell 1995–1996, Rule, Milke, & Dobbs 1992). Research conducted to determine how great a distance from their bedrooms nursing home residents would travel to access social spaces and under what conditions reveals

- *Residents who lived closest to social spaces (20 feet) utilized them more often than residents who lived in spaces farther away.*
- *Residents in shared bedrooms used social spaces more than residents who had private bedrooms.*

- *Residents visited spaces more often that had elements of novelty and continually changing features such as views from windows, bird feeders, aquariums, pinup boards, arrivals and departures of guests, and even shift changes of hospital staff.*
- *Residents walked further if they were going to participate in activities rather than to merely visit social spaces* (Pinet 1999).

We can use this information to create general guidelines for design planning for distance and social spaces for the elderly.

- *Plan bedrooms in clusters rather than in long double-loaded corridors.*
- *Locate social spaces close to bedroom cores; 20 feet is optimum.*
- *Locate activity spaces closer than social spaces to bedrooms because activity spaces bring residents out of their rooms.*
- *Design in a dynamic flexible manner. Provide for novelty and changes in scenes and activities.*

Lighting

Lighting is always part of visual privacy, and studies of the elderly and illumination confirm that lighting changes are powerful forces in the physical and psychological wellness of those who are confined to their rooms and often have light deprivation, mental impairment, or depression. Manipulation of light and lighting can be used to alleviate symptoms of depression, increase overall feelings of physical and psychological well-being and enhance the restorative experiences of privacy. However, the technique of lowering light levels to enhance the experience of privacy may not always be appropriate for older individuals. As we age, we may need up to one-third more light to be able to see accurately. Additionally, lowered light levels can diminish the vitality of cool colors. For example, many older individuals have

reduced sensitivity to colors at the blue end of the spectrum. Therefore, an environment designed with cool colors to enhance the experience of privacy may be perceived by the elderly as dull and gray. Older individuals also require higher contrasting color schemes due to the reduced ability to distinguish closely related colors.

The design considerations for age-specific privacy needs in healthcare facilities are but one part of a larger body of knowledge regarding how our privacy needs change with age. Designing for privacy for different age groups in a variety of environments is covered in-depth in Chapter 8.

INTERIOR DESIGN APPLICATION FOR HEALTHCARE PRIVACY

Designers must create healing environments that provide patients with the ability to choose the levels of privacy that they need within the functional restrictions that are a central part of healthcare design. We must provide for choice and control of environmental elements that enhance privacy whenever possible. We must create places of privacy for families, friends, and patients to retreat from observation and intrusions while remaining accessible to the medical staff. We must also provide places for the staff to get away temporarily to redirect their attention and to recover from stress and mental fatigue.

Design Elements: Three Sensory Components

Three sensory components of the environment are critical to privacy in healing environments: color, light, and sound. Each of the three has the ability to affect our individual physical and psychological health and well-being. When applied properly in the design, these components contribute to a healing environment that becomes good medicine in itself.

Color

Using a variety of colors is recommended for healing environments. If used properly, color variety can add visual stimulation and provide positive distractions in these settings. They can also communicate what levels of privacy may be expected in various areas of healthcare facilities.

Our individual physical and psychological reactions to different colors can affect the healing process. These reactions must be considered when using color to promote privacy in healthcare environments. We have learned that, in general, warm colors speed up the metabolism, encourage activity and interaction, and are helpful when performing physical tasks. Cool colors are calming, introspective, promote more passive behavior, and are helpful when performing detailed tasks. Research has shown that these very different effects are because red has a stimulating effect on the sympathetic nervous system, increasing blood flow to the muscles and boosting brainwave activity. This process accelerates heart and respiration rates and raises blood pressure. Conversely, a cool color such as blue stimulates the parasympathetic nervous system, which produces a calming or tranquilizing effect on the body (Grappell 1995).

Restorative private spaces in healing environments should be designed using appropriate combinations of warm and cool colors to communicate different levels of privacy in each space. Color symbolism and associations made between warm and cool colors can be used to indicate whether a space or area is public or private. Because we associate warm colors with activity and interaction, their use in wayfinding and in the design of more public spaces can communicate that an area is accessible and open. Because cool colors are associated with calming and more passive activities, they can communicate that an area is more private. For example, in the more public areas such as hospital lobbies and clinic waiting rooms, a predominant (but not exclusive) use of warmer colors such as rose, peach, and terra-cotta can encourage conversation and interaction among patients, visitors, and staff. As the spatial hierarchy leads patients and visitors from these areas to increasingly private areas, a greater emphasis on cooler colors such as blue and green can be used to create a calming, more private feeling.

The correct balance between warm and cool colors can help avoid monotony and provide appropriate levels of visual stimulation in all areas. An aesthetically pleasing combination of warm and cool colors such as rose and green or peach and blue can provide appropriate soothing/stimulating effects in healthcare environments and induce moods that help to support varying levels of interaction and degrees of privacy. (See **Figure 6.9**).

FYI   Neither monochromatic nor high contrast color schemes are effective in creating restorative private spaces in healing environments. Monochromatic schemes tend to be less visually stimulating and can quickly become boring in environments where patients must spend long periods of time. Although high contrast color schemes are helpful to distinguish shapes and forms and define objects—especially for the visually impaired—they may create too much visual stimulation, which can increase stress.

The physical and psychological effects of color schemes can be altered dramatically by variations in the value (the amount of white or black in a color) and chroma (the intensity or saturation of a color). Value and chroma can change a color's effect and meaning. A rich blue used to create a private environment can

Figure 6.9 Colors used to enhance privacy in healing environments should be chosen with consideration for their psychological effects and cultural symbolism.

Public Spaces: Lobbies, Reception Areas

Predominately warm colors to encourage interaction and communication, balanced by calming cooler colors

Public Spaces: Floor or Department Lounges, Surgery Waiting Areas

Predominately cool colors taken from nature to sooth, balanced by soft warm colors to enhance positive feelings

Patient Floor Corridors

Predominately cool colors taken from nature to symbolize entering private areas, balanced by soft warm colors to enhance positive feelings

Patient Rooms

Predominately cool colors taken from nature to calm and sooth, balanced by soft warm colors taken from nature used in artwork and accessories to enhance positive feelings

Patient Lounges

Areas of predominately cool colors taken from nature as a backdrop to colorful flowers, views of nature and artwork depicting nature

become cold if too much white is added so that it becomes a pale, light blue. The relaxing benefits of a cool color palette that is conducive to privacy will be lost if the cool colors lose their vitality. Conversely, a palette of fully saturated hues will compete for attention, increasing the environmental load so that the eye will have difficulty focusing upon any one color or area.

Color combinations found in nature are often the most pleasing (Fehrman & Fehrman 2004). Color schemes inspired by nature are familiar, and they represent one of the many qualities of nature that serve as a positive distraction: harmony. Our sense of color harmony and aesthetics is derived from our rich history of living in natural environments. This reassuring quality of nature-inspired color schemes provides an important balance of familiarity to the high levels of novelty inherent in most healthcare environments.

Any discussion of the effects of color on privacy, health, and well-being must also include a discussion of the effects of light. Color and light are inseparable and their effects are reciprocal.

Light

Restorative private environments benefit from abundant natural light and controllable artificial light. The importance of light to human health and well-being cannot be overstated. Light has been called the most important environmental input (after food) in controlling bodily functions (Birren 1969). The new science of photobiology, which studies the health effects of light, provides important research data about the effects of color and light on the body.

Natural light, which is made up of all colors in the visible spectrum, has the capacity to improve our overall health and resistance to infections by enhancing the immune system, increasing the amount of oxygen carried in the blood, improving the performance of the cardiovascular system, and increasing the amount of adrenaline in the body's tissues, which, in turn, enhances our ability to tolerate stress (Fehrman & Fehrman 2004). The body is also naturally receptive to the changing rhythms of daylight, which has been shown to enhance the healing process.

All healthcare environments benefit from a balance of natural and artificial light. Used correctly, natural light is a powerful positive distraction that has been difficult to replicate with artificial light. Daylight provides fascination because it is constantly changing in direction, intensity, and color. All living things respond to natural light. Trees reach for the light. Flowers turn toward the light, often so quickly it can be directly observed. Pets stretch their bodies to take in the full extent of a beam of sunlight streaming through a window. Birds become increasingly active and sing more frequently as natural light spreads over their habitat. Human beings are no less susceptible to the joys of natural light, and they benefit tremendously from exposure to natural light in healthcare settings.

However, since we spend 90 percent of our time indoors—or more when confined to a hospital—the effects of artificial light on our physical and psychological health and well-being must be given serious consideration by healthcare designers. Research conducted in 1974 to determine the effects of artificial lighting on fatigue reveal that standard cool-white fluorescent light increases fatigue (weariness, tiredness, and boredom) significantly more than full-spectrum fluorescent light. Cool-white fluorescent light—still commonly used in offices, institutions, schools, and medical facilities—also increases irritability, eyestrain, and headaches over full-spectrum light (Mass, Jayson, & Kleiber 1974). In addition to increasing fatigue, fluorescent light emits several types of potentially harmful radiation, at least one of which may be linked to the development of leukemia (Fehrman & Fehrman 2004). Newer models of fluorescent light minimize some of these harmful problems but do not eliminate them completely.

Incandescent light provides a healthy looking warm glow to a space and to people. Because incandescent light is most often used in homes, it significantly reduces the institutional feeling of a space, and it can enhance the feeling of privacy. However, incandescent light produces heat, uses much more energy than fluorescents, and has a relatively short lifespan. For these reasons it is used sparingly as general illumination in healthcare facilities.

Regardless of the type of lighting used, privacy is usually associated with lowered light levels. As light levels decrease we are less visually exposed, which enhances the feeling of privacy. Natural light can be shaded or it can be filtered using a technique called "radiant forest" in which light from the sun is filtered through the leaves of trees to produce the mottled effect of light and shadow experienced when walking thorough a forest on a sunny day. Radiant forest can be used also with artificial light sources to create an illusion of natural light in environments where natural light is not available. The radiant forest technique enhances feelings of fascination, which contributes to positive distractions. It also provides a feeling of enclosure necessary for privacy. (See **Figure 6.10**).

Although we have only just begun to discover the full potential of light to affect wellness and as a tool to enhance the benefits of privacy, a few general guidelines are possible.

- *Design buildings so that natural light enters from multiple directions: windows, skylights, clerestories, and atriums.*
- *Avoid constant, unchanging light levels.*
- *Create gradual increases and decreases in light levels from less private to more private areas.*
- *Design artificial light to mimic the visual effects of natural light.*
- *Whenever possible, adjust artificial light to natural daylight rhythms.*

Sound

Generally, when discussing sound as a component of healthcare environments or privacy, the focus is upon noise or unwanted sound. As discussed previously in this chapter, noise is a primary source of stress in healthcare environments causing frustration, irritation, and reduced tolerance for pain. Because noise makes it difficult to focus and concentrate, it is detrimental to privacy as well. Healthcare designers must make the reduction of noise a priority through the use of acoustical techniques and materials, appropriate space planning, furniture selections, and the use of sound masking. However, the reduction of environmental noise is not the only consideration to be made.

In 2003 the Health Insurance Portability and Accountability Act (HIPAA) mandated that virtually all healthcare organizations in the United States ensure greater protection of patients' private health information. This privacy law includes coverage of "oral communications" requiring that medical organizations provide their patients and customers with a level of speech privacy. Discussions among healthcare staff involving a patient's personal information, as well as confidential information read aloud from a computer screen or written document must not be overheard by others. This places even greater importance upon the control of sound in staff areas. As a result of HIPAA, many sound masking companies are now focusing on the development of sound masking devices to specifically mask voice transmission. Sound masking involves producing an electronically generated ambient sound that has the effect of canceling or masking other noises in the environment. When installed correctly, the masking sound is unobtrusive and goes virtually unnoticed. Voice levels may be further controlled by the use of dropped ceiling baffles and increased use of acoustical materials surrounding staff areas.

Natural sounds can also mask unwanted noise. Natural sounds such as moving water, birdsong, rain, and wind moving through trees and plants are especially effective in masking unwanted sounds of voices, traffic, and equipment. Moving water has been shown to be the most effective natural sound to calm and relax us while masking other noises. Soothing natural sounds are also positive distractions that can help to reduce stress and therefore aid the healing process.

Soothing music, discussed earlier in this chapter as a positive distraction, can have positive effects upon wellness and contribute to acoustical privacy. When coordinated to the rhythms of the body, music helps to control heart and respiration rates and lower blood pressure. As a positive distraction, music can facilitate relaxation, reduce pain, and even reduce the need for anesthesia (Ulrich 2000). Stress is further reduced when patients have control over the music. Music also provides sound masking, which, together with its

ability to provide positive distractions, enhances acoustical privacy.

Next, we will discuss privacy considerations and criteria for four specific healthcare spaces: lobbies (including reception areas and waiting rooms), patient rooms, staff areas, and emergency rooms. These areas have been chosen because they represent the three types of territories found in healthcare facilities (primary, secondary, and public), as well as needs for all types of privacy (solitude, intimacy, anonymity, and reserve).

Healthcare Lobbies, Reception Areas, and Waiting Rooms

A patient's first impression of the philosophy of care of any medical facility is formed in the lobby or reception area. Whether the facility is a medical office building, a hospital, or a facility for seniors, the design should inspire confidence by emphasizing comfort, care, and wayfinding. The high touch backlash in healthcare design is producing lobbies, reception areas, and waiting rooms that resemble more the hotel lobbies of the future rather than

Figure 6.10 The lighting technique called Radiant Forest simulates the quality of natural light as it is filtered through the leaves of a forest on a sunny day. Photo: Ambient Creations

Figure 6.11 Healthcare lobbies often resemble hotel lobbies. This view of the café in the Sky Ridge Medical Center in Lone Tree, Colorado, illustrates areas designated for intimate interaction. © Rion Rizzo/Creative Sources Photography. Architect: Gresham Smith & Partners, Nashville, Tennessee.

the institutional waiting areas of the past. Residential quality design elements in these spaces provide familiarity and reduce the stress associated with the novelty and uncertainty of medical procedures.

Interior designers are challenged to accommodate a variety of functions, activities, and needs in these areas, many of which require privacy. Intimacy is necessary for patients to communicate effectively and confidentially with healthcare staff in registration and admitting areas. Intimacy is also important for those who must wait together, while those who must wait alone sometimes desire anonymity. Both patients and visitors who do not want others to know the nature of their visits to the medical facility often need reserve. Solitude is sometimes necessary for those who must deal with difficult decisions or with grief.

Designing for privacy in healthcare lobbies, reception areas, and waiting rooms must include the three components of supportive design: control, social support, and positive distractions.

Control in Healthcare Lobbies

Designing for control to facilitate privacy in healthcare lobbies involves two considerations: 1) providing information for orientation and wayfinding, and 2) the ability to choose desired levels of social interaction. To provide a sense of control, information must be provided in a way that eliminates the confusion and feelings of helplessness that can contribute to stress. Incoming patients and visitors must be able to recognize effectively where they should go. **Redundant cuing** (the use of multiple elements to communicate information) should lead patients and visitors directly to the reception desk, admitting areas, and information centers. Examples of effective redundant cuing include consistent, graphically appropriate signage used together with color coding and material and lighting changes. Focal points can be used to draw people to

important areas in the lobby, reception area, and waiting rooms and to provide a visual marker for orientation.

Choices for social interaction and privacy require that large spaces be divided physically, visually, and acoustically into smaller, flexible territories. Sequencing these smaller territories from less to more private areas provides a variety of options for different levels of interaction. A hierarchy of circulation spaces should be established to connect these smaller territories to one another and to major functional areas within the larger space.

Primary circulation spaces should move people directly to and from major functional areas and around (not through) more private territories. Secondary circulation spaces should lead into the areas established as private territories. The most private areas should be located at the end or to the side of secondary circulation spaces.

A variety of seating types and arrangements within these smaller territories can provide further options. To accommodate intimacy, choose comfortable, lightweight, fully upholstered chairs and loveseats and place them in a sociopetal arrangement that focuses attention toward the center of the grouping. The grouping should be somewhat flexible to accommodate an additional chair if necessary. Fixed seating is not recommended because it severely limits flexibility and choice. Place sound absorbing materials near the source of sounds and lower the light levels in more private areas.

Additional ways to provide choice include using various sizes of tables with chairs to create an option for conversation, reading, working, or playing games. These tables should not be located adjacent to the more private areas. It is important also to provide seating for single visitors. Chairs and supporting furniture such as a table and lamp arranged in a semi-sociofugal pattern and placed near architectural features or against the walls provide seating options with important backup elements for people waiting alone. For example, four chairs arranged individually around a large support column will prevent eye contact and maintain a sociofugal arrangement. The smaller spaces within lobbies and waiting areas should not be too exposed nor too enclosed.

Alexander and his colleagues (1977) explain the importance of creating a balance between spaces that are too open to provide any type of privacy and those that are too closed to provide positive interaction. Describing the pattern called Half Open Walls, he writes that although an enclosed room provides control for certain activities, "it is very hard for people to join in these activities or leave them naturally. On the other hand, an open space with no walls around it, just a place marked by a carpet on the floor and a chair arrangement, but entirely open to the spaces all around it, is so exposed that people never feel entirely comfortable there" (p. 893). The solution, according to Alexander, is to create a space that is less enclosed than a typical room with four walls and a door, but much more enclosed than just a space within an open area. He explains, "A wall which is half-open, half-enclosed—an arch, a trellised wall, a wall that is counter height with ornamental columns, a wall suggested by the reduction of the opening or the enlargement of columns at the corners, a colonnade of columns in the wall—all these help get the balance of enclosure and openness right and in these places people feel comfortable as a result" (p. 894). These types of semi-enclosed spaces also create areas of prospect and refuge that allow visitors to achieve optimal physical and visual privacy while still allowing them to observe everything around them.

Social Support

The ability to interact positively with others in healthcare lobbies and waiting areas is dependent primarily upon acoustical privacy and sociopetal space planning. Acoustical privacy can be achieved by placing sound absorbing

materials near the source of the sounds or, as discussed previously, by masking sounds. Pleasant music is particularly effective to mask sounds in these areas. Natural plants can also be effective sound absorbers when grouped together densely in varying heights, some of which are at least four feet tall to create acoustical barriers and a sense of enclosure.

Considerations to create sociopetal seating arrangements that encourage positive interaction and conversation include flexible, comfortable seating as discussed above and the ability to establish desired personal space zones. Larger scaled lounge chairs provide for larger personal space zones. Chairs with high backs also increase the size of our personal space zones and provide a degree of both acoustical and visual privacy as well.

Positive Distractions

The condition of waiting for news about an ill or injured loved one can cause our psychological state to swing from the extremes of anxiety, fear, and stress to tedium and boredom. Positive distractions can help to relieve both extremes by

Figure 6.12 Walking the labyrinth at Johns Hopkins Bayview Medical Center can provide positive distractions and a sense of solitude for patients as well as for visitors and the medical staff. Photo taken by Sandy Reckert-Reusing.

redirecting our attention to something pleasant and interesting. Effective positive distractions for lobbies and waiting areas include artwork depicting nature; focal points, such as fountains, aquariums, and fireplaces; and both visual and direct access to nature or natural elements. Although the television is a distraction in these environments, it is not always positive. For this reason, televisions are not recommended in these areas of the healthcare facility. If, however, televisions are used in waiting areas, acoustical privacy must be considered, and individuals waiting in the specific areas in which televisions are located should have control over them.

A relatively new form of positive distraction used increasingly in healthcare environments is the labyrinth. (See **Figure 6.12**). These large maze-like patterns take their form from ancient circular mandalas found in many cultures and used as spiritual symbols, meditation tools, and symbolic pilgrimages. The most famous labyrinth is found on the floor of Chartres Cathedral in France where it is "walked" by Christians as a symbolic pilgrimage to Jerusalem.

Interior designer Victoria Stone specializes in designing labyrinths for medical facilities. Stone has found that the process of "walking the labyrinth" can be a very effective positive distraction. She explains, "By taking the labyrinth out of a religious setting, and placing it in a non-denominational healing environment, people of all faiths and religious traditions will have an opportunity to experience the spiritual support it provides when facing serious health problems. In the medical center setting, the labyrinth walk becomes as a holistic healing tool, a mind, body, prayer path. It is an experience that honors the whole person. With its holistic nature and simplicity of use, the labyrinth is an excellent tool for integrating spiritual self-care into a healthcare setting" (Stone 1999, p. 1).

Labyrinths can provide a sense of *solitude* without isolation. Their power to provide positive distractions is enhanced when placed in natural settings such as healing gardens.

The Emergency Department

The fears that accompany a visit to the emergency department can be some of the most stressful we may ever experience. Uncertainty about what is wrong, the general level of unfamiliarity, crowded conditions, rapid change, and lack of control are major contributors to stress in these environments. The emergency department process involves arriving, going through triage (to categorize the severity of the medical problem), registration, examination, diagnostic testing, diagnosis, and treatment. These activities take place in a variety of different spaces with a variety of different personnel. A traditional ER design arranges these spaces around a walk-in entry, an ambulance entry, and a large waiting room in the back of the hospital.

The nature of treating medical emergencies usually limits patient privacy to visual screening from observation by nonmedical individuals. However, because emergency departments treat all manner of injuries and illness from cuts and broken bones to heart attacks, strokes, and trauma, patients vary greatly in their needs for attention, interaction, and privacy. Designs usually focus on the need for visual and verbal communication between the medical team and patients and among the members of the medical team. However, concern for patient and family privacy in ERs is becoming increasingly important to the design of these spaces for hospital administrators, medical staff, architects, and healthcare designers.

The urgency for treatment of patients means that time spent waiting in emergency departments is often less than in other waiting areas of the hospital. However, the trauma and stress inherent in ER experiences often require a higher level of privacy.

Research indicates that ER patients perceive that they have greater auditory and visual privacy in rooms with solid walls than in those with curtains (Barlas, Sama, Ward, & Lesser 2001). Solid walls are often considered impractical in emergency departments with multiple patients. Although curtains allow for easy movement of people and equipment and for appropriate observation of patients, studies show that the perceived lack of privacy in curtained cubicles causes patients to feel reluctant about being examined or to share personal information with healthcare staff (Barlas et al. 2001). The challenge is to balance patient privacy needs with the needs of staff to observe patients directly and to move both people and equipment efficiently in emergency departments.

The newest, most patient-centered design concept for emergency departments is the all private ER. In these facilities, patients and families are accommodated in private rooms. Ball Memorial Hospital in Muncie, Indiana, is pioneering this concept. (See **Figure 6.13**). The new ER has 39 private patient rooms, each with comfortable seating for family and a television. When patients need complete privacy, families can wait across the corridor in a more traditional waiting area. Although this arrangement of spaces increases the overall size of the ER, there are many advantages. Patients are moved less often, which saves time and labor. Additionally, families can provide direct social support to the patients; families and patients have much more control over their environment; visual and acoustical privacy can be achieved; and the environmental load is lower, all of which can significantly reduce stress. The all private ER reflects the importance for patient-centered healing environments to provide privacy, to relieve stress, and to promote healing.

Patient Rooms

The first question to answer when designing patient rooms is are they single or double rooms? The debate over which is better, single or double patient rooms, is not new. Arguments for single rooms included concern about the transmission of infection in double rooms. Proponents of double rooms argue that the social and emotional support of a shared room is beneficial to patients' psychological health. Construction costs are lower for double rooms but costs involved in moving patients who have problems with their roommates are high. The bottom line is that patients prefer private rooms and the trend in hospital design to provide more single rooms reflects that preference. An article in *The Business Journal of Milwaukee* reports, "Semi-private

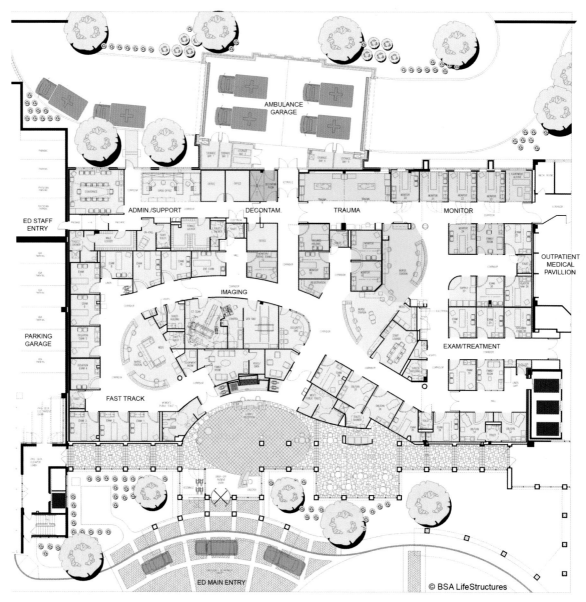

Figure 6.13 Floor plan of the "No Waiting Room" emergency department at Ball Memorial Hospital in Muncie, Indiana. © BSA LifeStructures.

LINK

If you want to know more about the preferences of the elderly in bedrooms in nursing homes, see Chapter 8, page 216.

rooms are becoming the exception rather than the norm. New construction projects are focusing exclusively on private rooms, and existing hospitals use semi-private rooms for single occupancy when volume is low, without charging a higher rate" (Mader 2002). Because patient rooms must accommodate both solitude and intimacy to provide the maximum benefits of privacy in the healing process, private rooms are usually preferred.

Patient concern for privacy and confidentiality has grown significantly in the last several years, resulting in the expectation and demand for private rooms. Healthcare administrators are accommodating that demand not only because private rooms appeal to patients, but also because they allow for a more cost-effective operation. The use of semi-private rooms is limited by the gender of the patients, infectious disease issues, and incompatibility among roommates (Mader 2002). These issues are not applicable to private rooms.

The most obvious quality of supportive design and privacy benefit that single rooms provide is increased control. When patients have control of environmental qualities such as light, temperature, telephone, access, music, and the television, they are able to get more rest and recover more quickly. When patients must share rooms, the challenge is to provide as much individual privacy and control as possible within a limited space. A private room is typically between 240 and 270 square feet, while a semi-private room is typically 300 square feet. It is, therefore, difficult to provide the same levels of acoustical and visual privacy in a room for two that is only a few square feet larger than a single room.

Design solutions that provide control and privacy in shared rooms include increasing the space between the beds and using an architectural element or implied thresholds to define the separate territories. For example, in rooms that are designed to be used permanently as shared rooms (as opposed to shared rooms that become private rooms when one bed is removed), half walls used together with cubicle curtains delineate territories and provide patients with the ability to control levels of visual privacy. Headwalls for each bed can be designed to provide a greater degree of enclosure with multiple sources of patient controlled light to accommodate the needs of the medical staff for examination and the needs of the patient for softer, more residential-like lighting. Curtains used to divide the bed areas should be made of thicker, more sound absorbing materials. Carpet provides greater acoustical privacy and is easier to walk and stand on, particularly for the elderly who feel more secure and confident on

carpet than on hard surfaces (Wilmott 1986). Research also suggests that visitors may spend more time with patients in carpeted rooms than in rooms with hard surface flooring (Harris 2000), which may enhance the social support component of patient rooms.

Modern patient rooms also provide more space for family requiring additional furniture such as glider-rockers, foldout sleeping chairs, and movable desks. Visitor seating should be lightweight and easily movable to accommodate changing social density and sociopetal arrangements. To create a feeling of territory, many healthcare facilities are treating the entrances to their patient rooms as if they were homes, with their own mailboxes, and even outdoor-styled furniture placed immediately outside the rooms where family can gather and relax (Monroe 2003).

Positive distractions should be integrated into the design of patient rooms. Although the television can be an important positive distraction, it should be balanced by other more high touch distractions. As discussed previously in this chapter, windows with views of nature are a powerful positive distraction that contribute significantly to the healing process. A window seat has the added benefit of providing prospect and refuge for ambulatory patients and their visitors. Art depicting serene natural environments as well as colorful plants and flowers also provide effective positive distractions. (See **Figure 6.14**).

Interior products are being developed to integrate the benefits of privacy with the capacity of nature to provide restoration and to promote healing. For example, window sized photomurals of nature can be attached to cubicle curtains or screens, and the patient is provided with earphones to listen to the ambient relaxing sounds of water, wind, birdcalls, and other natural sounds associated with the scene depicted in the photomural. When the curtain is drawn around the patient, and the earphones

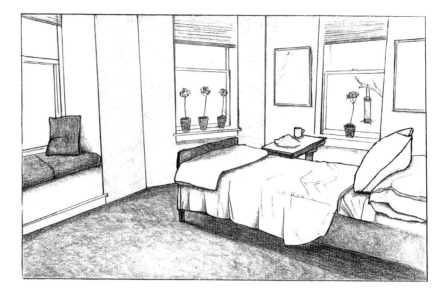

Figure 6.14 Patient rooms designed to provide positive distractions, including visual access to nature, also benefit from creating an area of prospect and refuge such as a window seat.

are in place, the patient may experience the deeper levels of solitude and relaxation that enhance feelings of well-being. Research suggests that two types of relaxation may be attributed to the use of this product: 1) psychological: feeling calmer, more serene, relief from anxiety, relief from pain, and ease of sleep; 2) physiological: reductions in blood pressure, heart rate, and respiratory rate (PIMHS 2004).

Staff Areas

The design of healing environments includes addressing the needs of the staff for control, social support, positive distractions, and privacy. A typical healthcare facility will have a variety of private and semi-private areas where physicians, nurses, therapists, and other medical and support staff work and interact with one another and with patients and their families. The staff requires spaces that support solitude for autonomy, contemplation, self-evaluation, emotional release, and rejuvenation. They require intimacy for social support, communication, and also for autonomy and emotional release. Positive distractions that redirect attention and relieve stress are important components of private spaces for healthcare staff and must be integrated into the overall design.

On a more immediate level, both physicians and nurses must have semi-private areas for writing in patients' charts and working on progress reports. This is best accomplished with designated sit-down writing areas at the nurses' station rather than in patient rooms. Multiple writing surfaces with a modicum of privacy such as half walls should be provided because physicians tend to make patient rounds at similar hours of the day and that creates high demands for desks at predictable hours.

Today, both men and women practice medicine, and often the work day extends into the evening, and in certain areas of specialty, through the night. Physicians who are sleeping "in the house" need private areas with separate sleeping rooms and bathrooms for men and for women. Today, many hospitals have staff lounges that adjoin private sleeping rooms. This arrangement is an example of using spatial depth to sequence staff areas from less to more private areas. To further increase spatial depth and feelings of privacy in the staff lounges and sleeping areas, the lounge can be located down the hall from patient areas. In this way, the staff will have more of a perceived "getaway experience." They are easily reachable but are usually behind an unmarked door. Amenities such as providing self-service or served food in these areas so that staff members do not have to use the public hospital cafeteria can also enhance feelings of being away.

Ulrich (1992) explains the need for private spaces, such as lounges for staff to alleviate the effects of stress. "Nurses and other healthcare staff experience stress and often burnout because their work is characterized by low control and high responsibility. One sign of a poorly designed work environment is the lack of adequate lounge or break areas. This shortcoming reduces the sense of control among staff and increases stress (and may contribute to higher turnover) by making it difficult to escape briefly from work demands" (p. 21).

Designers need to provide adequate lounge or break areas with a variety of flexible seating options and positive distractions. These "special" environments should vary in their levels of privacy. To provide the opportunity to choose the levels of interaction staff members have in these spaces and alleviate boredom, each lounge area should be designed as a unique environment with different color schemes, furniture types and arrangements, and artwork. Use lower levels of lighting, preferably incandescent, and avoid overhead fluorescent lighting. Whenever possible, bring natural light into these spaces. The staff should have access to indoor nature areas or outdoor gardens for optimal positive distractions.

Acoustical privacy is essential to protect the confidentiality of patient information, to allow for effective communication among the medical staff and between staff and patients and their families. As discussed previously, sound masking devices and acoustical materials placed near the source of voices are effective solutions. Lowered ceilings with acoustical baffles communicate visually that the area is more intimate and also block transmission of sound.

Half walls, partitions, screens, and plantings can enhance visual privacy. Changes in colors from a warm/cool balance in the more public areas to a cool/warm balance in the more private areas, and lowered light levels will enhance the experience of privacy in staff areas.

HEALING GARDENS

The final section of this chapter is devoted to a discussion of healing gardens as part of the total supportive healing environment. All types of gardens that provide access to nature can have positive effects on wellness, but healing gardens are designed specifically for this purpose. (See **Figure 6.15**).

Figure 6.15 Healing gardens provide opportunities for solitude, intimacy, and positive distractions. The presence of moving water is one of the most effective positive distractions and helps to mask other sounds to enhance solitude and intimacy. Elliot Kaufmann/ Beateworks.com.

Well designed healing gardens provide opportunities for solitude and for intimacy by creating places for social support and positive distractions. Healing gardens are particularly effective as positive distractions because they allow the user to have direct access to unthreatening natural environments. A significant body of knowledge (Marcus & Barnes 1999) supporting the idea that nature has unique abilities to foster healing and overall well-being has identified healing gardens as effective tools to provide relief from the awareness of the uncomfortable physical symptoms associated with illness, as well as actual relief from those physical symptoms. Additionally, this research shows that healing gardens have the capacity to foster relief from stress and depression.

Healing gardens are appropriate for all types of medical facilities. Used most frequently in designs for seniors and for Alzheimer's patients, healing gardens motivate residents who may have problems with wayfinding and place identification to go outside, walk, and interact with one another (McBride 1999). Children's hospitals are also increasingly designed with healing gardens to appeal to children's needs to explore, play, and fantasize as part of the healing process (Moore 1999).

The components of a healing garden should include (see **Figure 6.16**) the following:

- *a variety of greenery and flowers that stimulate our visual, tactile, and olfactory senses*
- *moving and still water*
- *areas of prospect and refuge*
- *a degree of enclosure*
- *shade and shelter from the elements*
- *a variety of viewpoints, focal points, landmarks, and seating options*
- *symbolic content*
- *mystery*

Interior designers and architects must work with landscape architects to create designs that integrate the interior spaces with the healing garden. Important considerations include the following:

Figure 6.16 This plan of a healing garden illustrates a variety of areas for different types of privacy and restorative positive distractions.

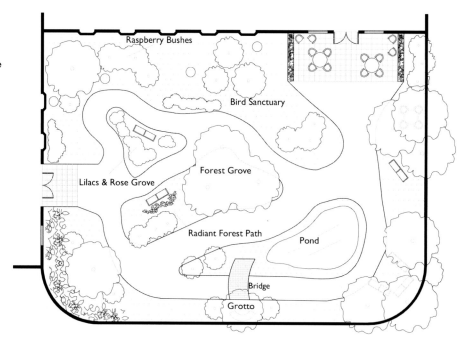

*   *Providing generous windows from interior spaces looking into the garden*
*   *Specifying windows with low sill heights*
*   *Using exterior overhangs to block glare*
*   *Providing distinctive thresholds between the interior and exterior*
*   *Providing a cloister to connect the interior with the exterior.*

People interact both actively and passively with outdoor areas, and the benefits that result from that interaction depend upon how the design supports their ability to have direct experiences with nature. While additional scientific studies are needed to explain the favorable influences of healing gardens on medical outcomes, it is clear from the existing research that healing gardens have the power to provide restoration from many of the symptoms of stress, depression, and the pain associated with illness and recovery. The unique opportunities that healing gardens provide all users within the healthcare facility to experience solitude and intimacy in a natural setting makes healing gardens an important element in designing for privacy in healing environments.

FINAL THOUGHTS ON PRIVACY NEEDS IN HEALTHCARE ENVIRONMENTS

Good design serves many functions. Among these functions are the wellness benefits associated with designing for privacy in healthcare environments. Good design also serves a symbolic function in healthcare environments. It conveys to patients and their families that the healthcare staff cares about their opinions, feelings, welfare, and comfort.

Healing is a holistic process involving physical, psychological, and environmental interaction. As we have learned in this chapter, considerations for privacy help to integrate these interactions. As healthcare continues to move into new areas of technology and rediscover traditional ways of healing, the role of the interior designer will necessarily expand. Hospital administrators, medical staff, architects, interior designers, environmental designers, and landscape designers will work together toward a common goal: to create supportive healing environments that integrate the built and natural environments to heal the mind and the body.

KEY CONCEPTS

1. Privacy has the ability to provide a refuge that has been shown to promote healing by providing rest, recovery, and contemplation.

2. The rediscovery of the connection between the mind and physical health has changed the way healthcare environments are perceived and designed. The new term, "healing environments," reflects the need for environments that help provide the positive emotional, physical, and cognitive effects upon patients that ultimately contribute to their overall health and recovery.

3. Choice and control (key concepts in designing for privacy) are essential considerations in the design of all areas of healing environments to help alleviate the stress and chaos often inherent in these settings.

4. The Theory of Supportive Design asserts that psychologically supportive healthcare environments reduce the environmental stress and support the patient's ability to deal with illness and procedural related stress by fostering three important qualities.
*   a sense of control over physical/social surroundings and access to privacy
*   access to social support from family and friends
*   access to nature and other positive distractions in their physical surroundings

5. Three sensory components of the environment are critical to privacy in healing environments: color, light, and sound.

ASSIGNMENT
DESIGNING FOR PRIVACY: SURGICAL WAITING ROOM

Learning Objectives:
- To analyze the privacy needs of a diverse population in an environment that varies in social density
- To formulate and apply design solutions that support the users' privacy needs to alleviate stress
- To consider cross-cultural similarities and differences in privacy needs and expressions of those needs

Learning Outcomes:
- Increased understanding of the designer's ability to affect people and the environment
- Increased understanding of human privacy needs and their relationships to other needs
- Development of skills in problem identification, analysis, and problem solving
- Increased understanding and appreciation of alternate points of view, such as age and culture

Description:
You have been asked to design the waiting room for families of surgery patients in a large children's hospital located in San Diego, California. The hospital administrators are interested in creating different types of waiting areas within the overall space to provide for the privacy and communication needs of individual parents waiting alone, couples, and larger family groups. The population served by this hospital is primarily a mixture of American and Hispanic cultures.

The waiting area is adjacent to an interior atrium with a healing garden, and the administrators want the waiting area to have direct access to the atrium. They do not want a television in this area but want you to provide other more effective positive distractions.

General Information:
- Ceiling height is 12 feet.
- An information desk (where the medical staff report the status of surgery patients for the families) must be centrally located. This desk is to be free standing (not a built-in) and must provide an acoustically private setting for families to talk on the phone with the medical staff.

Design Criteria:
Using the information from this chapter and chapters 1, 2, and 3, prepare for your clients an analysis of privacy needs, a concept statement, space plan, and a perspective sketch for the waiting area.

Analysis:
Prepare an analysis of privacy needs for the waiting room including

- The types of privacy to be accommodated and why
- The expected benefits of each type of privacy (Chapters 1 and 2)
- How choice and control can be provided to alleviate stress
- Personal space and territoriality considerations that provide opportunities for social support
- The appropriate physical characteristics to use to promote desired levels of privacy (Chapter 3)
- Possible applicable cultural norms and practices
- Appropriate types of positive distractions
- Considerations for an appropriate color palette to enhance privacy

Solution:

1. Prepare a statement that describes your analysis of the privacy needs for the waiting room and how you have designed the space to support those needs.

2. Prepare a detailed and annotated space plan that utilizes the physical characteristics of environments that support privacy.

3. Prepare a sketch of the space highlighting the information desk and adjacent seating.

4. Provide a color palette for the waiting area.

REFERENCES

Alexander, C. A.; Ishikawa, S.; Silverstein, M.; Jacobson, M.; Fiksdahl-King, I.; & Angel, S. (1977). *A pattern language*. New York: Oxford University Press.

Altman, I. (1975). *The environment and social behavior: Privacy, personal space, territory, crowding*. Monterey, CA: Brooks Cole Publishers.

Bame, S. I. & Wells, W. (1995). "Acoustical design features associated with noise level in health facilities: The case of dialysis facilities." *Journal of Interior Design*. 21. 2: 1–14.

Barlas, D.; Sama, A. E.; Ward, M. F.; & Lesser, M. L. (2001). "Comparisons of the auditory and visual privacy of emergency department treatment areas with curtains versus those with solid walls." *Annals of Emergency Medicine*. 2001, August, 135–139.

Becker, M. (2002). *The healing power of pets: Harnessing the ability to make and keep people happy and healthy*. New York: Hyperion.

Birren, F. (1969). *Light, color and environment*. New York: Van Nostrand Reinhold.

Byers, J. E. & Smyth, K. A. (1997). "Effect of music intervention on noise annoyance, heart rate and blood pressure in cardiac surgery patients." *American Journal of Critical Care*. 6. 3: 183–191.

Crawford, J. J.; Pomerinke, J. A.; & Smith, D. W. (2003). *Therapy pets: The animal-human healing partnership*. Amherst, NY: Prometheus Books.

De Angelis, T. (2002). "A bright future for PNI." *Monitor on Psychology*, 33: 6.

Evans, G. (2001). "Environmental stress and health." In A. Baum, T. A. Revenson & J. E. Singer (Eds.), *Handbook of Health Psychology* (365–385). Mahwah, NJ: Lawrence Erlbaum Associates.

Evans, G. W.; Maxwell, L. E.; & Hart, B. (1999). "Parental language and verbal responsiveness to children in crowded homes." *Developmental Psychology*, 35, 1020–1023.

Evans, G. W. & McCoy, J. M. (1998). "When buildings don't work: The role of architecture in human health." *Journal of Environmental Psychology*, 18, 85–94.

Evans, G. W. and Cohen, S. (1987). "Environmental stress." In D. Stokols and I. Altman (Eds.), *Handbook of Environmental Psychology* (571–610). New York: John Wiley & Sons.

Fehrman, K. R. & Fehrman, C. (2004). *Color: The secret influence*. New York: Prentice Hall.

Gillies, M. (1992). "Teenage traumas." *Nursing Times*, 88, 27, 26–29.

Grappell, M. (1995). "Psychoneuroimmunology." In S. O. Marberry (Ed.), *Innovations in Healthcare Design* (115–120). New York: Van Nostrand Reinhold.

Harris, D. (2000). *Environmental quality and healing environments: A study of flooring materials in a healthcare telemetry unit*. Unpublished doctoral dissertation, Texas A&M University, Department of Architecture, College Station, TX.

Heerwagen, J. & Orians, G. H. (1993). "Humans, habitats, and aesthetics." In S. Kellert and E. O. Wilson (Eds.), *The Biophilia Hypothesis* (138–172). Washington: Island Press.

Hilton, B. A. (1985). "Noise in acute patient care areas." *Research in Nursing and Health*. 8: 283–291.

Horsburgh, C. R. Jr. (1995). "Healing by design." *New England Journal of Medicine*. 333 (11): 754–740.

Hutton, A. (1999). *Drawing out the adolescent perspective on the design of an adolescent ward*. Unpublished master's thesis, Flinders University of South Australia, Adelaide, Australia.

Hutton, A. (2002). "The private adolescent: Privacy needs of adolescents in hospitals." *Journal of Pediatric Nursing*, 17, 1, 67–72.

James, A.; Jenks, C.; & Prout, A. (1998). *Theorizing childhood*. Cambridge, England: Blackwell.

Kam, P. C.; Kam, A. C.; & Thompson, J. F. (1994). "Noise pollution in the anesthetic and intensive care environment." *Anesthetic*. 49: 982–86.

Kaplan, S. and Kaplan, R. (1989). *The experience of nature*. New York: Cambridge University Press.

Kellman, N. (1995). "History of healthcare environments." In S. O. Marberry (Ed.), *Innovations in Healthcare Design*. (38–48). New York: Van Nostrand Reinhold.

Linton, P. E. (1995). "Creating a total healing environment." In S. O. Marberry (Ed.),

Innovations in Healthcare Design (121–131). New York: Van Nostrand Reinhold.

MacKenzie, H. (1988). Teenagers in hospital. *Nursing times*, 84, 32, 58–61.

Mader, B. (2002). "Private hospital rooms: the new norm." *The Business Journal of Milwaukee*. 2002. URL *http://milwaukeebizjournals. com/milwaukeestries/2002/11/11/focus2.html*.

Marcus, C. C. & Barnes, M. (1999). *Healing gardens: Therapeutic benefits and design recommendations*. New York: John Wiley & Sons, Inc.

Mass, J.; Jayson, J. K.; & Kleiber, D. A. (1974). "Effects of spectral differences in illumination on fatigue." *Journal of Applied Psychology*. 59: 524–526.

Mazer, S. & Smith, D. (1995). "Beyond silence: Music as environmental design." *Journal of Healthcare Design*. V: 151–161.

McBride, D. L. (1999). "Nursing home gardens." In C. C. Marcus and M. Barnes (Eds.), *Healing Gardens: Therapeutic Benefits and Design Recommendations* (385–436). New York: John Wiley & Sons, Inc.

Monroe, H. (2003). "Interior monologues." *Healthcare Design*, 3 (2): 31–32. PIMHS Newsletter (2004). Portsmouth Institute of Medicine, Health and Social Care, Issue 5. Portsmouth, UK.

Moore, R. C. (1999). "Healing gardens for children." In C. C. Marcus and M. Barnes (Eds.). *Healing Gardens: Therapeutic Benefits and Design Recommendations* (323–384). New York: John Wiley & Sons, Inc.

Naisbitt, J. (1982). *Megatrends: ten new directions transforming our lives*. New York: Warner Books.

Newman, B. M. & Newman, P. R. (1991). *Development through life: A psycho-social approach*. Chicago: Dorsey Press.

Noell, E. (1995–1996). "Design in nursing homes: Environment as a silent partner in caregiving." *Generations*, 14–19.

Pinet, Celine. (1999). "Distance and the use of social space by nursing home residents." *Journal of Interior Design*, 25, 1, 1–15.

PIMHS. (2004). "PIMHS Researchers attract further research funding." Portsmouth Institute of Medicine, Health and Social Care. *PIMSINFORM* 5: 2

Rule, B.; Milke, D.; & Dobbs, A. (1992). "Cognitive functioning and social interaction of the aged resident." *The Journal of Applied Gerontology*, 11, 4, 475–485.

Slee, P. T. (1996). *Child, adolescent and family development*. Adelaide, Australia: Harcourt Brace.

Suite Dreams Project. URL: *http://www.suite dreamsproject.org*.

Stone, V. (1999). "The evolution of the labyrinth into a spiritual healing tool." URL: *http://stonecircledesign.com/anim.html*.

Torrice, A. F. (1995). "Color for healing." In S. O. Marberry (Ed.). *Innovations in Healthcare Design* (140–150). New York: Van Nostrand Reinhold.

Turnock, C. & Kelleher, M. (2001). "Maintaining patient dignity in intensive care settings." *Intensive and Critical Care Nursing*. 17: 144–145.

Ulrich, R. (1984). "View through a window may influence recovery from surgery." *Science*. 224: 420–421.

Ulrich, R. (1992). "How design impacts wellness." *Healthcare Forum Journal*. September/October. 20: 20–25.

Ulrich, R. (1995). "Effects of healthcare design on wellness: Theory, and recent scientific research." In S. O. Marberry (Ed.). Innovations in Healthcare Design. New York: Van Nostrand Reinhold, (88–104).

Ulrich, R. (1999). "Effects of gardens on health outcomes: Theory and research." In C. C. Marcus and M. Barnes (Eds.). *Healing Gardens: Therapeutic Benefits and Design Recommendations* (27–86). New York: John Wiley & Sons, Inc.

Ulrich, R. (2000). "Effects of healthcare environmental design on medical outcomes." In Dilani (Ed.). *Design and Health: Proceedings of the Second International Conference on Health and Design*. Stockholm, Sweden: Svensk Byggtjanst.

Wilmott, M. (1986). "The effects of a vinyl floor surface and carpeted floor surface upon walking in elderly hospital patients." *Age and Aging*, 15: 119–120.

Wilson, C. C. (1998). *Companion animals in human health*. Thousand Oaks, CA: Sage Publications, Inc.

Yinnon, A. M.; Ilan, Y.; Tadmor, B.; Altarescu, G.; & Hersko, C. (1992). "Quality of sleep in the medical department." *BJCP*. 46. 2: 88–91.

CHAPTER 7

Privacy and Related Needs in Hospitality Design

Hospitality design involves both lodging facilities and food and beverage service. Perhaps no other design specialty offers so many options for the interior designer as does hospitality design. The multicultural influences and technology that characterize today's hotels and restaurants also present unique challenges for the interior designer.

Among these challenges is the need to design for privacy to accommodate diverse populations, functions, customs, and expectations. In this chapter we will examine applicable privacy theories as well as design considerations and solutions for privacy within the world of hospitality design. Although we will focus upon the specific considerations and solutions for hotels and restaurants, these principles also apply to the larger group of hospitality facilities, including bed-and-breakfasts, resorts, country clubs, athletic clubs, cruise ships, and casinos.

THE EVOLUTION OF THE CONCEPT OF HOSPITALITY

The concept of hospitality is ancient, rooted in early Greek and Roman ideals concerning the proper ways to receive and treat both strangers and invited guests in one's home. A place that is

"hospitable" is defined as one that is warm and convivial, providing shelter and rest. It is easy to imagine that these hospitable qualities would have been very important to early travelers. Today, more than ever, the human population is on the move for both business and pleasure. However, from ancient times to the present, the traveler is both vulnerable and dependent upon the generosity of strangers. This condition of travel must be considered carefully together with other functional and aesthetic requirements when planning hospitality facilities. Although originally the only "design" considerations for hospitality were for the basic physical needs for food, shelter, and safety for travelers, contemporary hospitality design has evolved over the last century to become an integral part of an enormous hospitality industry. The changes from designing for the largest common denominator to creating highly individualized designs to meet the diverse needs and expectations of the traveling public are profound. Today, the hospitality industry includes everything from small bed-and-breakfast establishments to large conference hotels, from roadside motels to cruise ships, and from fast food chains to luxury gourmet restaurants.

Modern travelers and diners have many choices today. Lodging facilities, once simple inns and taverns with a few rooms in the back or on the second floor, have evolved into icons, such as The Ritz, The Plaza, The Waldorf, and The Savoy. Some have become destinations themselves, such as grand resorts and Las Vegas casino hotels. Food and beverage facilities have grown from a mug of ale and a loaf of bread at a village tavern to elaborately themed environments of entertainment and exotic, gourmet fare.

DESIGNING FOR PRIVACY NEEDS IN HOTELS

Regardless of size or type, all hotels have two basic design similarities: 1) guest rooms tend to have standard sizes and similar furniture arrangements, and 2) all require a public space where guests can check in and out (Piotrowski & Rogers 1999). There are thousands of variations on these two areas of design, but all have in common the need to regulate interaction with others. The complexity of these needs and types of interactions also vary with the type of hotel, level of services and accommodations, and the theme. In this section, we will examine how these variables affect designing for privacy.

Changing Emphasis in Hotel Design

An exhibit in 2002 at the Cooper-Hewitt National Design Museum in New York City entitled "New Hotels for Global Nomads" examined the role of the hotel in the new world of travel and tourism, declaring that hotels are the "crossroads of our nomadic society" (Albrecht & Johnson 2002, p. 9). Within these structures we not only eat and sleep but also work, play, relax, enjoy entertainment, and escape the realities of life. As "global nomads" we interact with other travelers from all over the world, mixing diverse social customs with local experience and flavor. (See **Figure 7.1**).

In the companion book to the exhibit, authors Donald Albrecht and Elizabeth Johnson (2002) identify five themes that define the evolution of hotels from the mid-1800s to the present day, and they look at the future of hotel designs and functions. The five themes—urbanism, mobility, business, nature, and fantasy—provide insights about the changing emphasis of hotel design. Additionally, each of the five themes provides a framework for us to examine the privacy needs and expectations of today's travelers as well as those in the future.

Urban Hotels

Urban hotels serve the needs of visitors to the city. They also serve the city's need to provide gathering places for public ceremony and social interaction. Urban hotels often become icons of a city, defining the city's architectural vision and state-of-the-art building technology. American urban hotels were the first to open their common areas to the public, bringing the life and energy of the city inside their walls and creating what author William James called "the democratization of elegance" (Albrecht and Johnson 2002, p. 14). Today's urban hotels still function as private expressions of public gathering places. However, designs now tend to emphasize a blending of the more intimate and private boutique hotel (home-like comforts) with the traditional "see and be seen" opportunities of the grand hotel (meeting rooms, restaurants, and ballrooms).

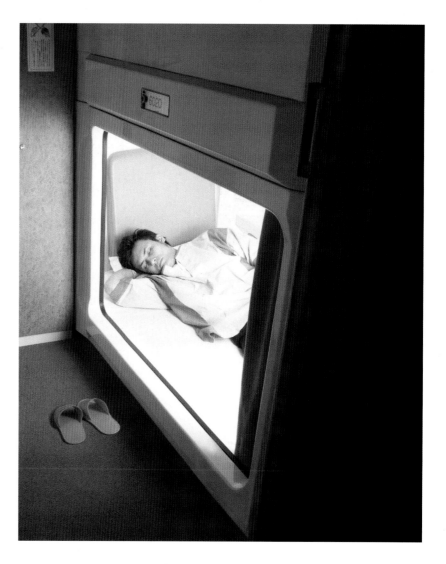

Figure 7.1 Tokyo's Capsule Hotel is an example of convenience at the expense of privacy. Coneyl Jay/Getty Images.

Hotels for Mobility

Hotels that cater to our mobile society first appeared along railroad routes in the mid-1800s to accommodate travelers taking advantage of the new freedom to travel and explore via rail. From the 1950s to the present day, hotels catering to our desires for mobility have become ubiquitous landmarks along U.S. highways. Today, new concept hotels are being designed to respond to the future of travel by car, bus, plane, ship, and even spacecraft. For example, the NASA Habitation Module is a model for a potential future hotel for space travelers reflecting decades of research into how to live and be productive in space. (See **Figure 7.2**). Considerations for territoriality

and privacy were central to these studies (NASA 1985), indicating the importance of these human needs to survival.

Business Hotels

Business has been a dominant reason for people to travel since ancient times. By the end of the 1900s some lodging facilities such as Statler Hotels began to cater specifically to the needs of the business traveler by offering special rooms for meetings, conventions, and places to display product samples. In 1954 Hilton purchased Statler Hotels, ushering in an era in

Figure 7.2 NASA Habitation Module still has a long way to go to provide the comforts of home. Courtesy of NASA Johnson Space Center.

which hotels played a key role in bringing together businesspeople, products, services, and customers. As the types and levels of interaction between hotel customers increased, the need to regulate that interaction for positive communication and for privacy increased also. Today's business hotels strive not only to connect business to people but also to provide guests with state-of-the-art communication technology and an environment that meets the business traveler's needs for rest and comfort.

Nature Hotels

The year 2002 was designated by the United Nations as the "International Year of Eco-Tourism," recognizing "that nature-based travel is the fastest growing segment of the tourism industry. Increasing by 20 to 30% per year, ecotourism is an antidote to the unintended consequences of travel itself: mass tourism to the world's most beautiful sites can destroy what it seeks to celebrate" (Albrecht & Johnson 2002, p. 27). Natural hotels respond to the need to escape the stresses of modern daily life. Originally these nature hotels were resorts located in beautiful wilderness areas designed to enhance the experience of nature using concepts of prospect and refuge and the symbolic associations of natural elements. Privacy was an important part of the natural hotel experience, but so too was the social component. People "getting away from it all," both to commune with nature and to enjoy the company of like-minded travelers, demanded designs that facilitated both activities.

The evolution of the natural hotel is in part the result of aging baby boomers who are less interested in the fun and sun travel experiences of their youth and, together with a growing segment of the overall population, are becoming increasingly environmentally aware. Other influences in the popularity of ecotourism include increasing awareness and concern for physical fitness and health (Ayala 1996). These factors have inspired the eco-resort, a place where travelers can personally experience and affiliate with nature without intruding upon it. Many of these eco-resorts offer the opportunity to experience wilderness solitude in the surrounding landscape. Ecotourism offers the opportunity for restoration and positive distractions by learning about one's surroundings within an environment that is ecologically, economically, and culturally sustainable.

Fantasy Hotels

Fantasy hotels respond to the universal human desire to escape reality. Traditionally, romance and sex have dominated the world of fantasy hotels. Technological innovation has also played a part in creating a fantasy world for retreat and escape. More recently, resorts designed around cartoon characters and casinos designed to reproduce ancient and exotic cities have become popular fantasy inspirations. The idea is to totally immerse the guests in the fantasy—whether it is a Disney scene or an Egyptian pyramid—so that they lose themselves in the experience and spend more money while escaping the reality of daily life. The role of privacy in these types of hotels is to enhance the escape experience while offering various opportunities for interaction.

High Tech/High Touch in Hotel Design

The high tech/high touch backlash discussed previously is a driving force behind the changing emphasis of today's hotel designs. The technology that drives our businesses and increasingly invades our personal lives is with us wherever we go. While this ever present technology makes many of the tasks that we must perform easier, allows us to communicate more effectively, and allows us to be instantly informed, it also adds

LINK
For an explanation of high tech/high touch, see Chapter 6, page 132.

to the stress and mental fatigue in our lives. As the relatively recent concept of working "24/7" implies, we rarely are far removed from the pressures of "taking care of business." The overwhelming response to the fast paced, technology driven world has been increasingly to seek a high touch balance. This balance inspires home-like qualities in guest rooms and hotel public areas and inspires new forms of the nature hotel.

The need to stay connected to technology may dominate our daily lives, but the need to feel comfortable, secure, and relaxed is not left at home when we travel. Today's hotels must accommodate both needs. When asked to rate the importance of a hotel's benefits, guests consistently emphasize comfort (Dube & Renaghan 1999). Research indicates that hotels that emphasize comfort and home-like elements increase business and greatly improve guest satisfaction (Siguaw & Enz 1999). This desire to make guests feel "at home" has become an important goal for hospitality designers. If hotels are to serve as our homes away from home, they must provide flexible, adaptable spaces that we can use for a variety of purposes. As discussed previously in Chapter 4, the comforts of home require the ability to achieve our desired levels of privacy for restoration, contemplation, self-evaluation, and to control interactions. Many of us have come to expect the same from our hotels as well.

Guest Needs and Expectations

Travel and tourism is the largest industry in the world, and we are an increasingly sophisticated traveling public. Once the destination and purpose of the visit is determined, travelers choose hotels based upon a variety of criteria, including perceptions of function, performance, convenience, services, and amenities. In the years since September 11, 2001, travelers also rate safety and security as higher priorities (O'Neill & Lloyd-Jones 2002). Today's travelers may fall into one or more of several categories defined by the purpose of the travel. They include business travelers, affluent travelers, traveling families, leisure travelers, and special needs travelers.

Business Travelers

Business travelers still constitute the majority of guests in the hospitality industry. A fully wired guest room, ample work space, a business center, good lighting, and great beds are among the top expectations of these guests. The overall quality of the physical environment rates high as an expectation of executive business travelers. A study of business executives using luxury hotel accommodations found that they rated pleasant, functional spaces significantly higher than elevated levels of personalized service (Mattila 1999). Business travelers also tend to develop loyalties toward one hotel over another based upon their past experiences.

Almost half of all business travelers in the U.S. are women, and their numbers are growing. The hospitality industry has only recently recognized the market potential in catering to female travelers who often have different needs and expectations of hotels than do male travelers. For example, women cite safety as their primary concern when traveling, while men rank safety as a lesser concern (Conner 1997). Women are more likely than men to incorporate leisure time into a business trip and to add a day or two to their trip to enhance the "get away" experience. Additionally, women take more international business trips per year than men and tend to stay nearly twice as long (McCleary & Weaver 1994). Responsive service is the number one expectation of women, who are twice as likely as men to order room service or to eat at the hotel restaurant (Witham 2000). The needs of female business travelers include various types of privacy accommodated by their rooms or suites, where visual separation or screening of the sleeping area from the work or conversation area is desirable.

Affluent Travelers

Unlike many travelers, affluent travelers appear to have been less affected by the desire to stay home after September 11. According to a Ritz-Carlton spokeswoman, "travel is not considered a luxury (for the wealthy) . . . it's a necessity. It's vital to their state of mind" (Engle 2003). Accommodations with views, room safes, pools, business centers, unobtrusive service, room refrigerators stocked with real food, and fine restaurants are some of the amenities expected by affluent travelers. However, this group of travelers values security and privacy even more than five-star luxury (Mann 1993).

Traveling Families

Family vacations have taken on a new dimension thanks to the creation of family suites, which provide unique spatial configurations, privacy, and entertainment for traveling families. In these suites, private parent bedrooms, semi-private children's rooms, and common areas equipped with kitchenettes and entertainment centers have replaced the single shared hotel room as well as the shared beds of the past. Family suites are now common in most hotels catering to families visiting theme resorts such as Disney World. The emphasis upon private but not isolated spaces for family members dominates the marketing campaigns for these hotels, reflecting an understanding that the ability to meet leisure travelers' privacy needs has become an important marketing tool.

Leisure Travelers

The needs and expectations of the leisure traveler are most often centered on comfort, which is largely dependent upon the design of the hotel (Dube & Renaghan 1999). Physical comfort in the form of residential style furniture, soft lighting, and private views all rate highly as amenities expected by leisure travelers. Interaction with different cultures is often an important part of the leisure travel experience.

A hotel catering to leisure travelers must serve as both a familiar haven and a symbol of the local culture, providing novel experiences for the guests.

LINK
How does the balance between novel and familiar elements affect our evaluations of environments? See Chapter 3, page 37.

Special Needs Travelers

Physical accessibility is not only required by ADA, but also expected by an increasingly mobile special needs public. Persons with disabilities and an aging population require that universal design principles apply to most public spaces and to a percentage of guest rooms. Space adjacencies as well as guest room and public space layouts that provide visual and acoustical privacy are important to provide special needs guests with the ability to control their environments and regulate interaction.

Privacy Theories Applicable to Hotel Design

We need privacy for a variety of reasons when we travel. The stress associated with the environmental load of new environments and the often uncontrollable interaction with strangers can take its toll quickly on our physical and psychological well-being. Crowded airports and airplanes, buses and trains, city streets, conference rooms, and tourist attractions can cause us to withdraw at a time when we would prefer to engage and interact positively with others. The inability to control our environments to regulate communication and to gain knowledge about our surroundings can add to the stress of travel. The unpredictability of strangers and a lack of understanding of social customs and norms can force us to maintain long periods of directed attention. The hotel can be a respite from these stressors. Interior designers must however, understand how people's needs for privacy are expressed in these situations so their designs accommodate guests.

Types of Privacy in Hotels

All four types of privacy may be required and accommodated in a hotel.

- Solitude *and* intimacy *may be found in the guest room, while intimacy is also accommodated in the lobby, restaurant, lounge, or other areas specially designed for personal interactions.*
- Anonymity—*being lost in a crowd—is often found in the busy common areas of the hotel.*
- Reserve *can be accommodated by a discrete staff, in-room services, private circulation paths, and the ability to maintain desired social, personal space zones.*

Environmental Load Associated with Novel Environments

Novelty can far outweigh familiarity when we travel. We look to the environment for cues to help us understand and make sense of our surroundings, but often the environmental load of a new place is too novel or is coming at us too fast to be able to organize it and respond appropriately. Travel, whether for business or pleasure, requires periods of directed attention to deal with this high environmental load. As we have learned, in order to maintain directed attention we often must screen out unnecessary or distracting stimuli. If we are screeners, we may automatically filter some of this stimuli on an unconscious level. However, if we are nonscreeners, we may look for characteristics of the physical environment that help us screen. If the physical environment does not provide the opportunity to screen effectively or to adjust it to our needs, our capacity for directed attention can be exceeded and we may experience mental fatigue. However, we still need to be able to call upon directed attention when circumstances require

LINK

For information about stimulus screening, see Chapter 3, page 41.

us to focus upon a task, especially when we travel. Although we often choose to travel for the purpose of experiencing novelty, we find that this experience is best served when we have the time and space to restore our capacity for directed attention and reflect upon what we have experienced. Places within the hotel that provide various types of privacy can help to restore that capacity.

As we have learned, privacy within a restorative environment can help us to recover from mental fatigue and regenerate our capacity for directed attention. Familiar elements allow us to take a break from directed attention. The universal appeal and restorative properties of nature can also provide involuntary attention, thus relieving mental fatigue.

Territoriality

Hotels are secondary territories. As guests, we do not own our rooms; we only occupy them temporarily. However, this temporary occupation creates a perceived primary territory. While we occupy the room, we have relatively exclusive control over access and use of that space. This is one of the reasons we want it to feel more home-like. As a primary territory, it serves as our sanctuary, a place of rest and safety. In our hotel room, to the extent that the design allows for it, we are in control of our environment.

Territoriality is also expressed in the common areas of the hotel. For example, we frequently place territorial markers such as baggage and reading materials to indicate our temporary occupation of a portion of a hotel's public space. However, because the common areas of hotels are often viewed as public—not secondary—territories, the social norms and customs used to communicate our marking of a portion of that territory may not be recognized or respected. These areas of a hotel require special design considerations to provide for the many levels of interaction, activity, and communication necessary to function effectively.

Personal Space

Our personal space bubbles often get larger when we travel. The close presence of strangers in a high load environment and the uncertainty that accompanies these close distances usually cause us to need more space than we might require normally. When strangers are in our intimate space zone (such as when we stand in a crowded hotel lobby or use public transportation in an unfamiliar city), more directed attention is required of us. If we are able to expand our personal space zone, we can focus less on the uncertainty that the presence of strangers causes, and we may feel less crowded.

We have different personal space needs for the public areas of a hotel than we do for the guest rooms. Interactions in the common areas of a hotel require appropriate distances for us to interact comfortably, safely, and effectively with strangers. If we are traveling alone, the public areas must provide places that allow us to maintain our desired personal space zones without isolation. If we are traveling with friends or loved ones, we should be able to communicate and interact in a hotel's public area without interference from others.

Our personal space needs in guest rooms vary based upon how many people are sharing the room. Guest rooms for multiple people should have adequate zoning of areas to define territory and provide appropriate personal space distances.

DESIGNING FOR PRIVACY CONSIDERATIONS AND CRITERIA FOR HOTELS

The type of services, amenities, and number and types of spaces offered by hotels vary considerably depending upon the type of hotel, its location, and, of course, its price. Our discussion of privacy needs will focus upon the two major types of spaces found in hotels: lobby/reception areas and guest rooms.

Lobbies: The Heart of the Hotel

The sizes, types, and number of public spaces within a hotel depend upon the type of hotel. Small, no-frills hotels may have only minimum public space while large conference or resort hotels may have as much as 20 percent of their overall space devoted to public areas. Although guest rooms take up most of the space in a hotel, it is the public areas that most often define a hotel and set it apart from its competition.

Lobbies are the central focus of hotels. It is here that the design theme is established, first impressions are made, and expectations are formed. (See **Figure 7.3**). Lobbies are gathering places and business settings. They also serve as circulation paths connecting the guests to the entire hotel. Lobbies can be extensions of the energy and atmosphere of the cities outside their walls or sanctuaries from that energy and atmosphere. Lobbies can be ceremonial, creating a feeling of entering another world, or they may be purely utilitarian. Whether small and intimate or large and public, the lobby is the heart of the hotel.

Although the first and most important consideration to be made in the design of a lobby is effective functioning for guests and staff, the complex relationships of interactions between people and their surroundings in the lobby present additional challenges for the designer. Designing for privacy is among the most fascinating of these challenges.

LINK
For more information about the physical characteristics that promote privacy, see Chapter 3, page 37.

Designing for Privacy in Lobbies

The environmental load is often high in a busy lobby. Social density (the number of people per unit of space) changes as people arrive, gather, and leave. Peak check-in and checkout times increase the social density and increase the environmental load. Stress may increase

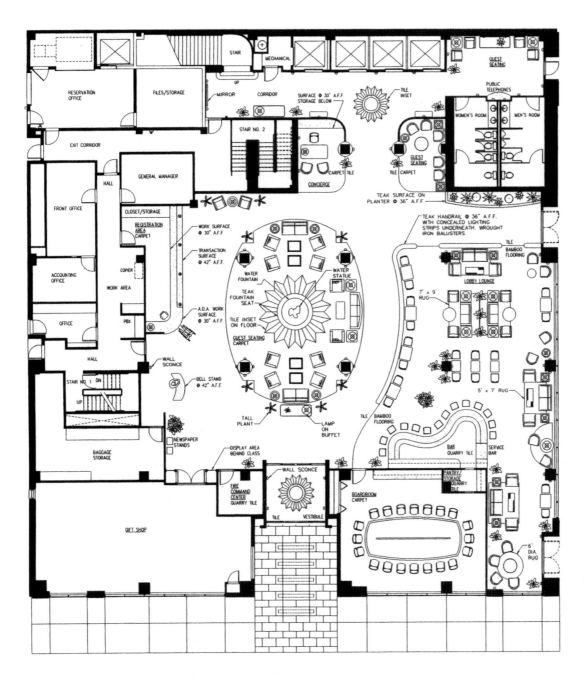

Figure 7.3 Lobbies are the guests' first impression of the hotel and set the tone for their expectations.

during these crucial times as guests orient themselves to the space, rush to catch transportation, and focus upon details requiring directed attention.

However, if well designed, high environmental loads in a hotel's public areas are not necessarily negative. The energy, anticipation, and excitement associated with arrival in a new

place, the movement and activities of various types of people, and the interaction with new people arouses our senses and can be pleasurable if the environment is designed to accommodate these experiences.

Characteristics of the physical environment that promote privacy in hotel lobbies include the following:

- *Sequencing spaces to create a spatial hierarchy for guests to progress from less private to more private spaces*
- *Using thresholds to define different territories within this spatial hierarchy*
- *Creating areas of prospect and refuge and stimulus shelters to provide opportunities to separate guests from the center of activity without isolation*
- *Creating a balance of novelty and familiarity to enhance the experience of a new environment while maintaining feelings of comfort and security*
- *Using color and light to define spaces and draw attention to them*

Designing for privacy in hotel lobbies requires zoning of activities to allow for proper circulation, effective communication, definition of territory, establishment of personal space, and control of interpersonal interactions. These zones include the Entrance/Orientation Zone, Reception/Front Desk Zone, Circulation Zones, Waiting Zones, Vertical and Horizontal Movement Zones, Conversation Zones, and Support Zones.

Entrance/Orientation Zone

This zone serves two important functions. First, it introduces a guest to the hotel, creating an important first impression. The entrance zone can establish, contradict, or reinforce a guest's expectations. Here, we pause to evaluate the immediate environment and determine (unconsciously) whether we will exhibit approach or avoidance behavior. The entrance zone must have certain qualities of familiarity to encourage us to approach. Universally recognized welcoming symbols such as warm light, pleasant music, and easy-to-understand signage increase the familiarity and therefore the approach qualities of the entrance zone.

The second function of this zone is orientation. We evaluate the elements of the environ-ment to determine where we are relative to where we have been and where we are going. The Kaplans' (1989) four predictors of environmental preference (complexity, coherence, legibility, and mystery) discussed in Chapter 2, provide insights for orientation and enhance the positive experience of this zone. For example, the space must have adequate environmental information (complexity) to enable guests to learn what is going on around them quickly. That information must be easy to organize (coherence) and contain familiar elements to help us understand and remember the informa-tion (legibility). Finally, the experience of the space is enhanced when the environment pro-vides hints that if we explore, we will discover new information (mystery).

We must be able to proceed directly through the hierarchy of spaces from the Entrance/ Orientation zone to the Reception/Front Desk Zone. Although the path should be direct, it can be configured to further enhance our experience of the lobby by using Alexander's (1977) pattern called Circulation Realms discussed in Chapter 3. As guests approach the reception desk, they may pass through thresholds (archways, columns, level changes, lighting changes) indicating progression away from public accessibility and into more private spaces. As each new "realm" is revealed, guests continue to form impressions and to further orient themselves.

Reception/Front Desk Zone

This zone is highly functional and the most critical point of interaction in the hotel. Social density and environmental loads change con-stantly and often dramatically within this zone as people check in and check out, often creating conditions of crowding. This zone should be designed so that guests can maintain desired personal space distances to alleviate crowding. It must also be designed so it will not appear to be a vague, uninviting, empty space during off-peak times.

Guests in this zone require *reserve*, the type of privacy that we require when we want to protect information about ourselves. To accommodate reserve, personal space distances must allow for effective communication without being overheard by others. Territory must be defined so that guests know where public spaces end and staff spaces begin within this zone. Acoustical and lighting applications are important design elements that can help provide for reserve in this zone. Sound absorbing materials should be used on vertical surfaces surrounding the reception desk so that staff and the individual guest can communicate effectively without raising their voices. Light levels should be high enough to be able to read and write effectively but not so high as to highlight the registering guest to the rest of the lobby.

While waiting to check in, guests can gain further information about the hotel through visual cues and signage. Qualities of mystery (partially concealed spaces, movement, sounds, changes in light), can promote the desire to explore other areas of the hotel and take the guests' minds off of waiting. Mystery can also serve as a positive distraction by redirecting guests' attention if they are feeling stressed or crowded while in the reception/front desk zone.

Alexander's (1977) pattern called Reception Welcomes You, uses an effective example to describe the importance of establishing an immediate relationship between the guest and the reception area: "A beautiful example we know of is the reception desk at Brown's Hotel in London. You pass into the hotel through a small, unassuming entrance, not unlike the entrance to a house. You pass through two or three rooms; then come to the central room in which there are two old writing desks. The receptionist comes forward from an inner office, invites you to sit down in a comfortable chair at one of these writing desks and sits down with you while you fill out the hotel register. The reasons most reception areas fail completely to have this quality, is

that the receptionist's desk is a barrier, so that the desk and equipment together help to create an institutional atmosphere, quite at odds with the feeling of welcome" (pp. 705–706).

The kind of design and personal attention described by this pattern may not be possible for large hotels that must deal with hundreds of guests each day. It may, however, influence the positions and design of registration desks so that even in large conference hotels, guests experience a sense of familiarity, intimacy, and connection with the hotel staff.

The concierge and bell captain are usually located within the Reception/Front Desk Zone. Their functions—to make the guests feel welcome, comfortable, and secure—are essential components of the experience of the many hotels. Placing their stations within this zone of activity makes them not only more convenient to locate, but also more subject to the changing social density of the zone. It is important to define the territory of the concierge with proper territorial markers such as distinctive desk and chairs, and changes in lighting, flooring, or other materials. The designer must also provide good acoustics so that verbal communications are easily facilitated and provide adequate circulation and waiting space so that personal space zones are not violated. The bell captain's territory should be defined by signage and located so that these staff members have exclusive control over access to guests' luggage.

Circulation Zones

Circulation zones are central to establishing areas of privacy, interaction, and activity within the lobby. These zones move people through the lobby to areas of interest and to other zones within the lobby. Beginning at the entrance, circulation zones connect guests to the places they need to go as well as reveal spaces where guests might want to go. The spatial hierarchy of the lobby is established by the configuration and nuances of circulation zones. For example, the path from the front desk (public area) to a quiet conversation setting (semi-private area) may take guests through or around a series of less private areas, enabling them to experience the different levels of privacy available to them within the hotel lobby. The path may lead past areas of novelty such as focal points, views, retail and restaurant areas, and art displays, encouraging guests to pause and to more fully experience the spaces.

Waiting Zones

These zones are temporary secondary territories where guests wait to meet others, for their rooms to be ready, or for transportation. Because they are areas of rapidly changing social density, they should be located away from more private areas of the lobby. The concept of prospect and refuge can be applied effectively to these zones so that guests who are waiting are not located in the middle of circulation zones creating a sense of exposure, but rather can see their surroundings clearly.

Vertical and Horizontal Movement Zones

These zones connect the lobby to the other areas of the hotel. They are circulation paths that move guests from floor to floor and within the spaces of each floor. These zones are comprised of elevators, escalators, corridors, and thresholds. Their utilitarian functions, code requirements, and the role they play in wayfinding dictate a great deal of their design criteria, including appropriate sizes and acceptable materials. These spaces, however, also serve an important function in creating privacy within hotels. As we move through these zones deeper into the hotel, the environmental load should lessen, familiarity should increase, and the spaces should become increasingly private. This can be accomplished by using materials with higher acoustical properties, lowering ceiling heights, adding implied and real thresholds, using darker valued richer colors, and lowering illumination levels.

Access to the zones leading to guest rooms should be visible from the Reception/Front Design Zone. Access to other major areas of the hotel can be revealed as guests move through the Circulation Zones within the lobby.

Conversation Zones

These zones are important regulators of privacy within hotel lobbies. Three types of privacy can be achieved in hotel lobbies: *intimacy*, *reserve*, and *anonymity*. *Intimacy* in this scenario involves interaction with friends, family, or acquaintances within the lobby. It involves personal, business, or casual conversations. *Reserve* involves the ability to converse while withholding certain information about ourselves. We use reserve when casually conversing with strangers with whom we do not expect to develop a relationship. *Solitude* is not physically possible in an area surrounded by people; we can, however, achieve *anonymity* if we are able to blend into the environment and are not forced to sit in major circulation paths.

Conversation areas should vary in size, configuration, type of furniture and materials, acoustics, color, and lighting according to the type of privacy for which they are intended. Intimate conversations between romantic partners or family members require acoustic treatments near the source of the sound (voices). This is often accomplished with high-back upholstered seating, lowered ceiling treatments, close sociopetal furniture arrangements, and lower levels of lighting that tend to lower voice levels. Cooler colors recede, especially under low light levels, making these areas less visually accessible from outside the area. Intimate conversation areas benefit also from the use of prospect and refuge.

Intimate conversations between friends and acquaintances are facilitated using the same basic criteria as between romantic partners or family. However, the degree of desired intimacy is usually less in these situations. Sometimes, when friends or acquaintances gather in the lobby to converse, they want to both see and be seen. They want to communicate effectively with one another but remain a part of the general activity of the lobby. To accommodate the desire to see and be seen while conversing intimately, the designer should place sociopetal seating arrangements near focal points and areas of interest and high activity. Circulation should be around but not through these seating arrangements. In this way, others will be drawn to the area but will not directly interact with those occupying the space.

Designing to accommodate reserve in conversation areas involves spacing and configuration of furniture so that *social personal space distances* of four to twelve feet can be maintained. From the close dimensions of this distance, conversation is relatively easy but personal contact is less likely. Lighting levels should be higher than in intimate conversation areas.

Designing for anonymity in conversation zones is actually designing for lack of conversation. A guest may want to get out of his or her room, observe what is going on, but not actively engage in conversation with others. To create anonymity within hotel lobbies, designers must always provide a backup element to prevent guests from feeling exposed. A single high back chair with a nearby table positioned in a corner or near an architectural element such as a column works well for this purpose. Sociofugal seating is appropriate in this circumstance so that guests do not feel compelled to converse. Similar to intimate conversation areas, prospect and refuge can be used to create a safe place from which to observe without being seen. Alcoves are especially effective for this type of prospect and refuge. Slightly lower levels of lighting so that the guest does not feel highlighted in the space help to preserve anonymity as well.

The proper relationship between enclosure and exposure as defined by Alexander's (1977) pattern Half Open Wall and discussed in Chapter 6 should be applied to the design of hotel lobby conversation zones as well. A degree of enclosure helps us establish territory and personal space zones, while a degree of exposure encourages interaction. The use of thresholds, partial walls, openings in walls, railings, columns, level changes, and lowered light levels all contribute to the feelings of enclosure without isolating guests from the rest of the lobby. (See **Figure 7.4**).

Support Zones

These zones include toilets, house phones, coat check, and other miscellaneous support functions. They should be located off the major circulation zones within the lobby. They should have familiar and easily recognizable qualities and be accessible but not directly open to conversation zones.

We now turn to the most private spaces within hotels: guest rooms. There are many types of guest rooms and their sizes and amenities can vary significantly from the minimal space and furnishings of an economy double bedroom to the expansive, well-appointed spaces of executive and resort suites.

Designing for Privacy in Guest Rooms

All guest rooms are, to some degree, perceived as a sanctuary from the outside world. The concept of the guest room as a sanctuary is as old as the first rooms offered to traveling strangers in early Christian monasteries. The universal qualities of sanctuary—a place of safety, a refuge, a shelter, a holy place, a place of asylum, and a place of protection—evoke images of environments where we can rest, rejuvenate, and feel secure. In all cultures, the place of sanctuary is reached through a series of spaces (spatial hierarchy) that grow increasingly private, mysterious, and meaningful. When these qualities are

Figure 7.4 Privacy in lobbies and other public spaces of the hotel can be accommodated by physical characteristics, such as thresholds, partial walls, and level changes. These characteristics provide feelings of enclosure without isolating guests from the rest of the lobby.

translated into today's hotel guest rooms, the experience is intensely personal and guests may return again and again. (See **Figure 7.5**).

The Guest Room as a Temporary Primary Territory

Guests tend to spend more time in their rooms than in any other area of the hotel. Crossing the threshold into a guest room for the first time can be a moment of high anticipation. This room is to be our home for the night or perhaps for much longer, and we have many expectations and requirements of this home away from home. One of the most important expectations and requirements is the ability to control access. Once inside our guest room with the door closed and locked, the space becomes our temporary primary territory. It is then that we explore, looking for those details that we expect to find, discovering details we did not expect, and adjusting the space to meet our needs.

Guest rooms designed as residential-like spaces provide options that allow guests to adjust certain elements to meet their needs while appealing to the travelers' universal needs for comfort, rest, security, and privacy. Examples of these options include window treatments that provide the opportunity to let natural light in the room but screen the guest from observation, multiple artificial light sources that allow the guest to adjust the ambient illumination of the room, and movable lounge chairs that can be rearranged to provide sociopetal seating for

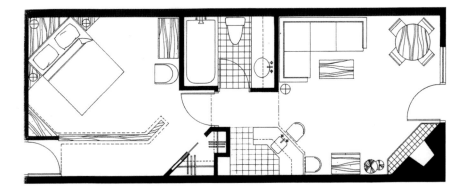

Figure 7.5 This floor plan illustrates several physical characteristics that can contribute to privacy in guest rooms. The use of partial walls and thresholds (lowered ceilings in the bath and eating zones) allow long, narrow guest suites to be divided visually into distinct territories.

conversations, individual reading, working, television viewing, and in-room dining for individuals or multiple guests.

Creating a Sense of Place

Generic hotel rooms, the kind that are the same wherever we go, follow a formula for layout and design with few opportunities to adjust the environment to meet our needs. Although they are more economical to build, generic rooms rarely provide a sense of place. The same room, with a slightly different color scheme, can be found in Los Angeles or in London.

Guest rooms, like all of the environments that we inhabit, should reflect their surroundings and create spaces that are both unique and specific. They should also be an extension of the local culture and geographic location. Yet the guest rooms must also provide the familiar elements expected and needed to create an environment that we can respond to instinctively and use without requiring a great deal of directed attention. The ability to be in our own guest room privately enjoying the inherently unique cultural, climatic, and visual qualities of the local environment is to experience the essence of a place revealed through personal experience. In this way, our guest room becomes not only our private sanctuary, but also a way to redirect our attention and experience restoration.

Physical Characteristics that Promote Privacy in Guest Rooms

Typically, interior designers need to provide for at least two types of privacy in guest rooms: *solitude* and *intimacy*. Solitude requires the need to be free from observation by others. To facilitate the need for solitude, designers must provide physical separation, visual and acoustical privacy, and the ability to control these three environmentally dependent qualities. Intimacy, whether with friends, lovers, family, or to facilitate private conversation with business associates, requires the same qualities as solitude, but it must also provide for the desired interaction among individuals.

Qualities of the built environment that promote privacy in hotel rooms include:

- *Creating spatial depth by increasing real or implied number of spaces that guests must go through to reach the most private areas of the room or suite (although spatial depth is limited in standard guest rooms, the use of thresholds can imply greater spatial depth in these types of rooms)*
- *Using real or implied thresholds to define territories within the room or suite (lowered ceiling heights or dropped soffits, arches, half walls)*
- *Creating areas of prospect and refuge and stimulus shelters to provide the opportunity to*

redirect attention (window seats, alcoves, half walls, and—in rooms that are not designed as accessible—level changes)

- *Using a balance of novelty and familiarity to enhance the experience of a new environment while maintaining feelings of comfort and security*
- *Using color and light to define spaces and draw attention to or away from areas* (See **Figure 7.6**).

Guest Room Layouts that Maximize Desired Levels of Privacy

Guest rooms should also be zoned to provide for efficient use of the space and to allow guests to establish territory and personal space. These zones often overlap or serve multiple functions. Although desirable, not all guest rooms will have all of the zones described below. Each zone has a specific set of functions, and each function has its own privacy requirements. When planning the guest room, it is helpful to think of the zones as activity spaces that can be sequenced from less private to more private. (See **Figure 7.7**).

Sleeping Zone

This zone includes the bed and bedside tables with adjustable light to accommodate reading or watching television. The sleeping zone is usually the focal point of the guest room and is a powerful symbol of sanctuary. Regardless of the other amenities, the bed is the ultimate familiar measure of privacy, comfort, and luxury. To provide for optimal privacy in this zone, the design solution should create a sense of enclosure. This can be achieved by using both novel and familiar elements. For example, the imaginative use of thresholds, alcoves, bed curtains, lowered ceilings, raised floors, half walls, decorative screens, rich dark colors, and intimate adjustable lighting all can add to the privacy of the zone. An emphasis upon cooler colors in this zone contributes to

the perception and achievement of relaxation. Cooler colors also contribute to visual comfort under the recommended warm, low levels of illumination.

LINK
For general guidelines about using light and color to enhance privacy, see Chapter 3, p. 57 and p. 58.

To enhance a feeling of prospect and refuge, a window with a view is essential in this zone. Flexible, controllable window treatments throughout the guest room should provide the opportunity to let in natural light while screening the guests from observation.

Working Zone

This zone includes a desk or multifunctional table with one or more chairs, telephone, outlets for electronic equipment, and adjustable lighting. The working zone should be placed near windows for natural light and to provide positive distractions to relieve mental fatigue via the view. If the view is poor or nonexistent, research has shown that artwork of aesthetically pleasing landscapes in rich colors can be an effective source to provide positive distractions (Ulrich 1993). Acoustical privacy is enhanced by placing sound absorbing materials near the source of sounds (telephones, fax machines, computers, and printers).

Lounging Zone

This zone includes comfortable seating for conversation, reading or watching television, and multidirectional adjustable lighting. The layout of this zone should be somewhat flexible to accommodate the needs of an individual guest or of more than one guest at a time. Ideally, in a shared guest room, the lounge zone should be visually and acoustically separated from the working and sleeping zone. In a suite, this is easily accomplished by the use of full or half walls or by

Figure 7.6 When designed with privacy in mind, the guest room can become a sanctuary. Preston/Schlebusch/Getty Images.

Figure 7.7 Guest room zones often overlap. By separating some zones and combining others and creating flexible, adaptable arrangements, privacy needs can be accommodated even in small guest rooms.

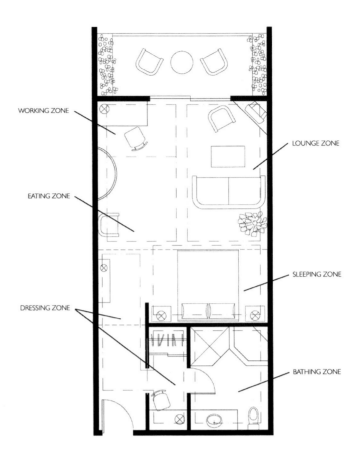

WORKING ZONE

LOUNGE ZONE

EATING ZONE

SLEEPING ZONE

DRESSING ZONE

BATHING ZONE

physical distance. In small rooms, the designer must rely on careful furniture placement, use of acoustical materials, and lighting to create or imply a separation. Slightly warmer colors than those used in the sleeping zone help to create a balance of warm to cool relationships and support the more interactive activities of this zone.

Dressing Zone

Designated dressing zones are a luxury usually reserved for higher priced suites. However, consideration should be given to enhance privacy for dressing in all shared guest rooms. Typically, this zone includes a closet, dresser, mirror, and luggage storage. Dressing is a private activity, even when intimate partners share the guest room. Ideally, this zone should be visually separated from the other zones but always physically adjacent to the bathroom zone. Because dressing is a transitional activity (getting ready for the day, for an evening out, or for bed), the dressing

area should provide adjustable, balanced light. Colors should be more neutral than in other zones to serve as a background for dressing and grooming activities. In addition to the clothing storage spaces, this zone should ideally be at least six feet in diameter and include a well lit full length mirror with space to lay out clothing, accessories, and jewelry.

Bathroom Zone

This zone includes the basic lavatory, toilet, and tub and/or shower with balanced adjustable lighting. The bathroom zone is usually more luxurious in upscale hotels. Elegant fixtures, surface materials, and special amenities add to the residential feel and comfort of the space. The arrangement of the guest room floors in most hotels locates the bathroom immediately inside the entrance to the guest room. This arrangement usually places the dressing area near the entrance door. While this arrangement is far from ideal from the perspective of sequencing spaces from less private to more private, it is a standard of hotel design that maximizes the placement of plumbing walls and minimizes construction costs. The designer's challenge in this type of space is to visually draw the guest past the entrance/bathroom/dressing area into the other zones of the room by creating greater spatial depth. This can be accomplished by using focal points, qualities of mystery, natural and dramatic lighting, and by layering color progressively using lighter valued colors at the room's entrance and gradually darkening the values toward the back of the space.

Natural light is usually preferred for grooming and applying makeup but the typical layout of spaces within the guest room makes it difficult to provide natural light in the bathroom zone. Balanced, adjustable artificial light with warm neutral colors provides the best background for activities in this zone.

Eating Zone

When provided for, the eating zone includes a range from minimal amenities such as a small refrigerator, coffee maker, liquor, and snacks, to a full service kitchen. The eating zone often appears to be an afterthought with refrigerators placed next to televisions and coffee makers taking up most of the vanity space in the bathroom. Ideally, the eating zone should be integrated with or adjacent to the lounge zone using built-ins designed to accommodate the appliances and supplies, and it should not interfere visually or acoustically with the more private zones of the guest room.

Access to Nature

Nature remains the ultimate getaway, and tourists increasingly demand that their getaway experience include the unique physical qualities of their destination's location and culture. Properly designed and integrated gardens, terraces, balconies, courtyards, cloisters, and outdoor rooms all can help to provide this experience and yield many of the restorative benefits found in more remote nature. This "nearby nature" is often marginalized as merely "landscaping" for hotels, reducing it to a recipe of grass, trees, flowers, and paths with little consideration for the deeper experiences and benefits that these environments can provide to travelers. The most important benefit of nearby nature in hotel design is to provide relief from too much directed attention.

Courtyards, especially if they are surrounded by a cloister-like structure that provides prospect and refuge, are very effective in bringing safe, nearby nature to guests. Courtyards are private open spaces that must not be too visually enclosed and must have multiple entrances if they are to be used effectively (Alexander 1977). The use of multiple courtyards—some small and some more expansive—can create *circulation realms* that connect interior spaces and lead the guest deeper into the heart of the hotel.

In Chapter 6 we discussed the significant benefits that healing gardens bring to patients in health care environments. As with healing gardens, the gardens of a hotel do not need to be expansive to be beneficial. They simply must be complex and mysterious enough to fascinate. If the hotel garden has this quality, it can provide a respite from directed attention. Rooftop gardens in city hotels are wonderful ways to provide prospect and refuge and the experience of nature when there is no space to accommodate a ground level garden. Both indoor and outdoor pool areas can be designed to integrate the symbolic restorative qualities of water with local plantings, views, and materials.

Balconies are frequently overlooked in their potential to provide nearby nature to guests in their rooms. Often, they are too narrow to do anything more than step outside of the guest room. They provide no options for use and offer little more than an escape route in the event of a fire. A well designed guest room balcony, however, can help reinforce the experience of a sense of place by providing a connection between guests in their rooms and their surroundings. If they are designed using the concepts of prospect and refuge, guests can experience nature without feeling exposed. (See **Figure 7.8**).

Our discussion of privacy needs in hospitality design now turns to restaurants and bars. These types of spaces are found in many hotels, and privacy considerations for restaurants and bars can be integrated with those for hotel lobbies.

DESIGNING FOR PRIVACY IN RESTAURANTS AND BARS

Public gathering places have always been a part of society in every culture. In medieval times travelers stopped at inns for basic food and drink, and to rest, tell stories, share information, and interact with both friends and strangers. Sharing food and drink in these gathering places

was a natural result of the desire to be hospitable in these settings. Communal eating served to bind people together and to create a sense of belonging in a world where the ability to identify and associate oneself with a group aided survival. The terms *banquet* and *feast* originated from these early gatherings and imply happy occasions of coming together to celebrate and share an abundance of resources. These communal dining experiences became associated with cultural and religious ceremonies and traditions, which continue today.

Today's restaurants, many of them with elaborate thematic "cuisine destinations," reflect the evolution of human civilization itself. Our mobile, technologically dependent society with people exposed to cultures, ideas, and cuisines from around the world has created a sophisticated palette and a demand for unique dining experiences. Restaurants still fill the need for public gathering places for social

Figure 7.8 Nature as a positive distraction can enhance the privacy experience in guest rooms. Bruce Forster/Getty Images.

interaction and the sharing of food. However, many of today's restaurants have become highly specialized to meet the diverse needs and expectations of an increasingly demanding public.

Eating Is Only Part of the Experience

Restaurants and bars are in the business of selling food and drink, but more significantly for interior designers, they also sell experiences. Many of us are motivated to go to restaurants and bars for reasons that far exceed the need for sustenance. Restaurants have become settings for life's events, for celebrations, and for ceremonies. A great deal of modern public and private life is played out on the stages that are restaurants and bars. From business meetings to marriage proposals to birthday parties or regular evenings out, restaurants and bars provide the settings where we share important parts of our lives with others.

Restaurants and bars are now often benchmarks for imaginative, innovative, daring designs that often rely upon a high degree of novelty to pique interest and promote an image. Many serve as stage sets for us to become our alter egos for a brief time. Others transport us to fantasy worlds and exotic lands. Still others create intimate settings rich in warmth and hospitality. Each type of restaurant and bar provides its patrons with opportunities to interact on many levels.

Privacy Theories Applicable to Restaurant Design

Privacy theories for restaurant design are similar to those for hotel design. Restaurants must be designed to balance the need for social interaction with the need to control that interaction. (See **Figures 7.9a** and **7.9b**).

Types of Privacy

Privacy can be a fragile and dynamic quality of restaurant and bar environments. The need to see and be seen is often in conflict with the need to interact intimately. Individuals dining alone may desire *anonymity* so that they can dine without being observed or recognized by others, or they may instead want to connect with others in the restaurant or bar. Sometimes couples may want to experience *intimacy* in an environment where they can focus exclusively upon each other. They may also want anonymity so that they will not be recognized or disturbed. However, other couples may want to participate in the larger public experience of the restaurant or bar. Groups of friends or business associates may want to converse without having to raise their voices or deal with distractions. On occasion, however, they may want to take a break from activities requiring directed attention and simply enjoy their surroundings. For these reasons, the interior designer must often create an overall environment made up of smaller spaces that can be adjusted to accommodate anonymity, intimacy, selected interactions, or maximum interactions.

Environmental Load

Restaurants and bars should be designed to create a particular environmental load that is appropriate to their image and function. High load settings surround patrons with a variety of sensory stimuli to create lively, dynamic environments. The colors, light, sounds, materials, patterns, scale, proportion, balance, and rhythm of interior elements can be manipulated in a variety of ways. They may be exaggerated, distorted, juxtaposed, and layered to produce highly complex, novel environments. Restaurants with high environmental loads encourage interaction on many levels. The novelty produces arousal, and the arousal encourages interaction together with the consumption of food and drink. The design emphasis is upon the high environmental load itself in these types of restaurants and bars, and that experience can sometimes require a great deal of directed attention. In designs of this type, intimate privacy is rarely a motivation for or an expectation of high load eating and drinking establishments.

Figures 7.9a and 7.9b
Privacy is enhanced in this restaurant by the use of real and implied thresholds. Careful space planning can provide visual and acoustical privacy without isolation. © Michael Moran Studio.

Restaurants and bars with lower environmental loads focus more upon communication among the guests as well as the experience of dining. Lower environmental loads require less directed attention than high load settings and therefore may be perceived as more relaxing and formal. A degree of familiarity helps to lower the environmental load and balance the novelty produced when we are surrounded by strangers.

Social density is an important part of the environmental load in restaurants and bars. The number of people in the space at any given time affects the environmental load. Even if we are going to a restaurant to have an intimate dinner, we usually prefer not to be the only ones in the room. The right number of people can create a level of anonymity that may actually be more conducive to an intimate dinner than the experience of being totally alone in the restaurant. However, as social density increases, levels of fascination, mystery, and uncertainty also increase, and we are focused less on intimacy and more on observation of and interaction with others.

Territoriality

Restaurants and bars are secondary territories used temporarily by those who do not actually own them. Often, neighborhood restaurants and bars are perceived as primary territories by the "regulars" who have "their" tables, booths, or stools at the bar. Owners often encourage this perception to inspire return business and customer loyalty. However, if the space provides no distinction between public and more private areas, and if all furniture is identical and arranged the same, territories are less easily defined.

Restaurants and bars that cater to a broader clientele may or may not provide the opportunity to create a temporary primary territory. Private dining rooms and relatively concealed booths can provide a high degree of privacy and a strong sense of territory in most restaurant settings. More often, however, designs emphasize a variety of flexible seating areas that vary in their degree of privacy.

Personal Space

Our needs for personal space in restaurants and bars vary greatly with our expectations, attitudes, and motivations. We generally choose a restaurant based upon what we hope to experience there. The type of restaurant and bar—its theme, colors, materials, seating types and arrangements, lighting, and acoustics—contribute to the ability to regulate our personal space zones in order to achieve our desired levels of privacy and therefore influence our expectations.

Our personal space zones also vary depending upon the environmental load of the restaurant or bar. For example, our zones may be much smaller when we go out to meet friends in a high load environment than when we are dining alone on a business trip. This is especially true for women. Crowded, high load environments provide less opportunity to regulate our personal space zones while lower density low load environments generally provide more space per guest, allowing for adjustment of individual personal space zones.

Approach/Avoidance Behaviors

For most restaurant and bar owners, the way to generate more profit is often equated with the ability to get more people eating and drinking. The term "turning the tables" in restaurant design refers to the rate at which patrons are seated, fed, and leave the restaurant. Theoretically, the more rapidly the tables turn, the more profitable the restaurant will be. This high-volume approach is rarely concerned with privacy. However, as we have learned, the ability to regulate interaction with others enhances our positive responses to most environments and determines, in part, whether we will approach or avoid environments. Restaurants and bars are no exception.

Mehrabian (1976) offers two recommendations for the design of the ideal restaurant and bar. He writes, "The first of these rules is that the various environments in our establishment must all cause approach, meaning, in this case, that people will enter, stay a while, enjoy themselves, and spend money in the process. The second rule is that people come from environments and activities widely differing in (environmental) load and may require recreational environments that compensate for the varying loads of their work setting" (p. 255). Later in this chapter, we will discuss some of the ways these recommendations may be accommodated.

Visual and Acoustical Privacy Needs in Restaurants and Bars

As discussed previously, the type of privacy that we seek most often in restaurants and bars is intimacy. Whether with loved ones, family, friends, or business associates, we interact in varying degrees of intimacy with others in these environments. These different degrees of intimacy require in turn varying degrees of both visual and acoustical privacy.

Visual Privacy

The desire to see and be seen is sometimes an important social motivation for going out to restaurants and bars. We often, however, also seek certain levels of privacy to converse and interact with selected others in these settings. Total visual privacy is rarely necessary to accommodate these privacy needs. When total visual privacy is required, private dining rooms, isolated alcoves, and areas of extreme prospect and refuge can provide for this need. More often, however, we want to be a part of the dynamic visual atmosphere created by others in the environment.

Physical barriers are not always necessary to achieve a degree of visual privacy. Lowered light levels and our line of sight (discussed below) within the restaurant or bar also affect visual privacy. When physical barriers are used to create the perception of privacy, care must be taken to ensure that conversations cannot be overheard. Visual privacy without acoustical privacy is rarely a desirable situation. Acoustical privacy is often more important in restaurant and bar environments than is visual privacy. While we may want to see and be seen by others, we may not want to hear and be heard by others. The right balance of visual and acoustical privacy contributes to the successful design of any restaurant or bar.

Acoustical Privacy

Acoustical considerations in restaurants and bars must be made for both airborne sounds (primarily voices and music) and impact sounds (feet and chairs moving on hard surface floors or silverware coming into contact with dinnerware, etc.). A lively acoustical environment, one that has a relatively high environmental load of sounds, is often desirable when the goal is to encourage interaction and to create arousal. However, more directed attention is required in these types of settings when we want to focus upon individual conversations. This is especially true for the elderly for whom background sounds can literally drown out individual voices.

As we have learned, long periods of directed attention produce mental fatigue, which can distract from the dining experience. Therefore, design solutions should include acoustical materials and spatial configurations that reduce sound levels in the areas designated as more private. The most effective way to reduce noise is to place sound-absorbing materials as close to the source of the sounds as possible. This means using carpeting and tablecloths for impact sounds and soft, textured fabrics on walls, soft chairs and seating, and acoustical ceiling treatments for airborne sounds. Lowered ceiling heights, half walls, and partial screening of private areas through the use of plants or suspended fabric panels help reduce sounds from adjacent areas.

Designing for Privacy Considerations and Criteria for Restaurants and Bars

Designing for privacy in restaurants and bars requires a variety of seating types, areas, and arrangements. In addition, restaurant and bar design should allow for a degree of flexibility to allow the spaces to be adjusted, furniture of appropriate scale and proportion to accommodate varying levels of interaction, appropriate circulation paths, flexible lighting, properly placed acoustical materials, and colors that encourage the type of interactions desired. In general, our design goal is to provide privacy without isolation.

Qualities of the built environment that promote privacy in restaurants and bars are similar to those for hotel lobbies: spaces sequenced to create a spatial hierarchy in which we progress from less private to more private spaces; thresholds to imply and define different territories; areas of prospect and refuge and stimulus shelters to provide opportunities to separate patrons from the center of activity without isolation, and the use of color and light to encourage or discourage interaction and communication.

Sequencing of Spaces

A well designed restaurant or bar contains a sequence of spaces of varying degrees of privacy. Each one of these spaces should be designed with an appropriate amount of enclosure according to its needs for visual and acoustical privacy. These spaces must be considered in relationship to one another and not as isolated areas. When properly designed, the sequence of spaces through which guests pass to reach their tables can enhance their expectations and arouse their senses.

Mystery is an especially effective way to draw people into the restaurant and create anticipation. By sequencing spaces so that patrons move through increasingly private and gradually revealed "realms" until they reach their tables, designers can create mystery and enhance perceptions of privacy.

Thresholds

Thresholds imply moving from one realm to another and are effective in defining territory in restaurants and bars. In addition to the more predictable types of thresholds such as doorways, arches, and columns, designers can vary ceiling heights and floor levels to create thresholds. We can also create alcoves as well as dramatically change color schemes, light levels, furniture styles, and can partially screen areas, which create transitions from one area or territory to another.

Prospect and Refuge

Areas of prospect and refuge are especially effective in allowing patrons to view and feel a part of the atmosphere and activities of the restaurant or bar without being disturbed.

Prospect and refuge add to the mystery of the setting by creating fascination among those for whom the prospect and refuge area is not accessible at that time. (See **Figure 7.10**). They may speculate about who is using the private area and want to return to experience it for themselves.

Stimulus shelters such as booths with very high backs can provide desirable areas of privacy especially in the midst of high load bar/lounge environments so that patrons can escape temporarily without physically leaving the bar itself.

Color and Light

Many designers and restaurant owners understand that warm colors (reds, oranges, and yellows) make both food and people look better and increase appetites. However, warm colors also speed up the metabolism and increase the environmental load by attracting attention, arousing diners, and contributing to higher noise levels. Because warm colors tend to direct our attention outward to the surrounding environment, they are less conducive to privacy than cool colors. Blues and greens tend to have a calming effect that causes us to be more inwardly oriented, so that we are better able to focus upon our dining companions and the food. Additionally, other diners are less visually drawn to areas of cool color, thus making these areas more private than areas using warmer colors.

Light can be manipulated to focus attention and increase arousal. Bright lights, moving lights, and intensely colored lights all attract our attention and can increase noise levels. Brighter lights create less intimacy and can help to "turn tables" more frequently. Lower light levels in certain areas will direct attention away from these areas toward the more brightly lit areas of the restaurant or bar. By adding sparkle to increase fascination and mystery and using soft, warm illumination with cooler colors, designers can further create an atmosphere of intimacy. Care must always be taken to ensure

Figure 7.10 Prospect and refuge creates not only privacy, but also mystery.

that enough illumination falls on the tables so patrons are able to read the menu and observe the quality of the food, yet not so much that it creates glare or inappropriately highlights the guests in private areas of the restaurant or bar.

Space Planning and Furniture Layout

One of the most important influences upon privacy in restaurants and bars is the seating arrangement. Placement of tables and chairs, booths, banquettes, and stools determines how territory is defined and personal space is regulated. Although ergonomic standards provide minimum spatial requirements for placement of furniture in restaurants and bars, these standards reflect only the physical space necessary to perform tasks. As we have learned, the physical space necessary for privacy is often very different from the typical ergonomic standards.

Circulation Patterns

A well designed restaurant or bar will have two major circulation patterns: one for the patrons and one for the staff. These patterns may overlap in certain areas but they should provide clear and distinctive paths to and from the most important areas of the restaurant or bar for each group.

Private areas should be located to the side of or at the end of circulation patterns. The more private the area, the further removed it should be from the guests' circulation pattern. However, if private areas are too far removed from staff circulation patterns, diners may be ignored or find it difficult to get waiters' attention. Circulation paths should be generous in the more private areas (four to five feet) to maintain acoustical privacy and allow waiters ample activity space near each private table.

Lines of Sight

Designers should mentally "sit" in every seat of the restaurant or bar and determine what the patron will see from that seat. Typically, the major concern is making sure that patrons do not have a direct line of sight to the kitchen or serving areas. However, when designing for privacy it is important to consider the visual exposure of private areas and the ability to make eye contact with others.

Direct lines of sight allow people to see each other clearly. Nonverbal communication can be quite intense through the use of eye contact and body language. While this type of setting may be very desirable in environments where people are seeking high levels of interaction, it is not conducive to privacy. To enhance privacy, designers should arrange seating and create visual barriers in ways that break up direct lines of sight. Indirect lines of sight can be accomplished by creating small, separate dining areas within the overall space and by the use of sociofugal seating arrangements (discussed below). Partial or full screening of an area using architectural or decorative elements, changing levels, thresholds, and lowered light levels can also break up direct lines of sight.

Indirect lines of sight can add to the mystery of the restaurant or bar. As with areas of prospect and refuge, partially screened or obstructed views of other areas may prompt patrons to want to return to the restaurant or bar to experience other areas.

Sociofugal and Sociopetal Seating

By using sociofugal and sociopetal seating arrangements, designers can significantly influence the levels of interaction in restaurants and bars. As discussed previously, sociofugal seating discourages interaction with others. The sociofugal placement of furniture around the periphery of rooms, in rows, or side by side makes it more difficult to communicate effectively. Sociopetal seating provides for better conversation by placing furniture at right angles, in a circle, or across from one another. Used in restaurants and bars, sociopetal seating focuses people toward the center of an area, while sociofugal seating focuses people toward walls, views, focal points, and one another.

LINK
For an explanation of the concepts of sociofugal and sociopetal space planning, see Chapter 3, page 55.

Figure 7.11 illustrates how sociopetal and sociofugal seating arrangements can be used to encourage interaction or to provide privacy. To encourage interaction, tables should be placed in an irregular, sociopetal arrangement so that patrons have to weave their way through and around the tables. According to Mehrabian (1976), this arrangement exposes patrons to one another and encourages eye contact. Lines of sight should be direct; therefore, there should be few physical or visual barriers. If the tables in these areas are round, more chairs can be added informally, increasing the social density. This arrangement is most appropriate in bars and lounges where patrons want high environmental loads and the opportunity to enjoy direct interaction with other people.

To create semi-private areas, tables should be arranged adjacent to, but not in the middle of, circulation paths. They should have a back-up element, which can be architectural (columns and half walls) or decorative (plantings and screens).

FYI   According to Edward T. Hall (1969), people seated directly across from one another at tables tend to assume a more confrontational posture, whereas people seated at right angles from one another tend to assume a more cooperative, conversational posture, which is more conducive to privacy. (See **Figure 7.12**).

Figure 7.11 To encourage interaction, tables should be placed in an irregular, sociopetal arrangement so that patrons have to weave their way through and around the tables. Courtesy of Graphisoft.

REAL GOODS RESTAURANT AND LIVING CENTER.
SCALE: 1/8" = 1' - 0"

Lines of sight should be indirect or semi-screened. The placement relationship of table to table in this type of arrangement is sociofugal, but the dining experience at each table can be sociopetal if seating is placed at right angles to encourage interaction between the individuals at each table.

Similar to semi-private arrangements, intimate areas should be sociofugal in relationship to the other areas of the restaurant but sociopetal in arrangement of seating at individual tables. To create the sociofugal arrangement, designers can place tables away from the central areas of the restaurant or bar around the periphery of the room along walls and near windows. Alcoves and areas of prospect and refuge also provide the physical separation without isolation desired for more intimate areas. Tables arranged toward focal points such as fireplaces, artwork, and fountains also can create a sociofugal setting, especially if they are semi-screened from the rest of the space. However, to maximize the intimate dining experience, seating at the tables should be placed at right angles.

Locating Fixed Features in the Space

Space planning considerations for privacy must take into account those fixed areas to which people are naturally drawn in a restaurant. Areas with beautiful views, a fireplace, fountain, the bar, or a stage for musical performances all tend to attract people. These areas also establish natural traffic patterns. If the designer is to use focal points and views to create a backdrop for private dining areas, these natural traffic patterns must be rerouted.

The placement of the bar can be very effective to direct traffic throughout the space. By placing a bar or any feature that can become a common destination for all guests in the middle of a space, circulation will be directed around its perimeter and toward its center creating a natural sociopetal environment. A bar placed against a wall directs traffic along its length creating a more sociofugal environment.

Because the bar is a common destination within the space, people often ignore designed circulation spaces and take the shortest route available, invading other's personal space zones to gain access. To avoid this situation and main-tain areas of relative privacy, the designer should anticipate the changes in social density around the bar area. Next, define the areas that draw people who come and go frequently from those areas that allow people to establish terri-tory in the space. This can be accomplished by using railings, half walls, columns, and other fixed features within the area to serve as a back-up element and create pockets of relative privacy within the overall space.

The configuration of the bar can also greatly influence levels of interaction. A long straight bar places guests directly next to one another, often within each other's personal space zones, but it does not encourage interaction. Bars with angles and curves provide options for varying degree of sociopetal interaction. (See **Figure 7.13**).

Furniture Choices for Privacy

Privacy and comfort go hand in hand. We cannot experience privacy while sitting in hard, open backed, uncomfortable chairs that physically expose us to others. Regardless of how carefully the designer has planned the space or considered the lighting, colors, and materials to facilitate

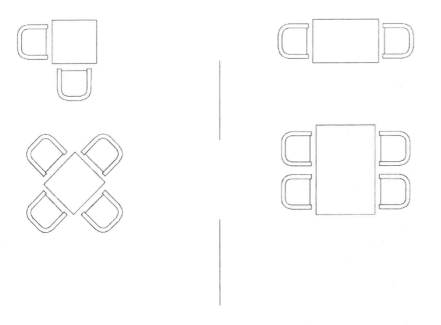

Figure 7.12 Sociopetal seating arrangements at tables are more conducive to intimate conservation if placed at right angles.

MORE INTIMATE   LESS INTIMATE

Figure 7.13 Long, straight bars do not encourage interaction and often place guests in one another's personal space zones. However, bars with angles and curves provide options for varying degrees of sociopetal interaction.

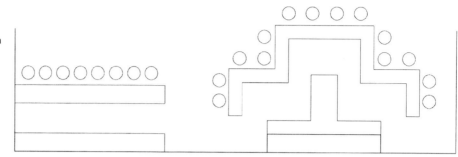

privacy in a restaurant or bar, the choice of improper furniture can undermine the privacy gained by the original design. To achieve privacy in a restaurant or bar we must not feel exposed or crowded, and we must be able to maintain our desired personal space zones. The table, seating, and adjacent circulation space form our territory while we occupy the space.

The most important furniture element to enhance privacy in restaurants and bars is the seating. Fully upholstered, high back chairs or booths can enhance both acoustical and visual privacy. Arms on chairs add to the ability to maintain personal space zones by creating a physical barrier between others and ourselves. The more generous the size of the seating, the more personal space we control.

Tables should be just large enough to accommodate the type of meals served and to provide adequate space for individual territories and personal space. Unlike a generously sized chair, a large table rarely adds to the ability to achieve privacy. As table sizes increase, the need to raise our voices to communicate effectively also increases. To help maintain acoustical privacy, large tables should be located in corners with additional acoustical materials used on nearby walls and ceiling.

The use of banquette seating (continuous built-in benches located along the wall with tables and chairs placed directly across from them) is one of the most effective ways to seat a large number of people in a small amount of space. This type of furniture arrangement is

Figure 7.14 Frank Lloyd Wright's design for this intimate room within a room created by the furniture and lighting brings diners together for conversation and defines their territory. Courtesy of the Frank Lloyd Wright Archives, Taliesin West, Scottsdale, Arizona.

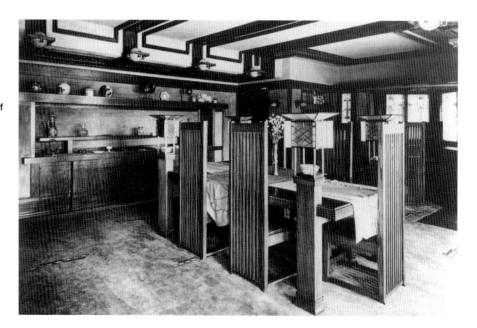

!APPLICATION!

Frank Lloyd Wright helped to define the concept of the residential dining table and chairs as a territory separate from the other areas of a space by placing extremely high backed seating around the table and anchoring lighting to the corners of the table. This arrangement created a room within a room, a very private setting for conversation and dining. (See **Figure 7.14**) Wright's intimate dining arrangement can be adapted to restaurant environments by using high back chairs and custom designed light fixtures.

There is a way, however, to modify banquette seating to maximize the use of wall space to accommodate the largest number of diners while still establishing territory, personal space and achieving a degree of privacy. As shown in **Figure 7.15,** the straight banquette can be angled or curved to change the line of sight and direct voices away from those sitting next to one another.

FINAL THOUGHTS ON PRIVACY NEEDS IN HOSPITALITY DESIGN

Hospitality design is an exciting, rapidly changing, and challenging area of interior design, and privacy is a growing area of consideration for these designs. The often thin boundaries between the public and private experiences of hotels, restaurants, and other spaces designated as part of the hospitality industry, create unique challenges for designers. Perhaps nowhere else do we find the opposing needs to interact and to withdraw from interaction so strongly expressed.

As designers and architects continue to examine the research findings that help us to understand and meet the diverse needs of "global nomads" and increasingly sophisticated diners, we gain new insights, and the needs for privacy become central to our considerations for function, aesthetics, and quality of life.

popular among restaurant and bar owners looking to turn tables quickly. This arrangement can be found in the most inexpensive as well as the most formal, expensive restaurants and bars around the world. It is however, rarely preferred by guests. This is because banquette seating is the epitome of mixed messages. It is a classic example of a sociofugal arrangement with people lined up side by side, modified by placing them directly across from their dining partner in a more sociopetal (albeit confrontational) position. This is high density dining that provides for virtually no visual or acoustical privacy and limits opportunities to establish territory and personal space.

Figure 7.15 Curved or angled banquette seating helps to establish personal space zones and territories.

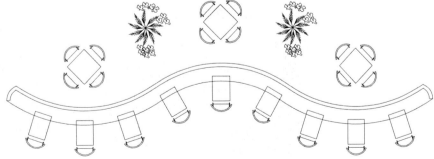

KEY CONCEPTS

1. Regardless of size or type, all hotels have two basic design similarities: 1) guest rooms tend to have standard sizes and similar furniture arrangements, and 2) all require a public space where guests can check in and out.

2. The stress associated with travel is often the result of high environmental loads and high levels of novelty.

3. All four types of privacy may be required and accommodated in a hotel: *Solitude* and *intimacy* in guest rooms, *intimacy* in the lobby, restaurant, lounge, or other areas specially designed for personal interactions, *anonymity* in the busy common areas of the hotel, and *reserve*, which can be accommodated by a discrete staff, in-room services, private circulation paths, and the ability to maintain desired social space zones.

4. Both territoriality and personal space are important privacy mechanisms that we use to achieve desired levels of privacy in hotels. Although hotels are secondary territories, guest rooms are usually perceived as primary territories for the time they are occupied. Personal space zones are usually larger when we travel to help regulate crowding and enhance feelings of personal safety.

5. Designing for privacy in hotel lobbies requires zoning of activities to allow for proper circulation, effective communication, definition of territory, establishment of personal space, and control of interpersonal interactions.

6. Qualities of the built environment that promote privacy in both hotel public spaces and guest rooms include spatial depth, real and implied thresholds, areas of prospect and refuge, a balance of novelty and familiarity, and appropriate use of color and light.

7. Guest rooms should also be zoned to provide for efficient use of the space and to allow guests to establish territory and personal space. These zones often overlap or serve multiple functions.

8. Privacy can be a fragile and dynamic quality of restaurant and bar environments. The need to see and be seen is often in conflict with the need to interact intimately. In general, the design goal is to provide privacy without isolation.

9. The type of privacy that we most often seek in restaurants and bars is intimacy. The different degrees of intimacy we seek in these environments require varying degrees of both visual and acoustical privacy.

ASSIGNMENT
PRIVACY FOR HOTEL GUEST ROOMS: CONCEPTUAL DEVELOPMENT

Learning Objectives:
- To identify and analyze guests' needs for privacy together with functional goals
- To explore conceptual design solutions that can be further developed into detailed finalized solutions
- To work as a team member to creatively develop design concepts

Learning Outcomes:
- Development of skills in problem identification, problem solving, and identification of user needs
- Development of skills in information gathering and analysis
- Development of ability to rapidly visualize concepts through sketching

- Development of space planning skills
- Greater understanding of the responsibilities and processes of working as a team member

Description:

This is a team assignment for two to three students, focusing upon developing conceptual skills for the design of two different types of guest rooms using the same general dimensions. The emphasis is upon generating several design concepts that emphasize the types of privacy required by the different types of guests. This assignment is to be completed entirely during one class period.

General Information:

1. The two types of guest rooms are
   - An executive guest suite in an upscale urban hotel in the U.S. catering to business travelers
   - A family resort suite in Hawaii accommodating four people

2. The suite is 26' wide × 20' deep

3. Ceilings are 9' high

4. Floor-to-ceiling windows and sliding door to a balcony (26'×6') running the width of the suite located on the south wall opposite the entrance

Analysis:

Using the designing for privacy information in this chapter and in chapters 1 through 3, analyze the privacy and functional requirements for each type of suite.

- Identify and describe in detail the types of privacy each type of suite must accommodate.
- Describe what your considerations to accommodate these types of privacy will be.

- Identify and describe in detail the functions that must be accommodated in each type of suite.
- Describe the guest room zones necessary to provide for the functions.
- Identify specific design requirements for function and privacy necessary for these zones (furniture, equipment, lighting).
- Identify and describe the possible physical characteristics that can be designed to support the function and privacy needs of each type of suite.

Solutions:

Using the information gathered from the analysis, create two conceptual designs for each suite (total of four designs) including

- Concept statement including your analysis
- Floor plan sketch
- Two interior elevations illustrating details that illustrate how privacy and function are accommodated
- Interior sketch illustrating how spaces or zones relate to one another visually (add color where applicable)

REFERENCES

Alexander, C. A., Ishikawa, S., Silverstein, M., Jacobson, M., Fiksdahl-King, I. & Angel, S. (1977). "A Pattern language." New York: Oxford University Press.

Albrecht, D. & Johnson, E. (2002). "New hotels for global nomads." London: Merrell Publishers Limited.

Ayala, H. (1996). Resort ecotourism: A paradigm for the 21st century. *Cornell Hotel and Restaurant Administration Quarterly 37, 5, 46–53.*

Conner, F. (1997). Security sells rooms. *Cornell Hotel and Restaurant Administration Quarterly, 37, 5, 54–61.*

Dube, L. & Renaghan, L. M. (1999). How hotel attributes deliver the promised benefits: Guests' perspectives on the lodging industry's functional best practices (part II). *Cornell Hotel and Restaurant Administration Quarterly, 40, 5,* 89–95.

Engle, J. (2003, February 2). While others fret, the rich travel on. *Los Angeles Times.* Reprinted in *Boulder Daily Camera.*

Hall, E. T. (1969). "The hidden dimension." New York: Anchor, Doubleday.

Kaplan, R. & Kaplan, S. (1989). "The experience of nature: A psychological perspective." Cambridge: Cambridge University Press.

MacKenzie, H. (1988). Teenagers in hospital. *Nursing Times, 84, 32,* 58–61.

Mann, I. S. (1993). Marketing to the affluent: A look at their expectations and service standards. *Cornell Hotel and Restaurant Administration Quarterly, 34, 5,* 54–58.

Mattila, A. S. (1999). Consumer's value judgments: How business travelers evaluate luxury-hotel services. *Cornell Hotel and Restaurant Administration Quarterly,* 40, 1, pp. 40–46.

Mattila, A. S. (2001). Emotional bonding and restaurant loyalty. *Cornell Hotel and Restaurant Administration Quarterly, 42, 6,* 73–70.

McCleary, K. W. & Weaver, P. A. (1994). Gender-based differences in business traveler's lodging preferences. *Cornell Hotel and Restaurant Administration Quarterly, 35, 2,* 51–58.

Mehrabian, A. (1976). "Public places and private spaces." New York: Basic Books, Inc.

NASA. (1985). *Living aloft: Human requirements for extended spaceflight.* NASA SP-483.

O'Neill, J. W. & Lloyd-Jones, A. R. (2002). One year after 9/11: Hotel values and strategic implications. *Cornell Hotel and Restaurant Administration Quarterly, 43, 5,* 53–64.

Piotrowski, C. M. & Rogers, E. A. (1999). "Designing commercial interiors." New York: John Wiley & Sons, Inc.

Siguaw, J. A. & Enz, C. A. (1999). Best practices in hotel architecture. *Cornell Hotel and Restaurant Administration Quarterly, 40, 5,* 44–49.

Ulrich, R. S. (1993). Biophilia, biophobia, and natural landscapes. In S. Kellert and E. O. Wilson, (Eds.). "The biophilia hypothesis" (pp. 73–137). Washington, DC: Island Press.

Withiam, G. (2000) Studying women business travelers. *Cornell Hotel and Restaurant Administration Quarterly, 41, 3,* 11.

CHAPTER 8

Age-Specific Considerations for Privacy

Life unfolds for all of us in stages. If we live a whole lifetime, we will experience a series of changes in ourselves and in our environment. We react to these changes and life itself against a backdrop of our culture, our age, our circumstances, and our values. In spite of differences, what we all share are timeless, universal needs. Privacy is one

of those needs. We experience privacy differently depending upon our age and upon the stage of life we are living.

CHANGING NEEDS FOR PRIVACY AS WE AGE

Privacy is a dynamic process throughout life. While there are many variables affecting our privacy needs besides age, privacy needs are age-specific and can change over the course of a lifetime. Research studies tell us those children as young as three years old have privacy needs crucial to their growth and development (Maxwell 1996). During the teenage years, adolescents probably display the most blatant needs for privacy of any age group. Young adults have new age-specific privacy experiences at school, at work, and in other environments where they interact with others as adults rather than as children. Privacy for adults

can be a hard-won victory, especially when they are still caring for children and at the same time caring for aging parents. This stage of life can last a long time, and the challenges of the experience heighten the need for privacy and respite. (See **Figure 8.1**).

As our minds and bodies age, privacy needs change also. Typically, our bodies tell us that we cannot run so hard or so fast anymore, but a lifetime of experience teaches us to value new opportunities. Aging adults have the time to savor privacy experiences such as intimacy and socialization, nature, contemplation, and restorative experiences. Later in life many of us will undergo health changes. Getting older and experiencing health problems can impact our autonomy and sense of control. Even if we remain in our homes, privacy needs shift when we must surrender part of our independence and ask for help with the activities of daily life.

Figure 8.1 Changing needs for privacy over a lifetime.

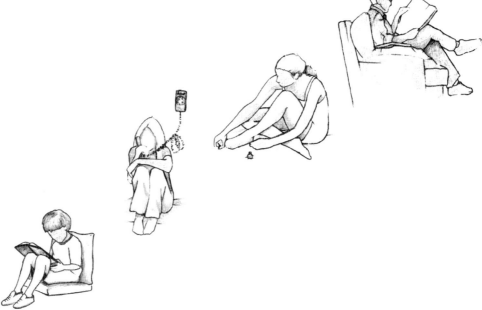

Sometimes our mental or physical status will require relocating to some type of continuing care retirement community. At this point, the dynamics of privacy change again. In a new environment often further away from family, communication and social interaction can take on new importance. At the same time during the latter years of life we need time to reflect on our past and on our life experiences, and this is often best accomplished alone. During these years many of us suffer the loss of our friends and our life partners. Privacy becomes critical to reflect on the implications of these profound events and to consider our own mortality. During this stage in life, however, the ability to interact with selected individuals also becomes critical to our overall health and well-being. Many of us may yearn for affiliation with others to soften our feelings of loss and desolation while some of us may need solitude for the experience. No matter what age we are, we never outgrow our need for privacy; it merely reshapes itself to the experiences of any stage of life.

These stages of life and the different nature of age-specific privacy needs are the subject of Chapter 8. We begin with an overview of the theoretical basis for understanding age-specific privacy needs. The scope of this text does not allow for considerations of every age group in every situation requiring privacy. Accordingly, we have chosen a variety of environmental settings with diverse privacy requirements. We have also provided *Links* to fuller discussions of privacy needs for different age groups in other chapters. Chapter 8 ends with a case study that validates the uses of privacy needs to improve the human condition, even in the face of **dementia** (moderate to severe decline of mental faculties).

THEORIES OF AGE-SPECIFIC PRIVACY NEEDS

When we accept the premise held by a number of people in different disciplines that our need for privacy has a biological basis (Boyden 1971, Westin 1967, Klopfer and Rubenstein 1977), then we begin to understand why the need for privacy manifests itself in people of every age and across many cultures.

Newell—A Systems Perspective

The systems perspective of privacy held by Newell (1998) and discussed in Chapter 2 maintains that there are cultural universals in place that promote our survival and development, and one of those is privacy. Although the experience of privacy may vary across cultures, there is a consensus among researchers that privacy is a dynamic therapeutic process and that we seek different expressions of privacy at different stages of our lives. Our motives for seeking privacy are often age-specific. For example, a small child wants the privacy and dignity of a closed bathroom door, and adolescents go to great lengths to separate themselves physically and psychologically from anyone older than themselves. A study by Newell (1998) found that while privacy experiences are universally restorative, the reasons for seeking privacy differ by age group. She found that younger people seek privacy on more of a need-to-escape basis, citing stressors such as responsibilities to other people, crowding, or abuse by others. The same study found that the participants over 30 years old wanted privacy for entirely different reasons, citing the need to do or achieve something. Newell, however, also found that the need for privacy across several cultures often arises from stress, grief, and fatigue in all age groups. Age, however, does sometimes skew the fatigue factor. In Newell's study, 60 percent of the group over 30 years old cited being tired as a major reason for seeking privacy, while only 20 percent of the younger group mentioned fatigue as a factor. Regardless of age or culture, two themes emerge consistently from Newell and others: that the most important factor in the privacy experience is not being disturbed and that the result of the privacy experience is the feeling of being more relaxed, less emotional, and refreshed. These factors contribute to the overall experience of restoration, which, as we have learned, is one of the most important benefits of privacy.

Children and Privacy

Children's privacy needs are a sharp contrast to adult privacy needs because young children live in the moment. For a child, privacy is a chance to inspect undisturbed a leaf with a worm on it. Privacy means hiding under the stairs and making up six imaginary reasons to be there. Or it may be staring out a window and redirecting attention to an outdoor scene that is more fascinating than the tame indoor activities that require directed attention. Privacy for a child does not necessarily require solitude because children have the ability, even more than adults, to lose themselves through redirected attention in the immediacy of an event. Nothing interests children more than the world around themselves. Like adults, children are attracted to environments that promise mystery and new information within a safe and predictable setting. Hiding, always a favorite activity, builds a child's concept of self as well as providing separation from parents within the safety of a known environment (Boschetti 1987). Hidden private places also furnish opportunities for prospect and refuge and reinforce the child's need for protection. (See **Figure 8.2**). Exploratory places bolster feelings of discovery and reinforce feelings of choice and control.

Sometimes it is not possible to have true privacy. Environments that have inadequate square footage for the social density within a space present challenges to restorative privacy experiences. We turn next to another aspect of privacy, the age-specific effects of crowding.

Crowding for Adults and Children

Achieving desired privacy is a positive experience, but there are often impediments such as age-specific perceptions of crowding. Both adults and children may experience crowding if their space is not large enough, but the physical environment affects adults and children differently. As we discussed in Chapter 4, for privacy, parents need away places and children need

Figure 8.2 The magic of hiding. Secret places provide opportunities for fantasy within a safe environment.

hiding spaces. Ideally, the residential interior should support the needs for adults' privacy and children's privacy.

Crowding at Home

Evans, Maxwell, & Hart (1999) found that adults in crowded homes have more social interaction than they desire, and consequently they withdraw. A result often observed in these studies is that parents in more crowded homes are less verbally responsive to their children, and they tend to withdraw more often from the children. In crowded homes, the act of social withdrawal often cannot provide the benefits of privacy because there are few if any private places in the home, and so withdrawal serves merely as a temporary escape. In this environment, the adults will find experiences of solitude or even intimacy difficult. Under acutely crowded conditions, if withdrawal is not possible, stress results (Evans, Rhee, Forbes, Allen, & Lepore, 2000). Evans found that parents in this study used impoverished language with the children. Impoverished language is the practice of using a minimal number of words to convey meaning, and Evans found that this in turn affected the children's cognitive development and progress in school.

Crowded conditions may affect children the most adversely because in acute residential crowding, the children's spaces are most often taken over by the family for other purposes (Maxwell 1996). For example, children of different age groups may share a bedroom or the bedroom may be located in a room used for purposes other than sleeping such as the living room. Children in these settings find limited space to perform functions such as personal grooming in private. Research studies (Saegert 1984, Sweaney 1986, & Maxwell 1996) report more anger among children in crowded homes, possibly an anger stemming from the lack of control and territoriality.

LINK

If you want to learn more about children's residential privacy needs, see Chapter 4, page 80.

Unlike adults, however, children in crowded residential environments are often able to use social withdrawal as a coping mechanism for positive privacy experiences. Even under the most crowded conditions, a small child can usually find a small place to hide and to dream. Additionally, most children seek out opportunities for outdoor play. The work of Evans, et al. (1996) and earlier studies (Saegert 1984) support the finding that children in crowded homes who have places to retreat to or who have easy opportunities to play outside suffer less and have fewer harmful effects from residential crowding.

Crowding for children is certainly not limited to conditions at home. Increasingly, young children are cared for outside their own homes. We turn next to an examination of crowding conditions in nonresidential settings.

Crowding for Children in Nonresidential Settings

In 2002, the U.S. Census recorded the percentage of mothers of young children who worked outside the home at 55 percent. Many of those children are cared for in child care centers (Maxwell 1996), and they may spend eight to twelve hours a day in these nonresidential settings.

A major national study of daycare facilities (Ruopp, Travers, Glantz, & Coelen 1979) found that group size is critical to children's intellectual and social development. In smaller groups (less than 15 children), "the children exhibited greater cooperation and compliance, more reflection and innovation, more verbal initiative, less aimless wandering, more involvement in activities, and less hostility and squabbles" (Maxwell, p. 499). Another extensive study with preschool children (Smith and Connolly 1980) found that less space per child reduced the amount of gross motor activity such as running, chasing, and rough-and-tumble play. The same study found a correlation between spatial density and social behavior. Children's social behavior was stable at about 25 square feet per child, but when density allowance dropped to 15 square feet per child, there was less group play and more aggression (Maxwell 1996).

LINK

For more information about social density and how it affects crowding, see Chapter 2, page 29.

The significance of these findings for privacy is that children in crowded environments will not have sufficient opportunities for restorative privacy experiences, and their cognitive and social development may suffer as a result.

LINK

For information about how prospect and refuge can enhance the experience of privacy, see Chapter 3, page 51 and Chapter 4, page 88.

CHILDREN'S NEEDS IN DAYCARE CENTERS

In a study of the design of daycare center environments (Trancik & Evans 1995), the authors explored the needs that children have in daycare centers and concluded that design elements can offer a type of protection for children to develop their competency and confidence in different areas. Selected needs that children have in daycare centers associated with privacy include control, complexity, mystery and exploration, and restoration.

Privacy and Private Places

Daycare centers are often organized in a communal manner providing public spaces and common areas for the greatest number of children. The space, however, needs to support both the experience of solitude as well as the varying degrees of interaction from small groups to public groups. Children need partitioned areas for small groups when the activity level of the whole group overwhelms them. They also need "stimulus shelters," small private places that provide opportunities to be alone, to play uninterrupted, to observe activities without participating (prospect and refuge), or to use emotions that they do not choose to share with other children (Trancik & Evans 1995). Children, because they are young and still growing, become fatigued throughout the day, and they need to have the option to seek out private places for rest and recovery. Adjacencies between public and private areas are always important for successful experiences of children's privacy. For example, if some of the children need naps and some of them do not, locating a sleeping area next to a group play area will not work (Trancik & Evans 1995). A properly designed spatial hierarchy as discussed in Chapter 3 will help to ensure the necessary levels of acoustical and visual privacy in these areas. (See **Figure 8.3**).

!APPLICATION!

DESIGN FOR PRIVACY

• Create a variety of spaces—public, semi-public, and private.

• Separate spaces spatially by activity. An area for reading or napping should be removed from spaces for eating or other group activities.

• Provide toilet stalls with privacy for the child but surveillance for the teacher by installing short louver type doors across stalls.

Trancik & Evans 1995

Control

Building to a child's scale is important for choice and control. The child should be able to open an (interior) door alone and to reach a light switch. This type of responsive environment allows children to develop self-identity, confidence and a sense of well-being (Trancik & Evans 1995).

Figure 8.3
Children's needs for privacy: choices between public and private space.

Children in daycare centers also need choices for their activities. For children who cannot yet read independently, a quiet room with one seating area works well for story time, but when children want to look at books on their own, they need individual reading areas. Well-designed private and semi-private spaces provide cues as to the intended usage. An area intended for quiet reading can feature a lowered ceiling height, ambient lighting, and reading alcoves with comfortable furniture and a variety of seating choices (Moore, Lane, Hill, Cohen, & McGinty 1990).

!APPLICATION!

DESIGN TO ENHANCE FEELINGS OF CONTROL

• Provide private space for children to dress and undress (swim suits, outdoor snow clothing) with sufficient space for comfort and ease so that they are encouraged to practice their dressing skills.

• Hang towels at a height that a child can reach easily.

• Provide responsive play equipment. On a climbing gym, different colored rungs painted at graduated levels let the child assess progress and develop climbing skills.

Trancik & Evans 1995

Complexity, Mystery, and Exploration

Complexity, mystery, and exploration in daycare environments maintain the child's sense of discovery in the settings where they may spend the bulk of their time. In new construction, often the architectural footprint of a daycare center is a square box that appears to have limited opportunities for complexity, mystery, and exploration. The interior of the space, however, always provides options to address the need for variety. Moveable partitions can help divide spaces by function, but they also are an easy and flexible way to vary the spatial complexity. Partial closure with moveable partitions can contribute to mystery with the promise of discovering new objects and places. Rooms with unusual shapes encourage children to explore and discover things that might be just around the corner. Interiors of daycare centers that have a blend of square, straight, and curvy indoor spaces and activity pockets within public areas keep a space fresh and open to a child's fantasies (Trancik & Evans 1995). (See **Figure 8.4**).

Restoration

As children go through their day, they are constantly acquiring information and learning from new experiences. This high level of activity makes growing children susceptible to mental fatigue, and mental fatigue can inhibit the learning process. Restorative opportunities for children provide feelings similar to adults' restorative experiences—the chance to get away, to experience feelings of time out or escape, and to return feeling refreshed. The nature of restorative experiences for children, however, is different (Trancik & Evans 1995). For example, most children have a natural affinity for animals, and watching the fish swim around in an aquarium or holding the classroom guinea pig is enchanting to most children. These activities provide involuntary attention, which contributes to the restorative experience. Animals can also serve as comfort when children are hurt or need a time out from interaction with their peers. Theme areas also can provide restorative experiences. Areas that provide stages for play acting or musical instruments satisfy fantasy needs and allow children to explore areas beyond the daycare setting without ever leaving the building (Trancik & Evans 1995). Some of the most satisfying restorative experiences for children come from the natural world. Nature is fascinating to children, and

Figure 8.4 Daycare center—different shaped rooms for exploration and discovery.

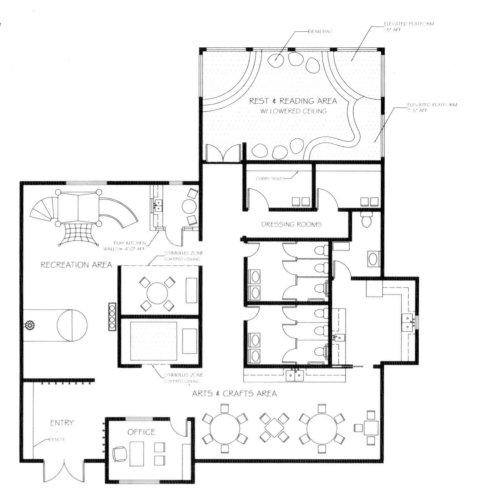

RESTORATIVE EXPERIENCES

• Close indoor/outdoor relationships are important, and windows placed at a child's eye level can enhance the connection with nature.

• In unpredictable climates, covered porches and courtyard spaces allow children to go outside despite rain or snow (see prospect and refuge, Chapter 3, page 51).

• If a daycare center is in a location that is removed from nature, installing a greenhouse or an arboretum can bring the outside in.

Trancik & Evans, p. 315

outdoor play, if it is imaginative, can become a restorative experience.

The process of a child's development moves along a continuum from helplessness and dependency to independence and maturity. For a number of years many children may move somewhat seamlessly from early childhood to the later years of childhood and to the experiences of public or private education. Expectations of appropriate expressions of privacy, however, change with age. For example, while a very young child has little sense of modesty, an elementary school child has long ago developed a certain level of sophistication for privacy experiences such as bathroom privacy and privacy for dressing and undressing. At the same time, in contrast to the pre-school child, the older child has stronger needs for privacy, and the concentration of directed attention as the level of conceptual learning increases. While childhood may be a smooth journey for many children, the next stage of life, adolescence, can present challenges to everyone involved in the experience.

THE ADOLESCENT EXPERIENCE AND THE NEED FOR PRIVACY

Adolescence is a time of explosive physical and emotional growth with rapid bodily changes and the accompanying changes in body chemistry. Although adolescents are children and usually still live with their families at this time, they are experiencing new awareness of themselves as individuals separate from the family experience. Adolescents sometimes tend to have unrealistic perceptions of themselves because of their strong age-specific needs for the development of self-identity. It is a searching, questioning time for many young people, a time that demands solitude, high affiliation and interaction with their peers, and to some extent, temporary exclusion of others older or younger than themselves. Most of these experiences require privacy or the intimacy of a small group.

LINK
To learn more about adolescents and privacy needs at home, see Chapter 4, page 80.

Adolescents struggle with new challenges at this stage of life. Typically, adolescents are self-conscious of their bodies and convinced that everyone is staring at them. They have a horror of being considered ordinary or typical in any way, and often they want little public identity with their families (Hutton 2002).

LINK
Adolescents have specific privacy needs in health care environments as well. See Chapter 6, page 141.

Privacy needs are enormous during adolescence. Designing for adolescents should begin with acknowledgment of and respect for adolescent needs.

- *Architectural privacy (walls and doors for real privacy)*
- *Private bedrooms (for territorial privacy and development of self-identity)*
- *Rooms or areas that allow semi-private (no adults) interactions with friends*

Architects and interior designers need to provide the maximum privacy for adolescents, even if the price is a trade-off in another area. For example, adolescents have critical privacy needs in their homes. (See **Figure 8.5**). Residential settings with high social density, tight square footage, or other constraints often would seem to work against providing private bedrooms for each child. For the adolescent, however, a tiny room, even if carved out of other usable spaces, fills an urgent need. Four walls and a door can provide opportunities for territoriality, contemplation, and restoration. A private room also affords opportunities for personalization of the space, a critical need in the adolescent's quest for self-identity.

We turn next to young adults, the age group defined as beyond adolescence, often living apart from their families, and involved in experiences of school and work.

PRIVACY NEEDS OF COLLEGE STUDENTS

For some young adults, the residential experience of living away from home in a college setting is an exciting experience, but it is also a time when privacy needs undergo changes that are age-specific as well as relevant to the new type of living arrangement. Typically, a young adult arriving at a university comes out of a family environment in which territoriality has been clearly defined by the cultural norms and practices within the structure of the family. In the college dorm setting or in shared apartment living, young adults live in a communal arrangement with less clearly defined territorial privacy.

The physical environment of the college dorm setting or other type of student housing can **either** enhance or frustrate privacy needs. For example, dorm rooms that receive more natural light are perceived as larger and less crowded than the same sized rooms that have little natural light (Evans, Lepore, & Schroeder 1996). Dorm rooms on higher floors are perceived as larger and more private (Kaya & Erkip 2001). A study of first-year university students who lived in residence halls found that when the residents were able to use a wide variety of successful privacy regulation mechanisms to avoid unwanted contact with their fellow residents, they were less likely to drop out of school by the end of the second year (Harris, Brown, & Werner 1996).

When high-rise dormitories are designed using long corridors with direct access into bedrooms, residents report feelings of crowding and stress. A study of modification of long corridor dormitories to shorter corridors with smaller subunits of rooms revealed that resident reports of unwanted social interaction dropped, and more pro-social behaviors were observed as well as less withdrawal (Evans et al. 1996, citing Baum & Davis 1980).

Additional studies tell us that anytime students are housed in a greater population density than was originally designed for the plan (such as tripled dormitory rooms intended for two people), they report their rooms as feeling cluttered, public, and chaotic. Students who experience perceptions of crowding in their dormitories are less satisfied with the residential experience and express negative feelings about the dormitory and about their neighbors (Kaya & Erkip 2001, citing Baum, Davis, & Valins 1979).

Conditions for the design of college dormitories are often not ideal. Many times designers must work with older buildings already config-

Figure 8.5 The luxury of privacy for an adolescent. © Richard Hutchings/CORBIS.

ured for institutional living. We must, however, apply concepts of privacy whenever possible in these settings, and in addition serve as educators about privacy needs for our clients. We move next to an examination of young adults' privacy needs in work environments.

PRIVACY NEEDS OF YOUNG ADULTS

Every generation believes in its own uniqueness. For young adults, that may be more reality than myth. They have grown up in a world redefined by technology. The "older" young adults (born between 1965–1976) grew up with television and saw the advent of the personal computer. The "younger" young adults (born between 1977–1982) have grown up in the electronic era and have had lifelong relationships with technology (Tapscott 1998, Rushkoff 1999). They spend hours alone in their rooms on their computers. Their socialization is often a computer-based activity of emailing their friends and making plans. These younger young adults are emerging from adolescence, and in today's world of rising prices for living and for higher education, some of them will still live at home.

Young Adults at Home

The younger adults still living in their parent's homes may have even stronger needs for privacy than when they were adolescents. They are no longer children, and they have their own lives. From the standpoint of territorial privacy however, they may "own" no more than they did as children—their own rooms. Their feelings of independence and self-identity are probably not particularly threatened because research studies (Beckmann 2000, Knoll & Ellis 2001) indicate that this generation, whether they live in their parent's homes or in their own homes, generally have boundless confidence in their own abilities, and consequently have strong feelings of achievement in areas of choice, control, and autonomy.

The older members of this generation are often living on their own and sometimes find themselves sharing space with a roommate or several roommates. This can present challenges to territorial privacy, particularly if the space is small and if people must share primary territories such as bedrooms. Sharing a bedroom for some of them is undoubtedly reminiscent of adolescence at home and/or college experiences away from home. Successful interaction in sharing residential space for young adults depends upon several factors. Respect for other people's privacy and using protocols can help make sharing space a workable experience. The most important factor, however, is the opportunity to effectively separate from others on occasion and to retreat to a private place. Like the crowding conditions in crowded homes that we discussed earlier in this chapter, if there is no private place at home, the young adult must seek out private places in other environments. For example, coffeehouses and other public spaces that provide semi-private areas for the patrons can help to satisfy privacy needs.

Young Adults at Work

While conditions of residential environments may present some privacy issues, young adults have had experience living in their parents' home or living with roommates at college. The new world that many of them have not experienced fully yet is the work environment. They are the newcomers, joining workers of varying ages, beliefs, and goals.

Preferences for Life and Work Experience

One of the major differences between young adult workers and older workers is in perceptions of privacy. For the older workers and the veterans of the work environment, the appreciation of privacy is sometimes tied up with status needs, and they may feel rewarded when they are given enclosed offices on high floors with windows and good views. For the young adults, although they voice preferences for private enclosed offices to accomplish specific tasks, in general they more often value access to and camaraderie with their peers in open collaborative work experiences (Beckmann 2000).

In a qualitative research study of ten focus groups conducted in five markets around the country as well as a second study of five focus groups (Knoll & Ellis 2001), young adults today express desires for life and work that have implications for privacy and related needs. This study found that they want to work in neighborhoods that offer things to do during breaks and after work, such as restaurants, bars, shops, or beaches. Other studies (Beckmann 2000, Weicker 2000), found that young adults consider having fun essential even at the office, particularly for reduction of stress. They want to be outdoors, and they believe that leisure is critical to health. Perhaps their desires for amenities, fun, and leisure stem from this generation's intuitive realization that stress is usually a harmful experience (Knoll & Ellis 2001). They express desires for integrated lives of work, home, and leisure, and they see a healthy seamlessness between life and work (Beckmann 2000, Knoll & Ellis 2001). As we learned in Chapter 4, the implications for privacy in this case are that lines are blurring between life and work, and the sociability of the home must be shared with the privacy needs for work. Problems for privacy in this case may or may not exist. If young adults can manage the hours spent at work, leaving enough time for family and life experiences, there may be no problem more complicated than finding a location for a home office. However, people of this generation tend to work hard, and if work becomes a consuming everyday event at home, they may find it difficult to give themselves the other experiences that they need for restoration and recovery.

Results of the ten focus groups' study (Knoll & Ellis 2001) found that young adults want easy access to work because they hate traffic and any type of commuting. They would prefer to walk, bike, or skateboard to the office. This desire for easy access to work may reflect several privacy needs. Certainly walking to work allows control, a sort of "driving the bus" experience. This generation also believes that doing several things at a time from anywhere can reduce stress. Walking to work while talking on the cell phone is an example of this belief. Being outdoors allows people to enjoy the restorative effects of nature, and arriving at work on a skateboard allows them to express their uniqueness.

Preferences for the Design of the Work Environment

The same studies that describe the preferences of young adults also focused on their design preferences in office environments. For people of this generation, many factors have influenced their perception of desirable working conditions. We have said that all of them grew up with television, and many of them have had electronic technology most or all of their lives. They have grown up connected to events on a global and immediate basis. They also have a more participative way of learning rather than the traditional listening to lectures and taking notes (Tapscott 1998). This type of learning may have been partially influenced by their life-long interaction with computers. Their work orientation tends toward collaborative work projects.

In the same study of ten focus groups (Knoll & Ellis 2001), young adults expressed their needs in the work environment.

* *They want open, light, airy workplaces that feel close to the outdoors or to the beach. Windows and natural light are important, and they want views of nature.*

* *They want the ability to personalize their space and ways to express their uniqueness, such as relaxed dress codes allowing for individuality, personalization opportunities, and the option of bringing their dogs to work.*

Each of these needs reflects qualities of privacy. The first need is expressed as a desire for redirected attention, and the second need is expressed as a desire for control and establishment of territory.

This generation's preferences for the physical design of the work space sometimes presents a conflict because of the inconsistency noted earlier between needs for privacy and their expressed preferences for collaboration. In the Knoll & Ellis study (2001), young adults stated that they want private offices to get their work done, to concentrate, and to have private phone conversations. At the same time, they express feelings of isolation in private offices if they are alone very long. Too much privacy does not feel right to this group because they crave interaction with others. While it might be tempting to believe that the new generation of workers has little need for privacy, these young people need privacy as much as any other generation. Their needs may be lopsided with heavy preferences for collaborative work, but it is often the heavy interactive nature of collaborative work that increases their environmental load and stresses them if there are no opportunities for privacy experiences.

Young adults express the belief that the work environment does not always support their needs. Focus groups by the Herman Miller Research Group (Beckmann 2000) with 18- to 21-year-olds collected information about young adults' impressions of the contemporary work environment. If we use privacy needs as a filter, the following issues are relevant. Their perception is that

- *Lack of personalization opportunities communicate corporate control.*
- *Cubicles represent a lack of individuality and lack of empowerment.*
- *Small spaces communicate lack of respect or employees not being valued.*
- *Private offices communicate status.*

Specific comments about open office planning reveal that to this generation, cubicles reflect low status. The Knoll & Ellis (2001) study affirms this finding, using some of the young adults' descriptive words: ". . . the cubicle is the symbol of everything 'old economy' in workplace design, evoking images of 'prison,' conformity, being a number or stamped with a barcode."

The cubicles are also unappealingly repetitive to them. When asked to draw their ideal office, most of the participants drew a spacious private office with amenities such as comfortable seating, a television, aquarium, and a mini-kitchen. The offices were homey in feeling featuring personalization, plants, and fun elements such as putting greens. Only time will tell if this group attains their dream offices. (See **Figure 8.6**).

Young adults today embody some of the values and status needs of the older generation, but their privacy needs are age-specific and linked to the influence of technology. In spite of their expressed preferences for private offices, they often work in open environments with little structure and few rules. Like any other age group, they can become overwhelmed. They need to regulate interaction with others. They need the restoration of privacy.

We also need to design responsive environments for them because they have a 24/7 mentality about work, and wherever they work needs to be flexible. We may find ourselves specifying day beds in the office for them and their dogs, and that is only if they have made an empowered choice to come to the office rather than to work

in another location. Or they may push the concept of alternative working experiences to heights we cannot imagine at this time. The future is theirs. Next, we turn to their parents.

THE BABY BOOMERS AND PRIVACY

The term *Baby Boomers* represents the generation born after the end of World War II in 1946 through 1964 (Dychtwald 1999, Beckmann 2000). This age group is the largest population group in the United States at the present time, numbering over 80 million people (Coile 2002).

Television and this generation grew up together. Many began watching television at the age of two; between 1948 and 1952, the number of television sets in U.S. households climbed from several thousand to 15 million. As children, baby boomers experienced other lives and places vicariously through television. From the beginning, the strengths and the weaknesses of this generation have been in their numbers. They are the generation who reinvented the workplace because they produced such a large class of skilled, professional workers. They have lived through tremendous upheavals in U.S. society, and today there are new roles to play for both men and women (Dychtwald 1999). It is not a life, however, without its trials and challenges to privacy.

Age-Specific Privacy Needs for Baby Boomers

Today, people of this generation often find themselves "sandwiched" between children still living at home and the care of their aging parents. This age group is stressed by successful but often demanding careers, the obligations to their adolescent children, and the responsibilities of caring for their parents. A recent ASID report (2001) estimates that relatives provide 70 to 80 percent of caregiving for older adults. The same report found that more than one-fourth of

Figure 8.6 A young adult's vision of the ideal office.

this age group expects to have a parent living with them in the future. Typical complaints of this generation include the feeling of being pushed and pulled by conflicting responsibilities with little time for themselves. Their lives require a lot of juggling, and they report high levels of stress (Dychtwald 1999).

Age-Specific Needs for Others in the Home

Interior design to provide privacy for this age group is also a juggling act because other age groups are involved. However, at this stage of life, parents and adolescents have a common goal: each group desires privacy from the other group. While the family still comes together for many events, both parents and teenagers need away places. The parents need quiet places to unwind, such as away rooms discussed in Chapter 4, to be alone or to enjoy intimacy with another person. The adolescents, as mentioned earlier in this chapter, need experiences of

privacy because while their own growth and development sometimes require solitude and contemplation, they also have very strong needs for intimacy with friends. Ideally, adolescents should have areas that are exclusively theirs, either permanently or temporarily. In the home, these are the years when residential space planning can include privacy areas for parents and adolescents remotely located from each other. Perhaps master bedrooms that are usually designated to parents are on other floors in the house.

This generation typically provides the care for their aging parents, and privacy needs are important for both age groups. Separate living quarters, if feasible, for older adults within the homes of their adult children can meet privacy needs, but not all homes or budgets will allow for this. In addition, the physical and psychological strain of caring for frail parents on a daily and time-consuming basis creates additional stress for overworked caregivers and provides little time for meeting other needs. Adult day-care centers can serve two functions: they get the older people out of the houses to interact with their age groups, and they indirectly provide respite for other family members. (See **Figure 8.7**). Next, we move to age-specific privacy needs for the next generation—people who have completed their work years in a specific occupation and have retired.

OLDER RETIRED ADULTS AND PRIVACY NEEDS

Retirement from employment in the past often meant a few years between work life and the beginning of ill health or death. Beginning in the last century, however, "advances in sanitation, public health, food science, pharmacy, surgery, medicine, and more recently wellness-oriented lifestyles" (Dychtwald 1999, p. 2) make it more certain that most of us will live for many years after retirement. Today, many of us are retiring at different times in life. The customary retirement age of 65 has shifted, both up and down, but many people are electing to finish a first career, retire, and move on to other pursuits.

These are the years that may sometimes have great potential for accomplishment as well as self-actualization. The relative affluence of a number of today's seniors makes them a dynamic group, interested in retaining control of their own lives within the privacy of their own homes. They have been dubbed the "wired retired" because they are the fastest growing group of Internet users today. Many of them acquired computer skills during the last part of their working years. They use computers, often handed down from their children or grandchildren, to interact with the family, to get healthcare news (Coile 2002), and to learn more about the world. The interactive use of computers allows seniors to stay connected with others, both younger people and friends their own age.

Figure 8.7 Social area in an adult daycare center provides recreation for seniors and respite for home caregivers. Courtesy of Allegheny Lutheran Social Ministries.

These connections provide the needed communicative and socializing experiences that studies (Kweon, Sullivan, & Wiley 1998) indicate can maintain well-being in seniors and older adults. For the seniors, too, the bonus is that all of this can happen without leaving home.

Aging in Place—Staying in the Home

Surveys in recent years (ASID 2001, American Association of Retired Persons [AARP] 1993) reveal that 71–83 percent of senior citizens want to age in place. **Aging in place** refers to remaining in one place lifelong, typically the home, but sometimes relocating to a type of continuous care facility that provides for the residents' changing needs as they age. Most seniors have a strong sense of place attachment to their homes and want to remain in their current residences as long as possible. If they need help caring for themselves, they want to receive that help in their own homes.

Remaining in the home for this age group as opposed to living in an assisted care facility is the ultimate age-specific privacy experience. Their emotional well-being is enhanced in familiar surroundings with the continuity of social relationships and long-established routines. Staying in the home represents having choice and control and avoiding what seniors often perceive as the loss of personal autonomy living in any type of facility with administrative controls (Golant 1999). This has implications for interior design privacy because of this group's strongly stated preferences to age in place. Interior design application will therefore have a strong residential orientation, whether it is in the seniors' homes, in the homes of their children, or in residential care facilities.

Age-Specific Privacy Needs in Residential Settings

Over a lifetime, senior citizens have experienced changes in their family structure. The large home that worked so well for raising a family is often too large and can feel a bit hollow for a couple. However, they usually want to stay, and they speak of making their homes more luxurious. A major research study conducted by ASID and others (2001) revealed that two in five older people want their homes to be more luxurious. It appears that at least part of the time, they are actually requesting amenities that enhance privacy experiences. For example, designers participating in this study made specific recommendations for this age group, and one was to "design bathrooms that are fun to lounge in, bathe in, and steam in" (p. 8). Other expressed preferences of the seniors were "an exercise room near the master bedroom" (p. 8) as well as guest suites with bedrooms and private baths.

A considerable body of research (Kweon, et al. 1998, citing others) indicates that seniors with strong social ties have better physical health and significantly higher levels of psychological well-being. Seniors living in inner cities often have lower levels of social interaction. If they live in high-rise environments in noisy, dilapidated conditions, research studies have shown that this generation often withdraws from nearby residents and fails to establish or maintain social ties. Providing secondary territories as we defined them in Chapter 2 such as halls, vestibules, and lounge areas allows transient access by all and encourages interaction and casual social relationships (Kweon, et al. 1998).

Many seniors in good health remain in their homes for a number of years. Often they have new-found freedom to organize their lives in a way that works for them, and they are able to experience privacy as well as socialization with others (Leibrock 2000, ASID 2001). Some seniors are not so fortunate if health issues arise, and independence and autonomy are no longer possible. Sometimes, even with family and other's help, older persons must seek out some level of assistance outside their own homes. Often that search leads them to a residential care facility.

Privacy Options in Assisted Living Facilities

Assisted living is a type of residential care home. The general interpretation of assisted living is a philosophy "that emphasizes some form of resident independence, autonomy, and privacy, and that endorses aging in place for the seniors in the facility" (Mitchell & Kemp 2000, citing AARP and the Assisted Living Facilities Association of America).

Assisted living facilities can often offer residents privacy options such as self-contained private apartments with kitchenette, bath, living, and sleeping area. Living with their own things and somewhat on their own can bolster older adults' feelings of territoriality as well as evoke memories and associations of being at home.

!APPLICATION!

PRIVACY IN ASSISTED LIVING

• The individual unit should be private, have a kitchenette, and be large enough to handle a family member for an overnight stay.

• The individual unit should have an accessible full bathroom.

• The individual unit should present as a complete housing unit rather than a hospital room.

Victor Regnier 1999

Design features such as lockable doors, individually controlled lighting, programmable thermostats, and their own personalization efforts enhance feelings of control and choices (Schwarz & Brent 1999).

Communicative Privacy Needs of Older Adults

We are social beings, and we need socializing experiences at all stages of life. As people age, their worlds can shrink with the deaths of people around them. Isolation is often an age-specific negative expression of privacy for older adults, and this is one disadvantage of remaining in their own homes. Assisted living facilities can offer the older person a variety of socialization experiences. Often the facility places a cluster of apartments in a single building with common areas of a parlor, community and craft room, and dining room. The closeness of the apartments encourages interaction and casual friendships. As we saw in Chapter 6, however, distances to social spaces become increasingly important for the elderly, and if the distance is perceived as "too far," residents will stay in their rooms (Pinet 1999). In addition, research (Mitchell & Kemp 2000) has shown that residents of care facilities place a higher priority on intimacy such as visits from family members, and the facility needs to provide rooms that allow for socialization with family or other residents. (See **Figure 8.8**).

LINK
To learn more about the recommended travel distances from area to area in residential care facilities to encourage social interaction, see Chapter 6, page 142.

THE SUNSET YEARS AND PRIVACY NEEDS

At the present time, 75 percent of the elderly population with disabilities receives caregiving exclusively from family members in the parent's or the adult children's home. Only 5 percent of the elderly are in nursing homes. Between now and the year 2004, however, Ken Dychtwald in *Age Power* (1999) feels that the number of people aged 80 and older will increase greatly, and many of them will require care on a daily basis.

Few of us can maintain our independence for a lifetime. Inevitably, for many of us, we must yield part of the autonomy and control that we have had for so long in exchange for the protection and safety by caregivers usually younger than ourselves. Some of us will move in a

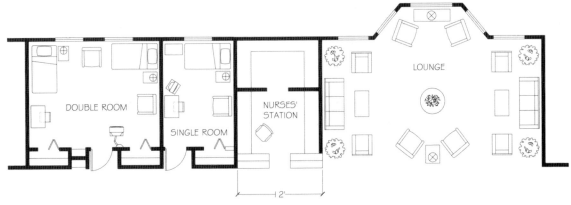

Figure 8.8 Assisted living—opportunities for socializing and receiving visitors.

continuum (aging in place) through the phases of assisted care. Others of us will relinquish our autonomy abruptly with the onset of acute illness or trauma. Whatever the pattern, moving into a care facility is a major life change. In nursing homes privacy options are limited because of the patients' health status but not impossible.

Privacy and Related Needs in Nursing Homes

For most frail elderly, moving from the home into an institutional facility such as a nursing home is an enormous life event. As Schwarz & Brent (1999) comment: "Life in a group setting introduces people to a heterogeneous, complex sociocultural system in a proximity that is very different from the places in which most residents lived before their institutionalization" (p. xvi). Older persons feel the lack of control almost immediately, particularly if they are placed in a facility against their wishes. Even if they are agreeable to living in an institutional setting, they are likely to experience feelings of separation from their former social network and a disconnection from their past. As Abeles (1991) observes: ". . . those with little sense of control may be more likely than others to adopt the 'sick role,' to prematurely withdraw from various daily activities, and to exhibit 'excess' disability" (p. 297).

One of the best ways to return a sense of control to the residents of any institutional setting is to allow them to make choices, depending upon the type of facility. Skilled care facilities, like elderly daycare centers, are organized and run according to the greatest number of common needs. There are, however, a number of choices that even older persons who are diminished mentally can make for themselves. These include choosing a roommate, selecting food preferences from a menu, deciding the time for meal hours, using laundry facilities, going outdoors, choosing hobbies and activities, having visiting and phone privileges, and sometimes even having a pet (Mitchell & Kemp 2000, Schwarz & Brent 1999). While these choices might appear insignificant to many of us, for an older adult encountering severe restrictions each day, these are opportunities for choice and control that can become life-enhancing options. (See **Figure 8.9**).

A research study (Michell & Kemp 2000) measured the perception of quality of life among residents with an average age of 81, some with cognitive skills intact and some with mental impairment. The study found that residents who participated in social activities had enhanced perceptions of quality of life, facility satisfaction, and showed extremely low levels of depression.

Figure 8.9 Zoning for territorial privacy in a shared nursing home bedroom.

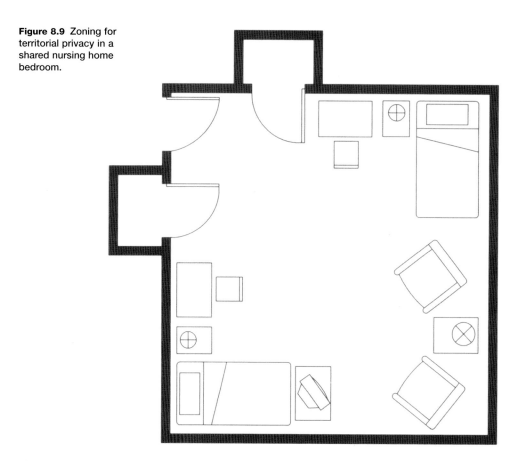

Loss of Privacy in Primary Territories

Perhaps the greatest loss to privacy in nursing homes is when residents must share their only primary territory—their bedrooms—with a roommate or with several others. In spite of the socializing aspects of rooming together, it seldom provides a positive privacy experience except in cases of close stable friendships or with married couples. A resident's last bastion of control in a care facility is the private bedroom. When residents must share rooms, they feel less at home in the room and have reduced opportunities for individual personalization.

They leave the room more often, possibly to give the roommate privacy, and exhibit "itinerant" behavior by roaming, going to the main lounge, to the nurse's station, and to the lobby. While roaming behavior is not necessarily a negative thing because it keeps the activity level of the residents high, and they are encouraged

to get out of their rooms and interact with others, nevertheless it may also reflect the lack of desired privacy opportunities. Studies consistently found that residents who share bedrooms go to other places for their privacy such as to the dining hall during off hours (Pinet 1999). They often demonstrate more agitation and irritability, sleep less, and require more medication. For persons with dementia, nonprivate rooms provide too much stimulation and a heightened arousal level (Morgan & Stewart 1998).

The Return of Privacy to Primary Territories

Morgan and Stewart (1998) conducted a study of persons with progressive dementia who were moved from semi-private rooms to individual private rooms in a special care unit (of the same nursing home). In the old unit, residents were frequently overwhelmed by noise and unavoidable social interaction. They clashed frequently with their roommates, had fairly severe sleep problems, and spent much of their time outside of their rooms roaming and displaying itinerant behavior.

Staff personnel and family members observed a number of lasting changes in behavior over the next year. Immediately after the move, time spent in the private rooms tripled from time formerly spent in shared rooms and stayed constant at each evaluation period. As their choices to have privacy and exercise territorial behavior increased, there was less itinerant behavior and less conflict between the residents, and the staff reported better sleep patterns with less medication administered at night.

Private Places for Alzheimer's Patients

At work, we take breaks; at camp, kids take naps; at home, we hide behind the newspaper or sit in front of the TV to shut others out. The difference is that those with dementia have lost that part of the brain that helps them control their impulses. If they get upset, they express it, while those who are more 'normal' have learned to keep it to themselves. Both situations are helped by having a place to go by oneself to cool down. Thus, private places contribute to residents' individual dignity and personhood.

Zeisel 1999, p. 122

If we look at people with dementia and their privacy needs in a cursory manner, we might assume that these people are not able to appreciate or to experience privacy because they are impaired. Morgan and Stewart's study, however, confirms that even persons with dementia need to be alone sometimes, and private places that residents can retreat to such as their bedrooms, a corner of a living room, or a garden can provide privacy. Experiences in private places can lower the arousal levels associated with some types of dementia and provide

respite. When family members visit, these areas have more of a home-like feeling and may conjure up memories of happier times in the past.

We end this chapter with a brief case study that illustrates the potential opportunities that we may have at any age and even with impaired health to exercise the timeless and universal need for privacy and interaction with others.

Case Study: Woodside Place

People who plan and design assisted care facilities have realized in recent years the importance of preserving the residential atmosphere because people, at any age, need to feel that they are at "home." Innovative projects such as Woodside Place, a facility in Pennsylvania for patients with Alzheimer's disease, have expanded upon the residential concept, allowing residents to choose when to eat, bathe, and go outdoors. The facility includes three houses, each with 12 residents. Each house has private rooms with half baths, living/dining rooms, kitchen, and communal shower rooms. The three houses are connected to a common core containing space for administration, a great room with sitting areas, craft room, music room, and television room (Hoglund & Ledewitz 1999). (See **Figure 8.10**).

From the beginning, the designers and planners of Woodside Place set communication and socialization as priority needs for the residents' experience. In spite of the residents' dementia, the researchers theorized that because memories of home are deeply rooted and archetypal, the residential orientation within a community structure would succeed. The Woodside research and subsequent occupation proved that sense of community is quite possible, even with dementia. At Woodside, residents socialize among the houses, using the common areas as a sort of town square or front porch. They display normal sociable patterns for this age group such as territoriality, repetitive

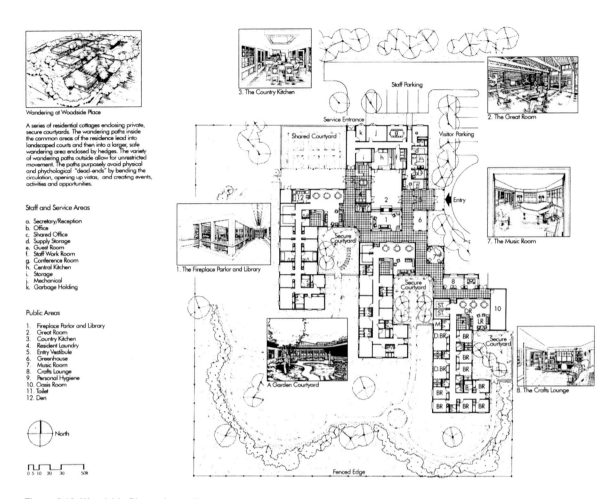

Wandering at Woodside Place

A series of residential cottages enclosing private, secure courtyards. The wandering paths inside the common areas of the residence lead into landscaped courts and then into a larger, safe wandering area enclosed by hedges. The variety of wandering paths outside allow for unrestricted movement. The paths purposely avoid physical and phychological "dead-ends" by bending the circulation, opening up vistas, and creating events, activities and opportunities.

Staff and Service Areas

a. Secretary/Reception
b. Office
c. Shared Office
d. Supply Storage
e. Guest Room
f. Staff Work Room
g. Conference Room
h. Central Kitchen
i. Storage
j. Mechanical
k. Garbage Holding

Public Areas

1. Fireplace Parlor and Library
2. Great Room
3. Country Kitchen
4. Resident Laundry
5. Entry Vestibule
6. Greenhouse
7. Music Room
8. Crafts Lounge
9. Personal Hygiene
10. Oasis Room
11. Toilet
12. Den

North

0 5 10   20   30   50ft

Figure 8.10 Woodside Place—Innovations in the design of Alzheimer facilities. © Perkins Eastman.

walking patterns, displays of homemaking skills, and hospitality efforts. The significance of this behavior for privacy and related needs is that, as Hoglund and Ledewitz comment, "these patterns imply a recognition of the public and private realms among some residents. While not all residents acknowledge it, the hierarchy of public and private spaces (sequencing) within the building appears to reinforce appropriate behaviors" (pp. 233–234). The residents spend less than 10 percent of their time in their bedrooms and spend a great deal of time in the public areas with other residents. Because of good staff planning of activities, the residents at Woodside Place spend three times as much time socializing as non-Alzheimer's residents of the main nursing home located on the same campus. This is a remarkable achievement for persons with Alzheimer's disease.

The staff at Woodside has found that gardens also can meet a number of needs for institutionalized elderly because of the healing qualities of nature and the outdoors. Healing garden activities are often part of deeply rooted archetypal memories, and the contact with nature can sometimes be a stabilizing force for persons with dementia (Zeisel 1999).

The innovations at Woodside Place have revealed that even among Alzheimer's patients, there are opportunities to enhance the quality of life and provide socializing as well as restorative experiences. The message for us is that we need to design intelligently for all age groups, no matter how severe their limitations, because they will be affected every day by the design decisions that we make.

FINAL THOUGHTS ON AGE-SPECIFIC PRIVACY

We have maintained throughout this book that experiencing privacy has important benefits for us at any age, such as enhanced feelings of well-being and the development of self-identity. We have learned also that the ability to achieve privacy and experience its benefits depends upon two interrelated concepts of privacy: choice and control. Some of the other benefits include personal autonomy, contemplation, rejuvenation, restoration, and creativity.

The universal need for privacy does not disappear at any age throughout life, but opportunities for specific privacy experiences may vary with the age group. Looking at life as a continuum, we can see that not all of the benefits of privacy can be experienced equally at different stages of life. For example, early childhood and old age are somewhat similar in their limited abilities to exercise choice and control. The busy middle stages of life permit more expressions of choice and control, but sometimes there may be fewer opportunities for solitude and contemplation. The privacy experiences of adolescents provide for degrees of choice and control, but because adolescents sometimes have more free time than adults, they may be able to enjoy richer experiences of solitude as well as intimacy with friends. There are trade-offs with every age. The one constant is that we all need privacy, and as with life, it has many facets.

KEY CONCEPTS

1. Privacy needs are timeless, but the types of privacy needs and experiences change throughout life.

2. Both adults and children need privacy, but the expressions of the privacy needs are different.

3. Crowding is a negative experience of privacy that affects both adults and children. In crowding, adults tend to withdraw and children often hide.

4. The privacy needs of young adults are linked to technological innovations and changes in lifestyles. Their attitudes and preferences are different from their parents'. They also have different expectations from work environments.

5. Older adults want to age in place, which usually means remaining in their homes. If this is not possible they will relocate to some type of assisted living facility. In this setting, except for extreme dementia, they still have privacy needs. They also have needs for socialization and communication.

6. There are age-specific trade-offs with privacy experiences. Not all types of privacy are achievable at all stages of life. The one constant is that we all need privacy.

ASSIGNMENT
OBSERVATIONAL STUDY: HIGH LOAD/LOW LOAD ENVIRONMENTS

Learning Objectives:
- To observe and analyze the similarities and age-specific differences in the ways people express their privacy needs in their primary territories
- To identify the physical characteristics of a space that can support or deny privacy

- To use designing for privacy information to formulate suggestions for improved privacy in primary territories

Learning Outcomes:
- Enhanced understanding about the relationship between human behavior and the built environment
- Development of critical and analytical thinking and skills
- Increased understanding of the similarities and differences of human privacy needs
- Development of skills in problem identification and problem solving
- Increased understanding and appreciation of alternate points of view

Description:
Choose two spaces that serve as primary territories, one belonging to you and the other belonging to someone in a very different age group from yours. These primary territories should serve similar functions. For example, one could be your private room at home, in an apartment, or the dorm, and the other could be the private room of an older individual in a nursing home.

Observation:
A. Observe the ways that privacy can be accommodated in each space.
- Physical characteristics, including architectural and interior elements that support privacy by providing choice and control
- Physical characteristics that provide visual privacy
- Physical characteristics that support acoustical privacy

B. Observe the ways that each space reflects the owner's desires for privacy.

- Territorial markers, including personalization
- Furniture arrangement, including sociofugal/sociopetal

Analysis:
Analyze these observations based upon what you have learned about age specific privacy needs from this chapter. Your analysis should answer the following questions:

1. Does each space provide adequate choice and control for the owner's desired levels of interaction with others?
2. What are the similarities in how each space provides for privacy?
3. What are the age-specific differences in how each space provides for privacy?
4. What suggestions would you make to enhance the experience of privacy in each space?

Solution:
Provide a written analysis and explanation of your suggestions.

REFERENCES
Abeles, R. (1991). "Sense of control, quality of life, and frail older people." In J. Birren, J. Lubben, J. Rowe, & D. Deutchman (Eds.), *The Concept and Measurement of Quality of Life in the Frail Elderly*. San Diego: Academic Press.

ASID. (2001). *Aging in place: Aging and the impact of interior design*. Washington, DC.

Baum, A.; Davis, G. E.; & Valins, S. (1979). "Crowding." In I. Altman & D. Stokols (Eds.), *Handbook of Environmental Psychology*, (533–570). New York: Wiley-Interscience.

Baum, A. & Davis, G. (1980). "Reducing the stress of high-density living: An architectural intervention." *Journal of Personality and Social Psychology*, 38, 471–481.

Beckmann, W. (2000). "Bigger than the baby boomer cohort: A new and different office worker geek." Zeeland MI: Herman Miller Research, Design and Development.

Boschetti, Margaret A. (1987). "Memories of childhood homes: Some contributions of environmental autobiography to interior design education and research." *Journal of Interior Design Education and Research*, 13(2), 27–36.

Boyden, S. (1971). "Biological determinants of optimum health." In D. J. M. Vorster (Ed.), *The Human Biology of Environmental Change*. Proceedings of a conference held in Blantyre Malawi, April 5–12, 1971. London: International Biology Program.

Coile, R. C. Jr. (2002). "Healthcare's new consumers." *Interiors & Sources*, (101–104).

Dytchwald, K. (1999). *Age power*. New York: Putnam.

Evans, G. W.; Lepore, S. J.; & Schroeder, A. (1996). "The role of interior design elements in human responses to crowding." *Journal of Personality and Social Psychology*, 70, 1, 41–46.

Evans, G. W.; Maxwell, L. E.; & Hart, B. (1999). "Parental language and verbal responsiveness to children in crowded homes." *Developmental Psychology*, 35, 4, 1020–1023.

Evans, G. W.; Rhee, E.; Forbes, C.; Allen, K. M.; & Lepore, S. J. (2000). "The meaning and efficacy of social withdrawal as a strategy for coping with chronic residential crowding." *Journal of Environmental Psychology*, 20, 335–342.

Golant, S. M. (1999). "The promise of assisted living as a shelter and care alternative for frail American elders." In B. Schwarz & R. Brent (Eds.), *Aging, Autonomy and Architecture*, (32–59). Baltimore: The Johns Hopkins University Press.

Harris, P. B.; Brown, B. B.; & Werner, C. M. (1996). "Privacy regulation and place attachment: Predicting attachments to a student family housing facility." *Journal of Environmental Psychology*, 16, 287–301.

Hoglund, J. D. & Ledewitz, S. D. (1999). "Designing to meet the needs of people with Alzheimer's disease." In B. Schwarz & R. Brent, (Eds.), *Aging, Autonomy and Architecture*, (229–261). Baltimore: Johns Hopkins University Press.

Hutton, A. (2002). "The private adolescent: Privacy needs of adolescents in hospitals." *Journal of Pediatric Nursing*, 17, 1, 67–72.

Kaya, N. & Erkip, F. (2001). "Satisfaction in a dormitory building: The effects of floor height on the perception of room size and crowding." *Environment and Behavior*, 33, 1, 35–53.

Klopfer, P. H. & Rubenstein, D. I. (1977). "The concept of privacy and its biological basis." *Journal of Social Issues*, 33, 52–65.

Knoll, Inc. & Ellis, C. B. R. Inc. (2001). "The new workplace: Attitudes and expectations of a new generation at work." East Greenville, PA: DYG, Inc.

Kweon, B. S.; Sullivan, W. C.; & Wiley, A. R. (1998). "Green common spaces and the social integration of inner-city older adults." *Environment and Behavior*, 30, 6, 832–858.

Leibrock, C. (2000). *Design details for health*. New York: John Wiley & Sons, Inc.

Maxwell, L. E. (1996). "Multiple effects of home and day care crowding." *Environment and Behavior*, 28, 4, 494–511.

Mitchell, J. M & Kemp, B. J. (2000). "Quality of life in assisted living homes: A multidimensional analysis." *Journal of Gerontology: Psychological Sciences*, 55B, 2, 117–127.

Moore, G.; Lane, C.; Hill, A.; Cohen, U.; & McGinty, T. (1990). *Recommendations for Child-Care Centers*. Milwaukee, WI: University of Wisconsin-Milwaukee Press.

Morgan, D. G. & Stewart, N. J. (1998). "Multiple occupancy versus private rooms on dementia care units." *Environment and Behavior*, 30, 4, 487–503.

Newell, P. B. (1998). "A cross-cultural comparison of privacy definitions and functions: A systems approach." *Journal of Environmental Psychology*, 18, 357–371.

Pinet, C. (1999). "Distance and the use of social space by nursing home residents." *Journal of Interior Design*, 25, 1, 1–15.

Regnier, V. (1999). "The definition and evolution of assisted living within a changing system of long-term care." In B. Schwarz & R. Brent (Eds.), *Aging, Autonomy and Architecture*, (3–20). Baltimore: The Johns Hopkins University Press.

Ruopp, R.; Travers, J.; Glantz, F.; & Coelen, C. (1979). *Final report of the national day care study: Children at the center*. Cambridge, MA: Abt.

Rushkoff, D. (1999). *Playing the future: What we can learn from digital kids*. New York: Riverhead Books.

Saegert, S. (1984). "Environment and children's mental health: residential density and low-income children." In A. Baum & J. E. Singer (Eds.), *Handbook of Psychology and Health*, 2, 247–271. Hillsdale, NJ: Erlbaum.

Schwarz, B. & Brent, R., (Eds.) (1999). *Aging, autonomy, and architecture*. Baltimore: The Johns Hopkins University Press.

Smith, P. K. & Connolly, K. J. (1980). *The ecology of preschool behavior*. Cambridge, MA: Cambridge University Press.

Sweaney, A. L. (1986). The perceptions of preschool children and their families' social climate in relation to household crowding. *Children's Environments Quarterly*, 3, 10–15.

Tapscott, D. (1998). *Blueprint to the digital economy*. New York: McGraw-Hill.

Trancik, A. M. & Evans, G. W. (1995). "Spaces fit for children: Competency in the design of daycare environments." *Children's Environments*, 12, 3, 311–319.

Weiker, J. (2000). Tech it easy, toys on tap help dot-coms recruit the 20-something. *Denver Post*, (pp. I-E, 8-E).

Westin, A. F. (1967). *Privacy and freedom*. New York: Atheneum.

Zeisel, J. (1999). "Life-quality Alzheimer care in assisted living." In B. Schwarz & R. Brent (Eds.), *Aging, Autonomy and Architecture*, (110–129). Baltimore: Johns Hopkins University Press.

Future archeologists, anthropologists, and historians will view the product of the labors of interior designers as clues to our society's political, social, economic, and ideological values. We should provide no less. In so doing—in creating the stuff of which history is made— we must not limit our role to that of passive recorders but recognize ourselves as active framers of that history. It is through critical thinking and the development of theory that we become participants in the shaping of the values manifested in the built environment.

MARCIA LEHMAN-KESSLER

CHAPTER 9

A Model for Designing for Privacy

Throughout this book we have discussed the ways that privacy theories may be translated into application. As all interior design students and professionals know, we arrive at our design solutions through a process that begins with programming, proceeds through conceptual design and design development to design implementation, and

finally to the completed design. Each step in the process has many considerations and operations that must be included if the design solutions are to be successful.

The Model for Designing for Privacy (see **Figure 9.1**) illustrates how privacy considerations can be integrated into each step and operation of the design process from programming to implementation. The three major phases of the design process are covered by this model: The Intelligence/Programming Phase, the Concept and Design Development Phase, and the Implementation Phase. This model is based upon the premise that humans have a universal need for privacy that must be considered in the design of all types of built environments. The three designing for privacy variables discussed in chapters 1 to 3—individual needs, environmental opportunities, and the interactions between the two—are integrated into this model.

The Designing for Privacy model also illustrates that all decisions should be informed by evidence-based design theories. **Evidence-based design** is the practice of grounding design solutions and decisions in a researched and documented knowledge base that includes the analysis and interpretation of research. This process provides information that helps designers predict, understand, and explain how our designs may affect the quality of human life.

THE INTELLIGENCE/ PROGRAMMING PHASE

The initial programming process begins with the Intelligence Phase in which we establish goals, gather and analyze facts, and determine needs. The model illustrates how these steps are accomplished using the theories and research-based information discussed in

226

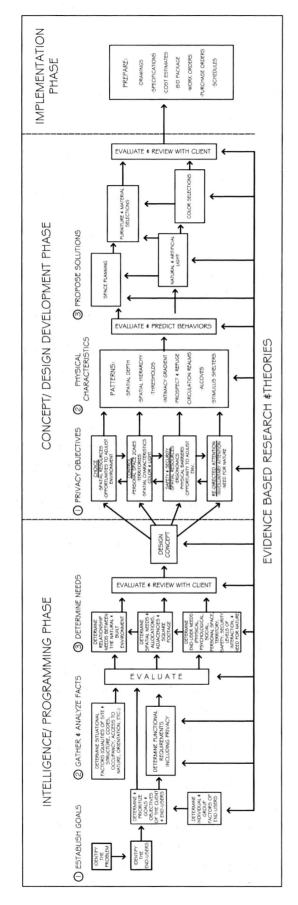

Figure 9.1 Evidence-based information informs each phase of the design process. Privacy considerations are made and evaluated often during each phase.

chapters 1 through 3. In the first step of this phase, using evidence-based research and theories, we establish goals by identifying the problem and the end users. Then we determine the individual and group factors of the end users that affect privacy needs. This information helps us to determine and prioritize the privacy goals and objectives of the end users and the client.

In the second step of the Intelligence Phase, we use the information gathered in the first step to determine the functional requirements—including the necessary types of privacy—to meet these goals and objectives. This includes determining the situational and regulatory factors, such as the physical qualities of the site and the structure, the applicable codes and standards, occupancy, and assessment of opportunities and limitations for privacy associated with the site and structure. The data collected from the first two steps of the Intelligence Phase yield information about the probable density levels and environmental load of the space. The first two steps of the Intelligence Phase are then analyzed and evaluated according to the applicable evidence-based research and theories for accuracy.

The third and final step of the Intelligence Phase is determining needs. Based upon the information analyzed and evaluated in the previous two steps, we are able to determine the end users' physical and psychological needs for the space, including needs for privacy, interaction, personal space, territoriality, safety and security, and positive distractions. This, in turn, leads us to determine and define spatial needs such as square footage, adjacencies, and space allocations. This last step in the Intelligence Phase is then analyzed again and evaluated according to the applicable research-based evidence and theories. The completion of the Intelligence Phase yields a program and design concept that informs the next phase of the Model, the Concept and Design Development Phase.

THE CONCEPT AND DESIGN DEVELOPMENT PHASE

The Concept and Design Development Phase of the model begins by identifying the physical characteristics that provide for the four major privacy objectives discussed throughout the book: choice, control, safety and security, and redirected attention. During this step we identify patterns (such as those developed by Christopher Alexander and his colleagues) described in Chapter 3 and in the four application chapters (chapters 4 through 7) together with the physical characteristics of those patterns that can be used to achieve the privacy objectives. After evaluation according to the applicable evidence-based research and theories and review by the client, this conceptual design informs the next step in this phase: proposed solutions.

Using the identified patterns and applicable evidence-based research and theories, solutions are formulated through space planning, lighting, color, and furniture and materials choices. Once again, these solutions are then analyzed and evaluated according to the applicable evidence-based research and theories and reviewed with the client.

THE DESIGN IMPLEMENTATION PHASE

The final phase of this model is the Design Implementation Phase, which includes the preparation of drawings, specifications, cost estimates and bids, as well as a schedule for construction and installation. Work orders and purchase orders are also issued during this phase. The model provides for evaluation of the details of the design in this phase to ensure that the drawings and decisions have not deviated from the concept. The Model for Designing for Privacy can be adapted to include and/or emphasize additional specific design goals by adding these goals to the first step in the Intelligence Phase and evaluating each subsequent step using applicable evidence-based research and theories.

THE ONGOING PROCESS OF EVALUATION

Figure 9.1 illustrates that there should be an ongoing process to evaluate how information from evidence-based design has been applied throughout the entire design process and in the completed design. **Evaluation** is a tool that informs us and supports evidence-based decision making in all phases of the project. There is often a misconception among designers that evaluation occurs only after a project is completed. Evaluation should, however, be an ongoing and integral part of the project from its conception to completion. We must integrate planning for evaluation into the design development, design documentation, and design implementation phases. This enables us to check to see how our decisions are informing and affecting the design process, and ultimately, the finished design.

For example, let's say that you are designing a surgery waiting room in a healthcare facility. One of the project goals is to reduce stress levels for the families of surgery patients. Evidence-based research involving the design of healing environments falls into five categories as described previously in this text: environmental stressors, control, social support, positive distractions, and access to nature. Using the evidence-based research and interpretations from this textbook you have become aware that privacy helps to relieve stress and that by defining certain characteristics of environments to provide privacy, you are able to include stress-reducing considerations in the intelligence/design programming phase of the project. Your design program now includes tested information that defines how to provide control, social support, positive distractions, and access to nature in the design. When applied to the design development phase of the project, this researched and documented information drives the design development by providing research-based solutions that meet project goals. Specific spatial configurations and adjacencies, relationships of natural to built elements, furniture choices and placement, light levels, color, and material choices can all be evaluated according to the research.

FINAL THOUGHTS ON PRIVACY FROM THE AUTHORS

The designing for privacy information discussed in this book is a synthesis of research, theories, and concepts from many disciplines, sciences, and philosophies. The suggestions for application of this information are the result of applying the creative, technical, and practical components of interior design to that synthesis. This process can enhance the value of our interior design solutions.

As with all design disciplines, the value of interior design is measured by its contributions to society. These contributions include providing healthy, safe, comfortable settings that function efficiently and that provide aesthetically pleasing experiences. These contributions are generally understood and recognized within the design disciplines and by the public. However, our contributions to society extend far beyond these traditional values to include a broad range of quality of life issues, including the need for privacy to promote physical and psychological health and to foster positive interactions and communication discussed in this book. As we develop an understanding for the need for privacy, we also gain insights into other important related needs. As a result, our ability to enhance the quality of life of those for whom we design grows, and we become valued for that ability.

When viewed as an essential component in the process of achieving quality of life, the universal need for privacy becomes an important interior design issue. Although there is no prototypical "private place," no design that meets all privacy needs, and no specific set of rules to follow in designing for privacy, interior designers can use the information presented in this book to create a framework within which to study and design for privacy. This framework allows us to conceptualize the built environment as a source for coping with the stress and crowding inevitable in our modern, rapidly changing world by providing for our diverse, multifaceted needs for privacy. It includes a deep understanding of the concept of privacy, its physical and psychological functions, our needs and goals for privacy, the mechanisms that we use to achieve desired levels of privacy, and the physical characteristics of environments that can contribute to privacy.

Interior design has the potential to profoundly shape our perceptions and our experiences in physical settings. Interiors are our most intimate experience of the built environment. As architectural and interior design historian Stanley Abercrombie (1990) explains, "Interiors surround us. We do not merely pass them on the street; we inhabit them. When we enter a building, we cease being merely its observer; we become its content" (p. 3). This intimate relationship between interior environments and human beings suggests that the discipline of interior design is a bridge between people and their physical environments.

In the past the concept of privacy was not always considered part of the scope of interior design services. Historically, interior design solutions began from an aesthetic basis. Later, functional and technical solutions became recognized as important contributors to interior design. In recent years, interior designers as well as people in related disciplines have begun to realize the importance of designing from a

basis of human needs. This approach, along with other factors of contemporary life, has increased the scope of interior design services over the last few decades, and today designers participate in design projects in ways that the previous generation could not have envisioned. Interior designers are undertaking new research, making new discoveries, and broadening the parameters of interior design services. All of us have witnessed technological explosions during our own lifetimes. Healthcare is delivered in new and innovative ways. Travel, once the luxury of a leisure class, is now part of daily life for many of us. Lines have softened between the workplace and the home and other remote locations. Our projects will have to reflect that fluidity of contemporary human life. Additionally, the consequences of a diminishing natural world and the inability for many of us to directly and regularly experience the restorative qualities of nature are not yet fully understood.

All of these experiences create needs for different types and levels of privacy. People need opportunities to control the physical and the built environment. This includes some degree of enclosure for privacy, personalization of individual spaces for territorial needs, and the ability to regulate social interactions by moving between places or manipulating personal space. Cyberspace has liberated us from the need to be together at the same time and in the same place, but as social beings we may be inextricably linked to places where we interact with others and where we retreat for privacy

We yearn for a connection to nature to sustain us in an increasingly technological and sometimes sterile environment. We need interesting visual and sensory experiences such as access to daylight and sunlight and indoor and outdoor stimuli. We have also learned that all of us need opportunities for restoration from the demands and environmental loads that constitute most of our daily lives. Places of tranquility—quiet, softly lit places with distant views serving as positive distractions—can fulfill these deeply felt needs.

Although there is no magic place that satisfies all needs for privacy and works for everyone, there is a commonality of human needs. We have needs rooted in our evolutionary past requiring that we have a degree of privacy, that we can regulate interaction with others, and that we are in alignment with the natural world. As designers and as members of this planet we must settle for no less.

Julie Stewart-Pollack and Rosemary M. Menconi
May 1, 2004

KEY CONCEPTS

- Evidence-based design is the practice of grounding design solutions and decisions in a researched and documented knowledge base that includes the analysis and interpretation of research.
- In the Model for Designing for Privacy, evidence-based design informs all phases of the design process.
- Evaluation is a tool that informs us and supports evidence-based decision making in all phases of the design process.

APPENDIX TO CHAPTER 9
APPLYING THE DESIGNING FOR PRIVACY MODEL IN THE CLASSROOM

In order to test the efficacy of the designing for privacy model in the classroom, the authors created a student project given to interior design students enrolled in a FIDER accredited program in the western part of the United States. Sponsored by publisher Fairchild Books, who provided awards for the top student projects, the purpose was to study conceptual design ideas and solutions that apply

the theories and principles of designing for privacy. Students had the option to design a residential space, a commercial space, or both types of spaces for their projects. Because the emphasis was upon conceptual design development for privacy, students were free to explore both architectural and interior elements that may support privacy needs. The projects were completed independently using information from this book without additional input from the authors or other instructors. We would like to share with you some of the results of these projects, illustrating how the model can be used to facilitate the integration of privacy considerations into the design process in the classroom.

The students applied the Model for Designing for Privacy to the three phases of the project. Consistent with the first Intelligence/Programming Phase, students were required to provide a programming statement explaining their considerations for the solution of the design problem. The statement included a brief description of the problem and the goals and objectives of the end users, including the applicable individual and group factors. The statement also described what the students believed to be the users' privacy needs and the situational factors that applied to the project based upon the evidence-based research and theories in the book. Students were required in their statements to identify the applicable privacy theories and types of privacy to be accommodated. This process produced a design concept for privacy that they further developed in the second phase of the model of Designing for Privacy.

In the Concept and Design Development Phase, students considered the privacy objectives for *choice*, *control*, *safety* and *security*, and *redirected attention* in the context of the types of privacy that they were designing to accommodate. They then identified the physical characteristics of the environment that could be used to support the desired privacy in their projects.

The Implementation Phase of the designing for privacy project included the preparation of annotated floor plans and renderings to illustrate the students' privacy solutions. These drawings as well as the design statements are discussed below.

DESIGNING FOR PRIVACY IN RESTAURANTS AND BARS: THE NAUTILUS LOUNGE

Using nature as a model, student designer, Seema Pandya created a small, intimate lounge by mimicking the internal chambers of a nautilus shell. She explains, "The main entrance as well as the toilets and sociopetal bar are located within the more social large curve of the shell shaped space. Intimate and private seating is tucked deeper inside the space. The curving of the inner wall automatically adds to a sense of mystery as the shape of the wall and the traffic pattern arouse the curiosity and guide one to explore the inner spiral." See **Figures 9A.1** and **9A.2** for illustrations of the application of the principle of design called *progression* used to create a pattern similar to Alexander's intimacy gradient by gradually raising and lowering spiraling wall heights to provide different levels of visual and acoustical privacy.

Alcoves located in the deeper "chambers" of the nautilus shell plan are delineated by thresholds that add to the sense of intimacy and mystery of these spaces. Each alcove provides adjustable translucent fabric panels to enable the user to control visual privacy while providing prospect and refuge. This conceptual design also uses the lighting technique called "radiant forest" discussed in Chapter 6 in which both natural and artificial light is filtered through the leaves of plants to create positive distractions and a sense of well-being.

DESIGNING FOR PRIVACY IN SHARED CHILDREN'S ROOMS: DEFINING TERRITORY

Student designer Miriam Hoffman used built-in beds to define territory and provide the prospect and refuge that young children prefer in the design of the children's primary territory within the design of a family home. She explains, "The sleeping nooks in both of the children's rooms are designed so that the children have their own personal private space. Each nook is raised off the ground, providing a distinct territory for each child."

See **Figures 9A.3** and **9A.4** for illustrations of how the sleeping nooks are designed to give children their personal views of nature. Personal space zones are easily defined and adjusted by this design, which provides ample common areas for interactive play.

DESIGNING FOR PRIVACY IN SHARED MULTIPLE USE SPACES: A LOFT FOR COLLEGE STUDENTS

Student designer Rachel Laessig responded to a challenge often faced by designers: to accommodate multiple activities and multiple needs for privacy in small, awkward spaces on a limited budget. She describes the challenge inspired by this real-life situation: "This space known as 'The Boulder Attic' is a loft shared by two college students who both have busy lives and conflicting schedules. The existing attic had no doors and therefore no means of separating two people. There was absolutely no concept of privacy, so designing the space involved creating a territory for each of the students and also a common area for the two to share. The design challenge for this space is to create both shared and private spaces between two people with a sense of privacy, comfort, mystery, and fun."

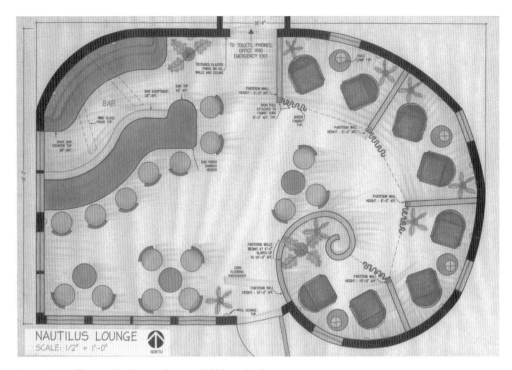

Figure 9A.1 The nautilus lounge is a spatial hierarchy in which one moves from less private to more private areas, created by mimicking the inner chambers of a nautilus shell.

Figure 9A.2 The nautilus lounge: The partition walls separating each individual alcove area begin near the bar at a height of four feet. Each proceeding partition wall progressively becomes taller until the last partition wall reaches the ceiling height of ten feet. As the walls grow increasingly taller, they create more physical, visual, and acoustical privacy.

Figure 9A.3 Shared children's rooms: Defining territory Each sleeping alcove is a defined territory to be personalized and controlled by each child. A central common area creates an interactive play area for younger children and is flexible enough to accommodate study areas as the children grow.

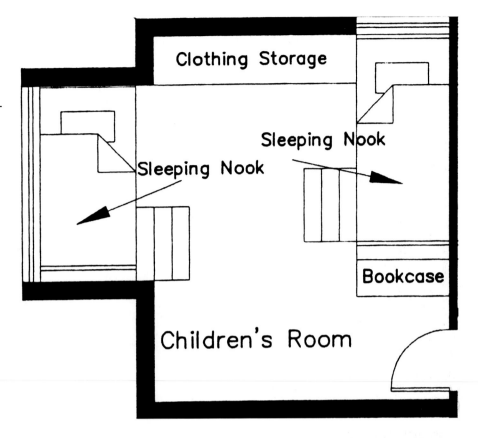

See **Figure 9A.5** for an illustration of a central common area defined by adjustable fabric walls that allow the spaces to be closed visually to clearly define primary territories. The fabrics also enhance acoustical privacy without the use of permanent barriers. This solution allows the space to be easily opened for entertaining. Flexible, movable furniture can be rearranged in a number of ways also to accommodate the changing levels of interaction desired by the roommates.

These conceptual design ideas for privacy illustrate some of the ways the Model for Designing for Privacy may be used in the class-room to examine and explore possible solutions for privacy during the design process. By using this model, we believe that design students and professionals can develop their abilities to identify and interpret privacy needs while enhancing the creative potential of those solutions.

REFERENCES

Abercrombie, S. (1990). *A philosophy of interior design*. New York: Harper & Row.

Lehman-Kessler, M. (1992). *Journal of Interior Design Education and Research*. 18 (1 & 2).

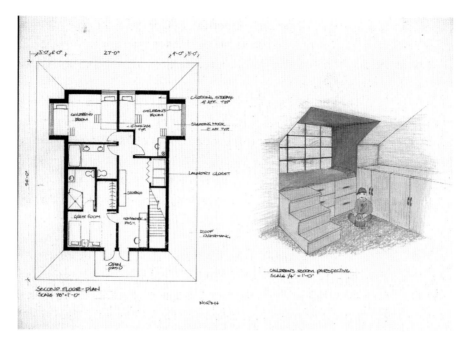

Figure 9A.4 Shared children's rooms: By using Alexander's pattern called "Window Places," the designer created stimulus shelters for each child offering prospect and refuge. Individual, personal storage areas for each child add to the ability to define and control primary territories.

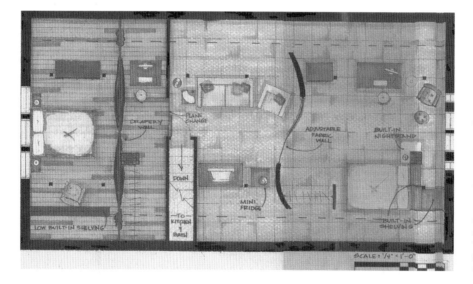

Figure 9A.5 Shared multiple use spaces: A loft for college students. The designer emphasizes the privacy objectives of choice and control and the adjustment of personal space zones and territories in this design for a shared loft space for two college students. This design solution relies considerably upon the appropriate use of interior materials to provide adjustable control of personal space, to mark territories, and to achieve desired levels of privacy.

GLOSSARY

achieved privacy   The actual amount of contact that we have with others as a result of our desired level of interaction.

acoustical privacy   The ability to protect information as it is being transmitted in face-to-face conversation or via telecommunications and the freedom from unwanted acoustical intrusions.

affiliation   The need to form friendships, to communicate and interact with others, to be part of a group, and to love.

aging in place   Remaining in one place lifelong, typically the home, but sometimes relocating to a type of continuous care facility that provides for the residents' changing needs as they age.

alternative officing   The practice of working away from the central office on a permanent basis.

anonymity   The freedom to be in public while at the same time free from identification or surveillance by others; the experience of being "lost in a crowd."

approach behavior   A positive response to an environment involving our desire to be in that environment, to explore it, and to interact with it and with other people.

architectural privacy   Objective physical privacy, usually requiring a door and walls.

arousal   Our level of attention, excitement, tension, and readiness to respond.

ASID   American Society of Interior Designers—the largest professional organization for interior designers in the United States.

assisted living   A type of residential care home with a philosophy that emphasizes resident independence, autonomy, and privacy.

ASTM   American Society for Testing Materials—an agency that reviews testing standards of materials.

avoidance behavior   A negative response to an environment that we perceive as unsupportive of our needs and performance of activities.

away room   An escape room, typically not intended for work, frequently set up to meet needs for solitude or intimacy.

BOSTI   Buffalo Organization for Social & Technological Innovation—a research team of consultants for the design of offices.

catharsis   An emotional release of tension and anxiety.

coherence   Patterns of elements in an environment that help provide a sense of order and direct our attention.

complexity   The amount of elements, features, or changes in an environment that affect the perceived environmental load.

concealment   Controlling social interaction by withholding personal information.

contemplation   Includes self-discovery and the ability to plan future social interactions where we feel free to express ourselves.

controllability   Perceived relationships between individuals and their environments that are essential to effective functioning.

creativity   The exploration of possibilities of expression and mental process that leads to ideas, theories, and artistic expression.

crowding   A psychological response to over-stimulation caused by too much interaction with others within a perceived limited space.

cubicles   An American modification of European office landscaping that utilizes partial height panels to enclose workstations.

dementia   Moderate to severe diminishment of mental faculties.

density   A physical condition involving space limitations and the number of people within that space.

desired privacy   Our subjective feeling about the ideal level of interaction that we wish to have with others at any given time.

directed attention   The type of attention required when we must focus and avoid distractions to effectively perform mental tasks. *Example:* studying.

emotional release   Relief from the pressures and stimulation associated with everyday life; the ability to withdraw from public view to release emotions.

enclosed or private offices   Single or shared office spaces with four full height walls, a ceiling, and a door, typically furnished with free-standing furniture.

environmental load   The amount or rate of information in an environment at any given time, also called **stimulation.**

environmental stress   A condition that occurs when the demands of the environment exceed our capacity to cope with or adapt to those demands from others, enabling us to choose the depth of communication that we desire.

evaluation   The process of evaluating how information from evidence-based design has been applied throughout the entire design process and in the completed design.

evidence-based design   The practice of grounding design solutions and decisions in a researched and documented knowledge base that includes the analysis and interpretation of research.

familiarity   Elements of the environmental load that are more familiar and better understood because we have encountered them before.

Haworth   A major systems furnishings manufacturer in the United States.

healing environment   A therapeutic environment that has a positive influence on the healing process. A healing environment incorporates design elements that reinforce privacy and control, positive distractions, and access to the patient's social support system.

Herman Miller, Inc.   A major systems furnishing manufacturer in the United States.

high load environments   An environment in which a great deal of novel, varied, intense, and complex information is contained or perceived at any given time. *Example:* a crowded emergency room.

hoteling   An on-site work practice of rotation workers using nonassigned workstations on a reservation basis.

human needs   The needs of workers that precede the functional needs for interior design. Selected human needs include privacy, place making, personalization, need for nature, and empowerment.

IFMA   International Facility Management Association—a professional organization for facility managers.

IIDA   International Interior Design Association—a professional organization for interior designers.

informational privacy (confidentiality)   A feeling of comfort that a confidential meeting will not be interrupted by the presence of other people or that confidential documents in the work space cannot be read by others.

inglenook fireplace   A wide, recessed chimney opening usually furnished with benches on either side.

intimacy   The need to be alone with others such as friends, lovers, or family without interference from unwanted intrusions.

involuntary attention   The type of attention that requires little or no conscious effort, a feeling of being in another world where we can experience fascination.

isolation   The process of separating ourselves physically from others by means of physical distance—going for a long drive alone, hiking deep into the wilderness, or walking along a deserted beach.

Knoll   A major systems furnishings manufacturer in the United States.

knowledge work   Abstract and symbolic work, result-oriented, relatively free of supervision. The work requires creativity and continuous learning.

knowledge workers   People engaged in creative and independent work, relatively free of hierarchical supervision.

legibility   Characteristics of an environment that enable us to understand and remember that environment.

limited and protected communication   Controlling the mental and physical distance that we keep from others, enabling us to choose the depth of communication that we desire.

low load environments   An environment in which the information rate is slower, more familiar, and less complex. *Example:* a spa.

mystery   Characteristics of an environment that provide us the opportunity to learn something that is not obvious or apparent when we first perceive a space.

nonscreeners   Human beings who tend to sense more stimuli within an environment and experience it as more complex and with a higher environmental load.

novelty   Elements of the environmental load that are unfamiliar to us.

office landscaping   A European design plan for the original open offices with no fixed walls and no enclosures around workstations.

open office plans   Often referred to as cubicles: workstations without fixed walls, utilizing acoustically treated panels for enclosure on two to four sides; typically furnished with panel-hung furniture.

panels   Demountable partitions, acoustically treated, used as "walls" to enclose workstations.

personal autonomy   Our sense of individuality and integrity; the freedom to separate from others, to be independent, and to think and act without coercion.

personal space   A portable territory, an invisible boundary that we put around ourselves.

personalization   The adornment, decoration, modification, or rearrangement of our built environment.

place attachment   Our feeling of connection to our physical surroundings.

primary territories   Owned and controlled exclusively by the occupants on a relatively permanent basis. The most commonly recognized primary territory is the home.

privacy   A process by which we control access to ourselves or our group and a condition of selective distance or isolation.

private spaces   Spaces designed for the sole function of individual activity.

protocols   Rules or guidelines that enhance the nature and level of privacy desired in the work environment.

proxemics   The study of how we use space to communicate based on social and cultural influences; the spacing or distance that we place between ourselves and others.

psychoneuroimmunology   The multidisciplinary study of the connection between the brain and the body's physical systems, particularly the immune system.

public territories   Available to anyone on a temporary basis. Public territories include beaches, parks, and most facilities defined as public.

recovery   Similar to rejuvenation but with a stronger sense of refuge and relaxation.

redundant cueing   The use of multiple elements to lead patients and visitors directly to a space such as a reception desk, admitting area, and information centers. *Examples:* consistent graphically appropriate signage, color coding, and material and lighting changes.

rejuvenation   The opportunity to recover from a personal social injury, injustice, or loss of self-esteem and to make plans for future social interactions.

reserve   The need to limit communication about ourselves, which is protected by the cooperation of others; verbally controlling information about ourselves such as withholding our feelings, opinions, and ideas rather than expressing them to others.

responsive environments   Flexible environments that provide the opportunity to alter one's surroundings to accommodate changing needs for togetherness and separateness.

screeners   Human beings who are better able to select what they respond to in an environment.

secondary territories   Temporary nonexclusive ownership such as the neighborhood bar or one's favorite table at the library.

self-actualization   The natural inclination that humans have to strive to fulfill their potential.

self-evaluation   The ability to process information, to plan and develop ideas, and to decide what we want to reveal to others.

social density   Changes in the number of people in a fixed space.

sociofugal spaces   A type of design for a space that discourages interaction and communication with others; supports needs for solitude or anonymity in a high density setting. *Example:* bar seating in a tavern.

sociopetal spaces   A type of design for a space that encourages interaction and communication with others; supports needs for communication. *Example:* seating at right angles, sidewalk café seating to mingle restaurant patrons with passersby.

solitude   The need to be alone and free from observation by others; refers to situations in which others cannot hear or see what we are doing.

sound masking system   Addition of background noise into the ceiling plenum or into the workstation at a decibel level higher than ambient sound.

spatial density   The same number of people occupying spaces of different sizes.

Steelcase Inc.   A major systems furnishings manufacturer in the United States.

stimulation   The amount or rate of information in an environment at any given time, also called **environmental load.**

stimulus screening   The process of selecting or filtering the environmental stimuli automatically on a conscious level according to our survival needs.

systems furnishings manufacturers   Companies that manufacture products for open office planning. The products include demountable partitions with electrical capacity, hang-on components, and panel-hung and free standing furnishings.

teleworking   An off-site practice of working from a remote location, often the home.

territorial behavior   A privacy mechanism in which we communicate to others that some part or quality of a physical space is "ours," belongs to us, or is under our control temporarily or permanently.

territoriality   A type of privacy in which we control a fixed geographical location by laying claim to it. *Examples:* office cubicle, desk at school.

territorial privacy   Having a place of one's own within the work environment; a feeling of ownership that contributes to the sense of self-worth and personal identity.

territorial markers   Symbolic or actual physical barriers and boundaries or objects used to communicate ownership and to personalize a space. *Examples:* fences, signs, and leaving a newspaper on our seat to save our place.

transcendent experience   An experience found in nature that is characterized by our strong positive feelings; overcoming the limits of our physical lives; a sense of timelessness and a sense of connection with the universe or a higher power.

visual privacy   A comfortable state in which workers can work without feelings of being observed and without the distraction of sudden movements and other unexpected sights.

virtual office   An off-site practice. The central office disappears, and workers work from a variety of nontraditional places—client's offices, airplanes, or the beach.

zoning   Delineating areas within a space as public or private by physical means such as enclosure or separation.

INDEX